HEROES
OF THE
FAITH

HEROES
OF THE
FAITH

Gene Fedele

BRIDGE
LOGOS

Newberry, Florida 32669 USA

Bridge-Logos
Newberry, Florida 32669 USA

Heroes of the Faith
by Gene Fedele
Design: Gene Fedele

Printed in the United States of America.

International Standard Book Number: 978-0-88270-934-5
Library of Congress Catalog Card Number: 2010923025

23 22 21 20   10 9 8 7 6 5

Dedication

To my wonderful and lovely wife, Kerri. Her beauty and virtue shine bright in daily devotion to her Savior and in every aspect of her life. As a wife, mother, and friend, she is a genuine example of Christian womanhood. I praise the Lord for her support, encouragement, and assistance in the research and writing of this book.

"Her children shall rise up and call her blessed; her husband also, and he praises her. Many women have done excellently, but you surpass them all."—Prov. 31:28-29

Reverend Charles Haddon Spurgeon, here shown as a young man preaching in the Metropolitan Tabernacle Church pulpit. London, England, March 26, 1861

CONTENTS

58   **Charlemagne (742-814):** *"By the sword and the cross," he became master of Western Europe. Through his enlightened leadership the roots of learning and order were restored to Medieval Europe.*

63   **Cyril (827-869) and Methodius (826-885):** *Today Cyril and Methodius are honored by Eastern and Western Christians alike, and the importance of their work in preaching and worshipping in the language of the people is recognized on all sides.*

65   **King Alfred (849-901)** *was a man who did more than any other to fight against the spiritual decay within the English church as well as against the Viking invaders. He established the English royalty, created the first English navy, authored English literature and ensured the survival of Christianity in England.*

69   **King Wenceslaus (907-935):** *The 19th-century Christmas hymn, "Good King Wenceslaus" is an allegorical depiction of the real-life 10th century King of Bohemia who was martyred as a lover of Christ and a provider for the poor and needy.*

71   **Olga (890-969) and Vladimir (956-1015)** *were called by the Lord to powerfully lead the Rus (Russian) nation from pagan ritualism to embrace the great religion of Jesus Christ.*

73   **Anselm of Aosta (1033-1109):** *Anselm's lot was cast in troublous times, but he fought against evil in cloister and in court, against corrupt monks, and against the worst king who ever wore the crown of England. He conquered them all because he triumphed through the grace of Christ.*

77   **Bernard of Clairvaux (1090-1153):** *In 1115 A.D. Bernard founded the monastery at Clairvaux. He and the monastery became a major center of spiritual and political influence.*

81   **Peter Waldo (1140-1217):** *In one sense, he was a protestant more than 200 years before John Huss. His followers, the Waldenses, began a reformation to which the latter Reformation of the 16th century would strikingly resemble.*

85   **Clare of Assisi (1194-1253):** *From her earliest years Clare seemed to have been endowed with the rarest virtues. As a child she was most devoted to prayer and to practices of mortification and devotion, and as she became a young girl her distaste for the world and her yearning for a deeper spiritual life increased.*

87   **Thomas Aquinas (1225-1274):** *Thomas Aquinas' extensive theological writings, along with his simple yet profound style of presenting the gospel makes him one of the most frequently quoted fathers of the Church.*

89   **John Wycliffe (1324-1384):** *Church officials feared to see the Bible in the hands of "commoners", but John Wycliffe believed the Word of God should be open to all people. His translation of the Scriptures from Latin to English was a milestone in biblical enlightenment and Church growth.*

93   **John Huss (1369-1415):** *In the remarkable providence of God, the work of John Wycliffe made its way from England to Bohemia and into the mind and heart of John Huss. This humble priest would stand against the formidable forces of the corrupt clergy and become an undaunted pioneer of Reformation in the 16th-century.*

97   **Johann Gutenberg (1400-1468)** *loved to read, but became impatient with the time-consuming process of book-making. His genius, faith, and passion for the spread of the Gospel propelled the events that introduced movable type and the first printing press to the world.*

101   **Savonarola (1452-1498)** *is considered by ecclesiastical historians as one of the four pre-reformers, along with Waldo, Wycliffe and Huss. Instead of fighting doctrinal errors, Savonarola focused on the practical implications of religion.*

103   **Albert Durer (1471-1528)** *is undoubtedly the greatest German artist of the Renaissance, but he is most well-known for his faith in Christ and his resolve to see his Savior honored and proclaimed through his life and his work.*

107   **Martin Luther (1483-1546):** *The world has rarely witnessed character and resolve as remarkable as that of Martin Luther. He was created by God to light the torch of the greatest revolution in the history of Christendom.*

112   **Hugh Latimer (1485-1555):** *"No one of the Reformers probably sowed the seeds of sound Protestant doctrine and preaching so widely and effectually among the middle and lower classes as Latimer, and no one was so well fitted to do it."—J. C. Ryle*

117   **John Knox (1505-1572):** *John Knox has become recognized as the most prominent figure of the Scottish Reformation. One of Knox's greatest accomplishments was through his writings, in particular his "History of the Reformation."*

120   **John Calvin (1509-1564):** *Among the great theologians to expound the doctrines of the Christian faith was John Calvin. He defended them against centuries of human error, and was the foremost thinker in Biblical learning, as well as in literary power.*

126   **Anne Askew (1520-1546)** *was martyred for her faithfulness to the Gospel of Jesus Christ. Her fine example of resolute faith and gentle piety gave courage to an entire generation of English Christians.*

131   **Joan Mathurin (1539-1560):** *This brave, young Vaudois woman chose to stand up against tyranny and die at the stake next to her loving husband, rather than deny her faith in Jesus alone for salvation.*

135   **Samuel Rutherford (1600-1661)** *was a non-conformist Presbyterian who would not be silenced by the designs of godless men. He preached with vigor, repentance and faith in Christ alone, and a nation moved to deeper piety and holy living.*

139   **Richard Baxter (1615-1691):** *The "holy Baxter" is renowned for his preaching, teaching, pastoral care and shepherding, as well as his renowned classic writings. In a stormy and divided age he helped point the way to "The eternal."*

143   **John Owen (1616-1683):** *You will find in Owen the learning of Lightfoot, the strength of Charnock, the analysis of Howe, the savor of Leighton, the glow of Baxter, the copiousness of Barrow, and the splendor of Bates.*

145   **John Bunyan (1628-1688)** *had the remarkable ability and biblical insight to view the Christian life in allegorical forms. Even his classic and immortal "Pilgrim's Progress" draws from experiences in his own life.*

150   **Isaac Newton (1642-1727)** *is generally regarded as the most original and influential discoverer of scientific principles and laws under creation. His understanding of light and color led to the invention of his telescope. This great man of God also discovered the law of gravity, calculus, and the three laws of motion.*

155   **Isaac Watts (1674-1748):** *The poetic gifts of the "father of English hymnody" was evident at the tender age of seven. He wrote more that 700 hymns in his lifetime, many that are regularly sung in services of Christian worship today.*

159   **John Brown (1676-1714):** *Rather than compromise their principles of civil and religious freedom the Scottish Covenanters, or "Martyr Warriors" were dragged from their homes and places of worship by the king's soldiers to face execution.*

161   **Jonathan Edwards (1703-1758):** *Over two centuries after Edwards' death, the great British preacher, Dr. Martin Lloyd-Jones, said of him; "No man is more relevant to the present condition (revival) of Christianity than Jonathan Edwards."*

165   **John Wesley (1703-1791):** *The Methodist revival cut across denominational lines and touched every class of society. England itself was transformed in the process. In 1928 Archbishop Davidson wrote that "Wesley practically changed the outlook and even the character of the English nation."*

169   **George Whitefield (1714-1770)** *was the most travelled preacher and one of the greatest evangelists of the 18th century. His diligence and sacrifice helped turn two nations back to God.*

175   **David Brainerd (1718-1747)** *lived only 29 years, but inspired many to follow Christ through his tireless missionary work in New England. His example of piety encouraged many into the mission field, such as William Carey and Henry Martyn.*

179   **John Newton (1725-1807):** *This former slave-trader became one of England's most prominent preachers. Today, John Newton is renowned for his inspiring hymn "Amazing Grace," which is probably the best known hymn ever written.*

183   **Richard Allen (1760-1831)** *was the pivotal leader and founder of the American Methodist Episcopal Church. He was born as a slave in 1760, bought his freedom, gave his life to Christ, and is now recognized as one of the great Christian leaders in American history.*

185   **Adoniram Judson (1788-1850)** *and* **Ann Judson (1789-1826):** *In 1812, Adoniram and Ann Judson set sail for India. These first American missionaries to evangelize Burma and translated the Scriptures into the Burmese language.*

5

189   **Horatius Bonar (1808-1889):** *A man of prose and poetry, Horatius Bonar was also a man of sorrow. Five of his children and his wife died during his lifetime. His deep faith and preaching of the Scriptures led many to saving faith in Christ.*

193   **Samuel Crowther (1809-1891):** *Once a victim of Muslim slave-traders, Crowther became free—not only in body, but in receiving the Holy Spirit—that he might become the first to minister the blessed truths of Jesus Christ to his native Africans.*

197   **Charles Dickens (1812-1870)** *frequently told his children about his precious Savior, Jesus Christ, making mention of Him in his letters to them. His most personal profession of faith was beautifully, and humbly expressed in his "Life of Our Lord."*

199   **Robert Murray M'Cheyne (1813-1843):** *"Among Christian men, a 'living epistle,' and among Christian ministers, an 'able evangelist,' is rare indeed. Mr. M'Cheyne was both. And without presumption, I say he was a 'disciple whom Jesus loved,'" says his friend and fellow minister, James Hamilton.*

203   **J. C. Ryle (1817-1900)** *is known as one of the most practical writers of Christian truth. Though dead he still speaks with poignant accuracy to the heart and mind of any who dare to read his books. The reader cannot help but be affected by Mr. Ryle's candid, yet urgent appeal to holy living.*

205   **Elizabeth Prentiss (1818-1878):** *Bearing her cross in this world with sweet resignation to the Lord, Elizabeth Prentiss has blessed and encouraged the hearts of thousands through her precious, Christ-centered writings.*

209   **"Fanny" Crosby (1820-1915):** *A stack of twenty hymnals together could hardly contain the number of Christian hymns written by Fanny Crosby wrote in her lifetime! Though many have been forgotten today, a large number still remain favorites of Christians all over the world.*

211   **Charles H. Spurgeon (1834-1892):** *The "Prince of Preachers," was also a gifted teacher, counselor, author, and philanthropist. More than any other individual of his time, he revived a sybaritic English society into God-fearing, Christ-serving people.*

217   **Dwight L. Moody (1837-1899)** *traveled in Europe and America, holding revival campaigns, and personally speaking with over 750,000 individuals. He preached to more than 100,000,000 people, and saw over 1,000,000 converted to Jesus Christ.*

221   **J. R. Miller (1840-1912)** *wrote more than seventy books, edited more than a dozen Christian periodicals, and pastored in a number of congregations. His ministry reached the hearts of hundreds of thousands and continues to reach millions more.*

226   **Amy Carmichael (1861-1951):** *Obedience, love, and selflessness were the marks of Amy Carmichael's life. Even after a tragic accident left her confined to the Dohnavur Fellowship compound, Amy blossomed as a Christian woman and writer.*

231   **Karl Barth (1886-1945)** *is considered by some to be the greatest Protestant theologian of the 20th century and possibly the greatest since the Reformation. More than any other, Barth inspired and led the renaissance of theology that took place from about 1920 to 1950.*

233   **C. S. Lewis (1898-1963)** *published 52 books, 153 essays, and a great many prefaces, letters, and book reviews. To this day, he remains one of the world's most popular Christian authors, with more than 1.5 million copies of his works sold each year.*

237   **D. Martyn Lloyd-Jones (1899-1981):** *Young and old, rich and poor, men and women, bright and dull, all seemed to come to hear the message of Jesus Christ put forth with a power and authority not often matched, by Dr. Martyn Lloyd-Jones.*

239   **Dietrich Bonhoeffer (1906-1945)** *was one of the few German Church leaders who stood up against Hitler in courageous opposition to his inhumane practices and anti-Christian beliefs.*

241   **Billy Graham (1915-present):** *Renowned evangelist and Baptist clergyman Billy Graham has been touching audiences around the world for over 50 years. A master of modern media, Graham has preached the Christian gospel through radio, television, film, and the printed word.*

243   **Joni Eareckson Tada (1950-present):** *The name "Joni" is recognized around the world. Overcoming the suffering and challenges of her paralysis Joni Eareckson Tada has ministered to the hearts of millions of people over the past thirty-five years.*

Elijah being fed by the ravens. Engraving from the Mother's Magazine (1856).

Author's Preface
Heroes of the Christian Faith

Among the multitudes of literary works that enrich our lives and encourage us in our Christian faith, few compare to the compelling biographical sketches of the many men and women who formed our heritage and paved the streets of history with truth and piety.

It is these apostles, kings, reformers, puritans, revivalists, suffering martyrs, and others, eminent in godliness, who have lit the sacred lamp that guides the feet of latter pilgrims through the trials of life in this world to that purer and more blessed abode in glory. In recollecting their lives, I am sobered by the fact that we owe so much of the religious knowledge and freedom we so cherish and enjoy today to those in ages past who did not succumb to the pressures of political, social, or ecclesiastical conformity, but rather endured trials and persecutions, and even death, that the precious truths of Christianity might go forth in victory. With this in mind, I have therefore endeavored to present just a few of these heroes of our Christian faith, whose lives and writings I pray will aid in your private meditation, family devotions, and eternal reflections.

For those who are being persecuted in the name of Jesus by the hands of godless men, in lands where professing Christ is a death sentence, may your heart find strength as you read of the sufferings and triumphs of those who have gone before you.

The lives of eminent Christian men and women in each generation from the Resurrection of Christ to modern day have been profiled here. Each short biography includes a general sketch of their lives, and the contributions they've made to the advancement of Christianity through the influence of their example and character as well as their literary works. My goal is to provide a concise, historical yet inspirational account of the activities, thoughts and writings of those individuals whom God chose to carry forth the gospel in powerful ways.

The utmost care was given to historical accuracy, but in some cases the records conflict. Subtle discrepancies in dates or of historical interpretation, therefore, are not easily addressed in such a short amount of space.

With any book that seeks to highlight a limited number of great and godly people among the thousands that might qualify, the final selection could be debated, and some might even disagree with the ones I've presented in this work. I submit that one could easily fill a dozen more volumes such as this one with the

"True biography," said one of Christ's faithful missionaries, "was never nor can be written. Fragrance cannot be put into picture or poem. There is a subtle evasive savor and flavor about character which escapes both tongue and pen. The very best things about such careers are unknown, save to God, and are among His secret things. Like Elijah, the best men hid themselves with God before they showed themselves to men. The showing may be written in history, but the hiding has none. And after studying the narrative of such lives, there remains a deeper, and unwritten history that only eternity can unveil."

stories of God's faithful men and women who have affected the course of ecclesiastical history.

In addition, this book is not intended to advocate any denominational or doctrinal position, but to demonstrate that, in the providence of God, there were those who had "not bowed the knee to Baal." Men and women, moved by the power of the Holy Spirit, have risen up at the appointed times in history to carry forth the truth of the gospel regardless of the obstacles and circumstances in the world around them.

During my research for this book I became further convinced that the succession of witnesses for evangelical truth throughout the ages remains unbroken, though it may not appear to be so in the dark ages of human history. In this book you will see that in generation after generation the people of God embraced their faith in Christ with great fortitude and courage and saw Him through the lens of the tribulations and challenges of their time.

The "Hall of Faith," as it's commonly referred to, found in chapter eleven of Hebrews records notable examples of faithful believers realized in the course of Biblical history. This "cloud of witnesses" as chapter 12 calls them, no doubt, could be added to in the godly men and women who have followed their example in the name of Jesus Christ.

We see a common thread of passionate love and devotion to the Son of God characterized in every one of these men and women. Not the murderous persecutions of the early Church at the hands of pagan Rome, nor the barbarian raids on medieval Christian kingdoms, not the martyrdoms of the Reformation, nor the relativism and easy-believism of the present day could daunt their resolve to do great things in the name of King Jesus. They are, indeed, "Valiant-for-Truth's" rising up to lead the forces of Christian truth and beauty to a lost and dying world!

The following pages present men and women of all ages. As you read through the biographies of these chosen saints, note that in each generation from the apostolic age to the present day the torch of divine truth was carried forward in splendor and passed on in victory.

Many know of the prophet Elijah and how he withstood the evil intentions of wicked Ahab and Jezebel. They know how he stood alone against 450 prophets of Baal, and how the one true God was revealed in a mighty way through the hands and faith of His servant. But this same Elijah, not long after, became greatly discouraged and pleaded with the Lord that he might die, thinking that he was the last remaining faithful one on the Earth. But the Lord revealed to him that he was not alone. *"I have left me seven thousand in Israel, all the knees which have not bowed unto Baal, and every mouth which has not kissed him"* (I Kings 19:18).

In his book *Elijah the Tishbite*, Dr. F. W. Krummacher speaks to this very passage of Scripture and confirms in such a blessed manner the purpose for this present work.

"We must never measure others by ourselves. If we seek more after the chief and essential matter, namely the contrite spirit and the genuine love of Christ and of the brethren, we shall perhaps number many as belonging to the flock of Christ, whom at present we are apt to overlook. Elijah, as we find, received an express revelation concerning the faithful in Israel and their number. The Lord unveiled to him the 'hidden church,' and it may be supposed how great was the astonishment of this man of God at learning that amongst the very people he had so severely accused, there were so many as seven thousand who had not bowed the knee unto Baal. He had regarded himself as the only light in the darkness of Samaria; and now, behold! a whole firmament of chosen souls is disclosed to his view, which the clouds of his weak faith had kept hidden from him.

"We have to be thankful that even still the Church is sometimes refreshed by such pleasing discoveries. Often, on the very spot where we expected to find only thorns and briers, we find a cultivation, like the garden of the Lord, and sweeter flowers that are likely to bloom in the more open places of Christendom."

We see in the pages of history, Christianity—like the sun struggling through the clouds of a dark day—calm, steady and resolute, continuing on its course. Though the storm-clouds may obscure its brightness for a season, nothing can impede its onward progress. At the present day, Christianity—triumphant over all the conflicts of centuries past—shines brighter, clearer, and with more healing across this vast world, than ever before.

This book is not intended to exalt individuals—for there is only one for whom such veneration is reserved—but to demonstrate what the mighty hand of God could do with humble men and women who have consecrated themselves to do His will.

"All the heroism which the annals of chivalry record pale into insignificance in the presence of the heroism with which the battles of the cross have been fought, and with which Christians, in devotion to the interests of humanity have met, undaunted, the most terrible doom.
—John S. C. Abbott

A standard format was the goal for each biography. Some are longer than others depending on the complexity of their lives and the historical setting surrounding them. Each was chosen for his or her contributions to the Christian faith as well as for the particular era of history in which the person lived. A short bibliography concludes each biography that readers may be further inspired by the lives and works of these pious Christians.

Another common thread that caught my attention in preparing this work was the fact that in the lives and conversions of so many of these men and women we see the influence and prayers of a godly parent or grandparent, particularly on the maternal side. What a testimony to our Lord's wonderful Covenant of Grace and fulfillment of His Word to all Christians in all generations that "the promise is unto you and your children..."

My prayer in presenting this volume of Christian biographies is that the Holy Spirit might bless unto your soul, and unto those in your family, these examples of Christian virtue, joy in suffering, persevering piety, and humble resignation before God.

May our Lord richly bless you.

Gene Fedele

The Apostle Paul, while under guard in Rome, addressing the Jewish leaders. (Acts 28)

The Apostle Paul *?-A.D. 64*

Voice of Christianity

The first generation following the Resurrection of Christ was one of marked contrast between the influences of wicked political and ecclesiastical leaders, and the piety and love of advocates and teachers of the new religion of Christianity. Paul, once a zealous member of the former class, became a central voice of truth, grace, and salvation through one God-man, the Lord Jesus Christ. His conversion was radical, as was his life in the service of the Redeemer. He withstood the forces of every evil opposition with the courage and fortitude of a King David, a Gideon, an Elijah, and a Jeremiah combined. Through the hand of the Almighty, the words and deeds of this man of God have indeed changed the course of humanity forever.

he sun shone at its highest and brightest across the midday sky over the desert highway leading to Damascus. A small caravan had left Galilee with a resolute purpose to affect the dispersion of this new, disruptive religious uprising connected to the "King of the Jews" who claimed to be God and was crucified for his "crimes."

Without warning, a light brighter than the noon sun, cascaded down from the heavens and with a force unknown rendered every man helpless and prostrate along the roadside. Among the small desert band was a man of religion, named Saul, a Pharisee of Pharisees, specifically commissioned to persecute the "seditious tribe of Christians," which he vigorously performed "breathing out threatenings and slaughter." For him, this day would be like none other, for God would speak to him like never before, even in all his years in the synagogues.

"Saul, Saul, why persecutest thou me?" came the powerful voice from Heaven.

"Who art thou, Lord?" answered the terrified Saul.

"I am Jesus whom thou persecutest," returned the voice. "Arise, and go into the city, and it shall be told thee what thou must do."

With that encounter the Lord changed Saul's name to Paul, to mark his new purpose in life—to proclaim the name of the Lord and Savior Jesus Christ, and renounce anything that was of the contrary. Paul was uniquely qualified and prepared by the Lord since his early days. Instructed in Mosaic law of contemporary Judaism, Paul would use his training and knowledge in a new and glorious mission to evangelize the world with the "good news" of a loving God who sent His Son to shed His blood on the Cross, that we might be saved from our sins. This wonderful truth deeply penetrated the heart and soul of the apostle, enabling him to go forward in confidence and faith.

This great apostle of Christ was born a Roman citizen, in the city of Tarsus, some time around the birth of Jesus. According to Jewish custom, he learned a trade before entering the more direct preparation for the sacred profession. The trade he acquired was

The passion and gifts of the Apostle Paul were refined in fires of suffering and persecution that he might pave the path for the future of Christianity.

the making of tents from goats' hair cloth, a trade that was one of the commonest in Tarsus.

Paul received his religious instruction in Jerusalem under the learned Gamaliel, who recognized his greatness at an early age. Convinced of the errors of Christianity, the young Pharisee consented to the stoning death of Stephen in the city square. His desire for the extermination of the Christians grew until his encounter with Christ on the Damascus road.

During his missionary journeys he travelled more than 10,000 miles, displaying almost superhuman energy and endurance. He suffered every trial imaginable—stonings, shipwrecks, beatings, imprisonments, and humiliations, in order to spread the gospel. One could say the successes Paul experienced as a missionary, writer, evangelist, preacher, theologian, and sufferer for the truth, could be found amidst his own words found in his first letter to the Church at Corinth, *"I have made myself a servant to all, that I might win the more ... I have become all things to all men,*

The conversion of Paul on the road to Damascus, as depicted in a 19th-century engraving by the famous artist Gustave Dore. "And he fell to the earth, and heard a voice saying unto him, 'Saul, Saul, why persecutest thou me?'" (Acts 9:4).

that I might by all means save some" (1 Corinthians 9:19-22).

Paul founded churches in twenty cities during his missionary tours, yet it was at Corinth that he experienced his greatest challenges as well as victories.

When Paul first put his pen to papyrus, he had been a Christian for more than fifteen years. His letters, which now comprise more than two thirds of the New Testament canon, reflect the passionate illumination of the Holy Spirit. His letter to the Romans has had a profound impact upon our understanding of sin and grace, predestination and faith. Wherever reformation has come to the Church the ideas of Paul's Epistle to the Romans have played a leading part.

Paul's fortitude and faith enabled him to transcend the cruelties of the enemies of Christ and become a pillar of the Christian Church and the whole of Western civilization.

The events surrounding Paul's death are not without question, but it is commonly accepted that he was beheaded with a sword near Rome in A.D. 67, during the reign of Emperor Nero, just a few years before the fall of Jerusalem in A.D. 70. His martyrdom was but the culmination of a life "poured out as a drink offering" to his Lord Jesus Christ.

Ignatius *30-117*
Divine Lamp of the Early Church

It has been aptly recorded that the first century following the Resurrection of Christ was one of great tribulation for the people who embraced Him as God and Savior. The pleasure-seeking dictatorial Roman Emperor Nero began the persecution in A.D. 64 when he blamed the great fire that destroyed half of Rome on the Christians. The Apostles Peter and Paul, among thousands of other Christians, perished in the ensuing persecution. A few decades later, Emperor Trajan sought to perfect the universality of his dominion with one religion. He decreed, therefore, that the Christians should unite with their pagan neighbors in the worship of the gods. What followed in the courageous life of Ignatius of Antioch was instrumental in strengthening the first generation of Christians to persevere and gain victory in their faith, even in the face of death.

At the time Trajan had succeeded to the throne of the Roman Empire, Ignatius, the disciple of John the Apostle, a man in all respects of an apostolic character, governed the Church of the Antiochians with great care. All the sterling qualities of the ideal pastor and a true soldier of Christ were possessed by the Bishop of Antioch in a preeminent degree. When the storms of persecution from the Roman Emperor poured down upon the Christians of Syria, they found their faithful leader prepared and watchful. Though Ignatius had formerly escaped the fury of Emperor Domitian, he resisted not the proclamation of Trajan, who condemned him to the wrath of fierce lions in the arena.

Ignatius Theophorus was appointed by the Apostle Peter to succeed Eusebius as bishop of Antioch. He was the first to speak of the Church as "catholic," meaning "universal." Antioch is also noted as the place where the followers of Christ were first called Christians.

It was the one great wish of the chivalrous soul of Ignatius that he might receive the fullness of Christian discipleship through martyrdom. For he inwardly reflected that the confession that is made by martyrdom would bring him into a yet more intimate relationship with the Lord. After continuing a few years longer with the Church, and, like a divine lamp, enlightening everyone's understanding by his expositions of the Scriptures, he was finally called to die for Christ.

During his interrogation, Trajan asked, "Dost thou then carry within thee Him that was crucified by Pontius Pilate?" Ignatius replied, "Truly so; for it is written, 'I will dwell in them, and walk in them.'" Then Trajan pronounced his sentence, "We command that Ignatius, who affirms that he carries about within him 'Him that was crucified,' be bound by soldiers, and carried to Rome, and there be devoured by the beasts for the gratification of the people." When the holy martyr heard this sentence, he cried out with joy, "I thank thee, O Lord, that Thou hast vouchsafed to honor me with a perfect love towards Thee, and hast made me to be bound with iron chains (which he referred to as "spiritual pearls"), like Thy Apostle Paul."

After having spoken thus, he clasped the chains about him with delight and prayed for the Church, commending it with tears to the Lord. The cruel soldiers then savagely carried him away to Rome, to furnish food to the bloodthirsty beasts.

More than one of the early church writers identifies Ignatius as the young child whom the Savior called to himself and set in the midst of the apostles as described in Mark 9:36.

As he was being led into the amphitheater he was met by many of his brethren who sought to secure his release. But he entreated them to not "envy his hastening to the Lord." We have Ignatius's own words, given in a letter that he wrote to his dear friend Polycarp of Smyrna while on his death march, "...nearness to the sword is nearness to God; to be among the wild beasts is to be in the arms of God; only let it be in the name of Jesus Christ. I endure all things that I may suffer together with Him, since He who became a perfect man strengthens me."

The character of Ignatius, as revealed from his own writings and also those of his contemporaries, is that of a true athlete of Christ. The honor of Christian, bishop, and martyr was

well merited by this energetic soldier of the faith. An enthusiastic devotion to duty, a passionate love of sacrifice, and an utter fearlessness in the defense of Christian truth were his chief characteristics. Zeal for the spiritual well-being of those under his charge breathes from every line of his writings. He was ever vigilant lest his fellow saints be infected by the rampant heresies of those early days. And he prayed continually for them that their faith and courage would not grow weak in the hour of persecution and death. In every sense, Ignatius was a pure pastor of souls—the good shepherd who lays down his life for his sheep.

The Colosseum of Rome was the sight of hundreds of first century martyrdoms.

Key Writings of Ignatius: 1. *Epistle of Ignatius to the Ephesians;* 2. *The Epistle of Ignatius to the Magnesians;* 3. *The Epistle of Ignatius to the Trallians;* 4. *The Epistle of Ignatius to the Romans;* 5. *The Epistle of Ignatius to the Philadelphians;* 6. *The Epistle of Ignatius to the Smyrnaeans;* 7. *The Epistle of Ignatius to Polycarp;* 8. *The Third Epistle of the Same St. Ignatius;* 9. *The Epistle of Ignatius to the Tarsians;* 10. *The Epistle of Ignatius to the Antiochians;* 11. *The Epistle of Ignatius to Hero, a Deacon of Antioch;* 12. *The Epistle of Ignatius to the Philippians;* 13. *The Epistle of Ignatius to Mary at Neapolis, Near Zarbus;* 14. *The Epistle of Ignatius to St. John the Apostle;* 15. *A Second Epistle of Ignatius to St. John.*

Worth Reading: *Vindiciae Ignatianae* (1846); *Corpus Ignatianum* (1849); *Apostolic Fathers,* by Bishop Lightfoot (1907); *Early Church: From Ignatius to Augustine,* by George Hodges (1915).

Polycarp *69-155*
"Angel" of Christian Truth

In the perilous times of the early Church, martyrdom was almost as common as conversions. Yet those of genuine faith were taught to never seek martyrdom or to avoid it when the only choice is to deny Christ. The heathen believed it was not possible for a true Christian to deny his Lord. Through his martyrdom the heroic Polycarp set the example from which believers drew strength and courage to face their own ordeals.

he interest attached to the life of the great Bishop of Smyrna arises not only from the simplicity and strength of his personal character, but from his close connection with the apostolic period, and the light that his career and writings throw upon the New Testament Scriptures. He was the principal link between two great eras of the Church's history. On the one hand, he was a pupil of the Apostle John. On the other, he was a teacher of Irenaeus, who in turn, became a chief representative of the Church's literary activity in the latter part of the second century. Through this very important period, therefore, Polycarp carried on the testimony both to the records and the substance of the Christian faith. From the apostles he received the doctrine, and in unquestioning faith he transmitted it, without any attempt at analysis or speculation. His confidence in the gospel was based not on elaborate reasoning, but on the experience of a lifetime; and the power and value of his convictions were attested by a martyr's triumphant death.

Polycarp was not merely an illustrious teacher, but also a preeminent believer, whose martyrdom all desired to imitate, as having been altogether consistent with the Gospel of Christ.

His pupil Irenaeus gives us one of the very few portraits of an apostolic man that are to be found in antiquity, in a few sentences: "I could describe the very place in which the blessed Polycarp sat and taught; his going out and coming in; the whole tenor of his life; his personal appearance; how he would speak of the conversations he had held with John and with others who had seen the Lord; and how he made mention of their words and of whatever he had heard from them respecting the Lord." Thus he unconsciously tantalizes our reverent curiosity. That such conversations were not written for our learning. But there is a wise Providence in what is withheld, as well as in the inestimable treasures we have received.

Irenaeus further tells us that "Polycarp was instructed by the apostles, and was brought into contact with many who had seen Christ." In fact, in A.D. 110, Polycarp experienced a lasting encounter with Ignatius that had a profound effect upon his mind and character. The elder "father" and fellow student of John the Beloved urged his younger associate to maintain a brave and hopeful spirit amidst the conflict already begun. In the time following, before the martyrdom of Ignatius, the two exchanged warmhearted letters of truth and encouragement.

One afternoon, while resting in his home, Roman soldiers broke in and arrested Polycarp. He asked that he might pray before being led away. His words moved even the hearts of those who were commissioned to affect his execution. When he reached the arena, the Proconsul pleaded with him to renounce Christ, that he might be set free, but Polycarp's resolve was firm.

"Eighty-six years I have served Him. He has never done me wrong. How then can I blaspheme my King who has saved me?" was the reply of the aged saint.

They did not nail him then, but simply bound him. And he placed his hands behind him, and being bound like a distinguished ram taken out of a great flock for sacrifice, and prepared to be an acceptable burnt-offering unto God, looked up to Heaven, and said, "O Lord God Almighty, the Father of thy beloved and blessed Son Jesus Christ, by whom we have received the knowledge of Thee, the God of angels and powers, and of every creature, and of the whole race of the righteous who live before thee, I give Thee thanks that Thou hast counted me worthy of this day and this hour, that I should have a part in the number of Thy martyrs, in the cup of thy Christ, to the resurrection of eternal life, both of soul and body, through the incorruption [imparted] by the Holy Ghost. Among whom may I be accepted this day before Thee as a fat and acceptable sacrifice, according as Thou, the ever-truthful God, hast fore-ordained, hast revealed beforehand to me, and now hast fulfilled. Wherefore also I praise Thee for all things, I bless Thee, I glorify Thee, along with the everlasting and heavenly Jesus Christ, Thy beloved Son, with whom, to Thee, and the Holy Ghost, be glory both now and to all coming ages. Amen."

At that last word the torch was applied and the fire instantly rose high, but the flames seemed to arch themselves around their victim. Seeing that the fire had failed to do its work, the officer charged upon Polycarp and pierced him with a sword. The eminent saint then gave up his spirit. It was more a day of triumph than one of tragedy. So this brave and true man of God received his "crown of life."

Key Writings of Polycarp: *The Epistle of Polycarp to the Philippians*

Worth Reading:: *The Encyclical Epistle of the Church at Smyrna: Concerning the Martyrdom of the Holy Polycarp*

"Eighty-six years I have served Him. He has never done me wrong. How then can I blaspheme my King who has saved me?" was the reply of the aged saint, Polycarp, as he stood before his persecutors.

Justin Martyr *103-163*
The First Christian Philosopher

The Romans established the colony of Neapolis after the destruction of Jerusalem in A.D. 70, and Justin's father apparently was part of the colonial administration. But in spite of such pagan Roman leaders as Gallio and Nero, the gospel was dispelling the gross darkness of first century philosophies and beliefs. The post-apostolic age saw its first great Christian philosopher and author in Justin, the founder of theological literature.

lavius Justinus (Justin Martyr) was a Gentile, born in the Roman colony of Neapolis in Samaria, near where Jesus had once spoken to the Samaritan woman by the well (John 4). Justin thirsted after truth and righteousness and would finally drink of the water Jesus offered. He was the first Christian philosopher and theologian after the apostles, explaining Christianity in terms familiar to the educated Greeks and Romans of the second century.

Justin gave his life in ardent defense of the Christian faith against pagans, Jews, and erring Christians. He taught in Rome and wrote works that equipped Christians for generations to come.

Before his conversion to Christianity he studied in the schools of the philosophers, searching after some knowledge that should satisfy the cravings of his soul. At last he became acquainted with Christianity and was at once impressed with the extraordinary fearlessness that the Christians displayed in the presence of death, and with the grandeur, stability, and truth of the teachings of the Word of God. Regarding his conversion, he states in his *Apologies,* "When I was a disciple of Plato, hearing the accusations made against the Christians and seeing them intrepid in the face of death and of all that men fear, I said to myself that it was impossible that they should be living in evil and in the love of pleasure."

From this time on he acted as an evangelist, taking every opportunity to proclaim the gospel as the only safe and certain philosophy, the only way to salvation. He believed that all truth was God's truth. Borrowing from John's treatment of the Word (*Logos* in Greek) in his gospel, Justin taught that any truth in the Greek or pagan philosophies was the Word or *Logos* reaching out to sinful humanity. He believed Plato's God was the God of the Bible and that Socrates was a Christian before Christ.

But the courageous and heroic pleadings of the man were for a despised people with whom he had boldly identified himself. The intrepidity with which he defended them before wicked men and godless leaders, whose mere impulse might punish him with death, was undaunted. Justin's spirit with which he exposes the shame and absurdity of their inveterate superstition are characteristics which every instinct of the uncorrupted soul delights to honor.

He wore his philosopher's gown after his conversion, as a token that he had attained the one true philosophy—Christianity—the only philosophy that lasts and triumphs over all.

It had been more than a hundred years since the angels had sung "Good will to men" at the humble manger. And that song had been heard for successive generations, breaking forth from the lips of sufferers on the cross, amidst the lions, and through the blazing flames upon the stake. Thousands of men, women, and children—withdrawing themselves from worldly pursuits and living among the ordinary and humble lot of the people— were inspired by it to live and die heroically and sublimely. Here they exhibited a superiority to revenge and hate entirely unexplainable by mere human means, praying for their enemies, and seeking to glorify their God by love to their fellow men.

One day, while walking by the sea, contemplating Platonic ideas, Justin met an old man who patiently talked with him of the weaknesses in Plato and about prophets more ancient than the Greek philosophers who told the truth about God and foretold the coming of Christ.

Justin Martyr confronted his heathen contemporaries like a Daniel. The "little stone" smote the imperial image in the face. He told the professional philosophers on a throne how false and shallow is all wisdom that comes not from the Scriptures, and that is not capable of reaching the masses. He exposed the impotency of even Socratic philosophy; showing, in contrast, the regenerating power in the works and words of Jesus. It was the mission of Justin to be a star in the West, leading its "wise men" to the cradle of Bethlehem. To the hideous calamities forced against the Christians he sometimes answered, as did the other apologists, by taking the offensive and attacking pagan morals.

Justin paid the price for his convictions. Not only did he teach Christianity as the ultimate truth and write in defense of the faith, he also defended Christ in public discussions. Two men he publicly debated in Rome were the heretic Marcion and the Cynic philosopher Crescens. The fourth century historian Eusebius suggested it was a plot by Crescens which brought Justin and six of his students to the attention of the Roman prefect Rusticus around the year 163. When these Christian believers refused to sacrifice to the Roman gods as demanded, they were condemned, scourged, and beheaded. Standing a firm witness to Christian truth even in death, Justin gained the name "Martyr" by which he continues to be known to this day.

Justin's *Apologies* are characterized by intense Christian fervor, and they give us an insight into the relations existing between heathens and Christians in those days. His other principal writing, *Dialogue with Trypho*, is the first elaborate exposition of the reasons for regarding Christ as the Messiah of the Old Testament, and the first systematic attempt to exhibit the false position of the Jews in regard to Christianity.

Key Writings of Justin: 1. *First Apology of Justin*; 2. *The Second Apology of Justin*; 3. *Dialogue of Justin with the Jew Trypho*; 4. *Justin's Hortatory Address to the Greeks*; 5. *Justin on the Sole Government of God*; 6. *Fragments of the Lost Work of Justin on the Resurrection*; 7. *Treatise Against the Jews.*

Perpetua *185-211*
Martyr of the Early Church

The most famous and complete record of early Church persecutions is found in "Foxes' Book of Martyrs," originally published in the late 16th century. The suffering and death of this courageous young lady along with hundreds of Christ's faithful servants is thus recorded.

he martyrdom of Perpetua and Felicitas at Carthage was one of the memorable events of the persecution of the early Christian Church.

Perpetua was a Roman lady of exalted birth, and highly educated, who had become a Christian at an early age. Her friend, Felicitas, was a young Christian bride, about to become a mother. The parents of Perpetua were pagans, as were her two brothers. She was only a twenty-six year old wife and mother with an infant child.

She was arrested and thrown into prison for refusing to follow Roman edicts of worship to pagan gods. Her aged father, who loved Perpetua, tenderly prostrated himself upon his knees before his daughter, and with tears gushing from his eyes, pleaded with her to save her life by sacrificing to the gods. She remained firm. A large crowd assembled at her trial. Her father brought into the court her little baby and entreated Perpetua, for the sake of her child, to save her life. He hoped that the sight of her child would cause her to relent and renounce Jesus. The public prosecutor, Hilarien, then said to her:

"In mercy to your aged father, in mercy to your babe, throw not away your life, but sacrifice to the gods."

"I am a Christian," she replied, "and cannot deny Christ." The anguish of her father was so great that he was unable to restrain loud expressions of grief, and the brutal soldiers drove him off with multiple harsh blows. "I felt the blows," says Perpetua in a brief memorial, "as if they had fallen on myself." Perpetua was then condemned to be torn to pieces by wild beasts.

"When the day for the spectacle arrived," says Perpetua, "my father threw himself on the ground, tore his beard, cursed the day in which he was born, and uttered piercing cries which were sufficient to move the hardest heart."

Both Perpetua and Felicitas were doomed to the same death. The two victims were led into the arena of the vast amphitheater, where they were to be cruelly gored to death by bulls. The rising seats that surrounded the amphitheater were crowded with spectators to enjoy the spectacle.

Imagine descending into the dark, damp dungeons opening into the arena. Here in this den are growling lions, gaunt and

Perpetua was an example of Christian resolve and courage, choosing to suffer and die with a clear conscience and truthful lips, rather than live life in denial of her Savior, that she might live with Him forever in glory.

fierce. Next to it is a den of panthers with glaring eyes. They have been kept starved for many days to make them furious. In another cell of stone and iron, which the glare of the torch but feebly illumines, is a band of Christians—fathers, mothers, sons, and daughters. They are to be thrown tomorrow into the arena naked, that they may be torn to pieces by the panthers and the lions, and that the hundred thousand pagan spectators may enjoy the sport of seeing them torn limb from limb, and devoured by the fierce and starved beasts.

In one of these cells Perpetua and Felicitas were confined. In another were several wild bulls. Within the amphitheater was congregated all the wealth and fashion of the city—vestal virgins, pontiffs, ambassadors, senators, and in the loftiest tier sat a countless throng of slaves. Carthaginian ladies, presenting the utmost delicacy and refinement, competed with men in the eagerness with which they watched the bloody scenes.

To these two women the thought of denying their faith was worse than the prospect of death in the arena. They felt the power of the Spirit to persevere, regardless of the consequences.

Perpetua and Felicitas were escorted from the prison to the arena "joyfully as though they were on their way to Heaven," records one witness.

In the center of the arena there was suspended a large network bag of strong fine twine, with crevices so large as to afford no covering or veil whatever to the person. Perpetua was first brought into the arena, young and beautiful, a pure and modest Christian lady. She was led forth entirely divested of her clothing, that to the bitterness of martyrdom might be added the pangs of wounded modesty. A hundred thousand voices assailed her with insult and derision. Brutal soldiers placed her in the transparent network. There she hung in mid-air, about two feet from the ground, as if floating in space. Then the burly executioners gave her a swing with their brawny arms, whirling her in a wide circle around the arena, before they departed.

The two women called out verbal affirmations of their love for each other, as well as encouraging words to "Stand fast in the faith." The iron door creaked upon its hinges, and flew open. Out from the dungeon leapt the starving bull, with flaming eyes, bellowing, and pawing the sand in rage. He glared around for an instant upon the shouting thousands, and then caught a glimpse of the maiden swinging before him. With a bound he plunged upon her and buried his horns in her side. The blood gushed forth, and she was tossed in the air. The shrieks of the tortured victim were lost in the hundred thousand shouts of excitement.

This scene cannot be described. It can hardly be imagined. Lunge after lunge the bull plunged upon his victim, piercing, and tossing, until the sand of the arena is drenched with blood. Her body swung around, a mangled mass. Felicitas in the meantime is compelled to gaze upon the scene, that she may taste twice the bitterness of death. She was next placed in the suspended network, and in the same fiery chariot of martyrdom ascended to Heaven.

Cyprian *200-258*
The Ignatius of the West

Living in the atmosphere of persecution under imperial edicts of Roman Proconsul Aspasius Paternus and often in the immediate presence of a lingering death, the professors of Christianity began falling away from the faith. This grieved Cyprian and called him into action, which ultimately cost him his life. One year after his return from exile, he was called again to renounce Christ. Instead he remained firm in his faith and was therefore sentenced to die by the sword. To this edict his reply was, "Thanks be to God!" After removing his garments and praying, he was martyred before a huge crowd of followers and entered into the presence of God.

yprian (Thascius Caecilius Cyprianus), bishop of Carthage and an important early Christian writer, was born at the beginning of the third century in North Africa, where he was educated from his early childhood. He died a martyr's death at Carthage, September 14, 258. His original name was Thascius, but at his baptism he took the name Caecilius in addition in memory of the presbyter of that name who was used by God to affect his conversion. He belonged to a provincial pagan family and became a teacher of rhetoric. In his desire for deeper holiness he gave a part of his fortune to the poor, imposed upon himself austere penances, and devoted himself to the study of the Bible and earlier Christian writers.

Cyprian was a staunch defender of the Presbytery and an advocate for incorporating the gifts of the laity into the life of the Church.

His ordination and his elevation to the episcopate rapidly followed his conversion. With some resistance on his own part, and not without great objections on the part of older presbyters, who saw themselves superseded by his promotion, the popular urgency constrained him to accept the office of Bishop of Carthage in 248, which he held until his martyrdom.

The breaking out of the Decian persecution in the year 250 induced Cyprian to retire into exile for a time, and his retreat gave his detractors occasion to sharply attack his conduct. During this year he wrote many letters from his place of concealment to the clergy and others at Rome and at Carthage. He controlled, warned, directed, and exhorted, and in every way maintained his responsibilities as Bishop in his absence, in all matters connected with the well-being of the Church.

It seemed though that his efforts produced little fruit and therefore he appears to have returned to his public duties early in June 251. Then followed many letters between himself and Cornelius, Bishop of Rome, and others, on subjects connected with various schisms and with the condition of those who had been perverted by them. But a terrible plague soon broke out in the city for which the Christians were blamed, thus igniting fresh persecution.

It was not long before Cyprian was arrested and brought before the Proconsul, where he was threatened to conform to the worship of the Roman gods. Instead, he publically confirmed his faith in the one God and Christ as the Savior of his soul. He was banished as a result, but returned to Carthage in 258, only to be arrested by the governor, who ordered him to be beheaded. After the sentence was passed, a crowd of his fellow Christians said, "We should also be killed with him!" Therefore, a number of his fellow worshippers were martyred along with him.

In his theology he was very much a standard-bearer of the "catholic" system as it was known to the Nicene Fathers. However, of all the Christian fathers, he is the most clear and comprehensive in his conception of the body of Christ as an organic whole, in which every member has an honorable function. Popular government and representative government, the legitimate authority and place of the laity are all embodied in the catholic system as Cyprian understood it.

The finest work written about this eminent saint was by his personal friend and deacon, Pontius, titled *The Life and Passion of Cyprian, Bishop and Martyr.* Pontius speaks of his beloved master thus: "There are many things which Cyprian did while still a layman, and many things which now as a presbyter he did—many things which, after the examples of righteous men of old, and following them with a close imitation, he accomplished with the obedience of entire consecration—that deserved well of the Lord.

"He [Cyprian] taught that we should do whatever Job had previously done, so that while we are doing like things we may call forth a similar testimony of God for ourselves. He, condemning the loss of his estate, gained such advantage by his virtue thus tried, that he had no perception of the temporal losses even of his affection. Neither poverty nor pain broke him down. The dreadful suffering of his own body did not shake his firmness. His house was open to everyone who came. No widow returned from him with an empty hand, no blind man was unguided by him as a companion, none faltering in step was unsupported by him with a staff, none stripped of help by the hand of the mighty was not protected by him as a defender."

Cyprian's most important work is his De Unitate Ecclesiae. This work makes the one episcopate, not of Rome, but of the Church at large, the foundation of the Church.

Key Writings of Cyprian: 1. *De Unitate Ecclesiae*; 2. *The Opera of Cyprian*; 3. *The Epistles of Cyprian*.

Worth Reading: *Cyprian's Works*, by J. Pearson (1882); *Cyprian, His Life, Times, Work*, by E. W. Benson (1897); *Life and Times of Cyprian*, by G. A. Poole (1898); *Cyprian the Churchman*, by J. A. Faulkner, (1908); *The Letters of Cyprian of Carthage* (translated by G. W. Clarke, 1984).

Constantine *280-337*

The Founder of Christian Freedom

For three hundred years following the Resurrection of King Jesus, Christians had been persecuted for their faith, even unto death. As an instrument in the hands of God, Constantine the Great ended this tyranny, enabling Christians to worship freely. One by one he conquered the enemies of Christ, revoking anti-Christian decrees, and established a freedom of religion that redirected the stream of history for centuries to come.

This bust of the Emperor Constantine, which is located at the Palazzo dei Conservatori in Rome, may well have been part of the huge statue of the emperor that was erected in Rome in 313 shortly after his victory over Maxentius, which Eusebius mentions in his Historia Ecclesiastica.

lavius Valerius Constantinus (Constantine) was born at Naissus in Servia, the son of a Roman officer, Constantius, who later became Roman Emperor, and Helena, a woman of remarkable, humble and pious character. At the death of his Father, Constantius, in 306, he was immediately proclaimed Emperor of the Western empire.

He undoubtedly belongs to the men of the third century whose military career paved the way to higher political position, but Constantine's course took a different path than any of his contemporaries or predecessors.

Constantine had acquired serious inclination toward the Christian faith from his mother. But his religious position in adult life was left obscure until his famous battle against Maxentius who first urged a war on Constantine in an attempt to secure sole headship of Rome as its emperor. The course of the battle was the vehicle God used to open his heart to Christianity. Eusebius faithfully recorded the life-changing events surrounding Constantine's conversion in his *Historia Ecclesiastica.*

In October of 312, Constantine and his troops were on the march to meet the impressive forces of the tyrannical Maxentius. While on the journey, Constantine had opportunity to consider the fact that the victor would gain control of the most powerful nation on the face of the Earth. The impact of this reality drove him to his knees in prayer to the God of the Christians. He recalled the example of a pious mother and a Christian people whose resolve for truth was unwavering even in the face of persecution. He pleaded for God to stretch forth his hand in aid, and while engaged in this act of devotion, he observed a remarkable appearance in the clouds. A cross with the inscription *In Hoc Signo Vinces,* or "By this thou shalt conquer," emerged in wonderful distinctness before his eyes. He took it as assurance that he would win the battle. His entire army was also witness to the sign.

Constantine can rightfully claim the title of Great, for he turned the history of the world onto a new course and made Christianity, which until then had suffered bloody persecution, the religion of the State.

Ancient coin of
Constantine I. His
laureate and helmeted
bust facing left.
Struck A.D. 310-312.

That night he received a dream that confirmed to him that he was dealing with the one and only true God. This experience convinced him that he should do battle in the sign of Jesus Christ, and his warriors carried a monogram on their armor that incorporated the first two Greek letters of the name Christ, chi (X) and rho (P). The brave army, its shields now adorned with the sign of Christ, pushed on toward Rome. The opposing forces met near the bridge over the Tiber called the Milvian Bridge, and in a bold assault Constantine overpowered his adversary. Maxentius' troops suffered a complete defeat. The tyrant himself lost his life when he drowned by the weight of his own armor while retreating. Amidst the rejoicing shouts of the populace Constantine marched into Rome, where by senatorial order an arch of triumph was erected in his honor.

Constantine's gratitude to the Lord for the victory was convincing. After concluding matters in Rome, he left in 313 for Milan, where he met Licinius, and gave to him his sister, Constantia, in marriage. The two emperors had deliberated as to what would be advantageous for the security and welfare of the empire and had taken into consideration the service that man owed to God. They discussed Christianity in relation to Church-State issues and ordered that Christian worship was henceforth to be tolerated throughout the empire. This decree is known as the Edict of Milan. Christians and all others were granted freedom in the exercise of religion—everyone might follow the religion that he considered the best. With this edict they hoped that "the deity enthroned in heaven" would grant favor and protection to the emperors and their subjects.

The "Chi-Rho monogram combining the first letters, "X" and "P", of the name of Christ (CHRISTOS), a form that had not been used by Christians before, was made one of the tokens of the emperor's standard. In addition, this ensign was placed in the hand of a statue of the emperor at Rome, the pedestal of which bore the inscription: "By the aid of this salutary token of strength I have freed my city from the yoke of tyranny and restored to the Roman Senate and people the ancient splendor and glory."

The Roman world was now divided into two portions, with two emperors—Constantine in the West and Licinius in the East. Gradually rivalries sprung up between them, and it became apparent that the empire was not long for accommodating two rulers. Licinius' great increase of power was heightened to such a degree that he became insolent and sought to emulate Constantine. He reckoned with Christianity only for external reasons and on the religious side had always persisted in the pagan religion and superstition, so much so that he provoked his imperial colleague to war. After two strenuous campaigns, separated by a delusive interval of peace, Licinius was vanquished in a decisive battle at Chrysopolie, September 18, 323. Thanks to the intercession of Constantia, the victor guaranteed him his life under oath and granted him Thessalonica as residence. The deposed emperor, however, sought to create a new insurrection by secret alliances with the Danubian barbarians. Con-sequently he was found out and condemned to death by the senate as a public enemy and rebel, and was executed as such in 325.

By renouncing belief in any of the gods of Rome, Constantine lived in a monotheism whose Christian import is confirmed by the fact that he not only provided complete freedom to Christianity in his kingdom, but also allowed Christianity to be observed in his palace.

The emperor conferred with spiritual counselors and through them became more intimately instructed in regard to Christianity. The influence of Hosius of Cordova had a profound impact on his spiritual growth, and maintained a high position of trust with him for many years.

Shortly after his defeat of Licinius, Constantine made Constantinople the capital of the empire, and in A.D. 324, Constantine finally achieved full control over an undivided empire. He then relocated the imperial headquarters to Byzantium and changed the name of the city to Constantinople. With his gifted energy he took every measure to enlarge, strengthen, and beautify it. For the next ten years of

The scene of Constantine's vision of the Cross of Christ, strengthened him in battle and ultimately led to his conversion. Nineteenth-century engraving from 1883 edition of History of Christianity, by John S. C. Abbott.

his reign he devoted himself to promoting the moral, political, and economical welfare of the empire and made provisions for its future government. It is popularly believed that he made Christianity the official religion of the empire because of his personal convictions. There are some who contend, though, that his actions were not so much inclined from religious convictions as they were actions merely intended to harness the power of "God" for the benefit of the state. Nevertheless, he issued edicts recommending the universal observance of the Lord's Day. He abolished all the laws that forbade Christians when dying to bequeath their property to the Church. And he forbade the cross from ever again being used as an instrument of punishment.

Though his intentions were righteous, Constantine's move created a top-heavy structure that would quickly depart from its original purity. It became a Church beholden to the state, out of touch with the needs of its members and concerned primarily with its own comfort.

Constantine had won the civil war, but the battles within the Church would prove to be more elusive for him. The main trouble he faced was the Arian controversy. This debate over a central Christian doctrine of the Trinity was larger than he imagined.

After much debate and sharp contentions, Constantine decided it was time to settle the controversy and restore unity in the Church. In 325 he summoned key bishops and Church representatives to join him at Bithynia for what would be the first, and arguably the most famous, council in the history of the Christian Church—the Council of Nicaea.

For the next two months of proceedings, the emperor participated in the controversy. He eventually fell on the side of the Cappadocean's saying, "For the decision of 300 bishops must be considered no other than the judgement of God," and against Arius, calling him, "that shameless servant of the Devil."

Though peace and freedom of religion was granted for Christians under the reign of Constantine, it was a mixed blessing. The fires of persecution experienced in the first three centuries kept the Church pure, but the Edict of Milan opened the doors for anyone to "join." This resulted in multitudes embracing Christianity, not because of a sense of sin and work of the Holy Spirit in the heart, but from a pursuit of popular interest and worldly gain.

The Arch of Constantine (A.D. 315) was erected in honor of the first Christian Emperor's victory over Maxentius at the Milvian Bridge (Soxa Rubra) in A.D. 312, just north of Rome. The arch served as the triumphal entryway to the Forum, through which victorious generals passed on their way to the steps of the Temple of Jupiter Optimus Maximus located on the Capitoline.

About Easter 337, a serious disease overtook Constantine, which soon developed into a dangerous illness. The warm baths of Helenopolis proved ineffectual, so in the certainty that his end was near he went to Achyrona, a suburb of Nicomedia, and before an assembly of bishops he read aloud his resolution to receive baptism, which he would have preferred to receive in the waters of the Jordan. He was baptized by Eusebius of Nicomedia and died a few months later.

Worth Reading: *Historia Ecclesiastica,* by Eusebius of Caesarea; *Life of Constantine,* by Averill Cameron (1999); *The Christianity of Constantine The Great,* by T. G. Elliott (1996); *The Conversion of Constantine and Pagan Rome,* by Andrew Alfoldi (1948).

Athanasius *295-373*
Defender of Orthodoxy

Athanasius ranks high as an author, though he would not have attained so high a place had it not been for the epoch-making war that he waged upon Arianism. During his illustrious ecclesiastical career, he effectively fought against the forces of error with compassion and fortitude, which helped form the Nicene Creed and secure it for generations to come.

In the midst of the Egyptian metropolis of Alexandria, and near the close of the third century, a youth was born, who by the grace of God was destined to rank with the highest Christian teachers of all ages, especially in giving form and definiteness to the convictions of the Church respecting the divine greatness of the Son of God. Of the lineage and early years of the great theologian, no authentic particulars have reached us. From his own account, it appears that his family was in straitened circumstances. His training and education render it probable that his parents were Christians, while the name bestowed upon him increases the likelihood of the supposition. For Athanasius, a synonym of Immortality, expresses, in a way not infrequent in that generation, the dearest hope of the followers of Christ.

The years in which the young Athanasius passed from infancy to childhood witnessed the outbreak of fierce persecution of the Church, under the Emperor Diocletian. From the age of six to that of sixteen, the lad must have become familiar with the cruelties, terrors, and heroisms of that fearful time. The Bible was a forbidden book, and its copies were confiscated. Christians could only meet for worship in secret places. Multitudes were thrown into prison, many were mutilated or put to death. One teacher of Athanasius at least was martyred during this persecution, and in the last year before the edict of toleration, Peter, the Bishop of Alexandria, was called to lay down his life for Christ. Peter was succeeded, after a short interval, by Alexander, a man of deep convictions and dauntless resolution, who had already marked the character and abilities of Athanasius, and had undertaken his religious training.

He became an attendant in the Catechetical School, and was educated under the eye of Alexander, of whom he afterwards became the companion and secretary. His eulogist, Gregory of Nazianyum, says that "Athanasius attained an extraordinary knowledge of the Scriptures. His mastery of the Bible is evident in all his works."

In A.D. 367 Athanasius' Easter Letter recognized the New Testament Canon, listing the same books of the Bible as we have today.

By this time, Constantine had succeeded to the imperial purple, persecution ceased, and outwardly the Church was at peace.

While the young Athanasius was yet a student, Alexander was engaged in a contest over the doctrine of the Trinity with Arius, a presbyter and minister of an Alexandrian church. Alexander insisted on the unity of the Godhead, while Arius maintained that Christ was an originated being, above all other created beings, but inferior to the Father. In 320, a synod of more than 100 bishops condemned Arius' doctrine, and expelled him from the Church.

The matter did not end there, the controversy heated and the Emperor Constantine, desirous for ecclesiastical peace, pleaded for reconciliation. This led to a convocation of bishops called to consider the issue, and in 325 the Council of Nicea convened. Hosius of Corduba presided over the deliberations. Many who had suffered in the great persecution were present, with scarred faces, sightless eyes, or maimed limbs, "bearing in their bodies the marks of the Lord Jesus." Arius was there to plead his own cause—an elderly man, tall, haggard, worn with asceticism, quiet and plausible in speech, with the light of fanatic earnestness in his eyes. On his side was the courtly Eusebius, with sixteen other bishops, all told. The great majority of the brethren were already bent on maintaining the orthodox faith. Chief among them was the aged Alexander, whose utterances had begun the conflict, and the youthful Athanasius was by his side, strong and slight, restless and active, with strongly-marked features, auburn hair, and eager, gleaming eyes. The young deacon from Alexandria soon became the master-spirit of the assembly.

The Council of Nicea discussed many topics, but the one great question was paramount. Before all things it was needful to meet the questions now raised concerning the Son of God: Who and what is He? The life of the Church through all generations depended upon the answer to be given. That there was need of a definition, marked a distinct stage in the progress of religious thought. After much debate, the propositions of Arius were rejected and the Nicene Creed was drawn up. In this great declaration of the council, the most significant part was the phrase describing the Son of God as "of one substance" with the Father (greek: *homoousios*). Defending this doctrine became a matter of life and death, which became evident in subsequent contests. Athanasius, with a wisdom beyond that of his contemporaries, believed with an intensity of conviction that was proof against all the changes and agitations of a stormy life that in the defense of this doctrine lay the grand secret of the faith. It is to his steadfastness that by God's blessing we owe a great deal of the power of evangelical Christianity.

Shortly after the council, Athanasius became Bishop of Alexandria where he established a refuge for the monks and

"It will matter little to the faithful what their sorrows may have been in this vain world, since no trace of them will remain when they enter on that ineffable peace which is in store for them in the life to come."
—Athanasius

"Others are content with caring for parts of the Church entrusted to their charge. Thou carest for the whole, as much as for thine own portion of it. Thou dost not omit occasions for deliberating, admonishing, and writing letters, bearing the best counsels."
—Basil of Caesarea, in a letter to his friend Athanasius

a missionary church. Still Arius persisted and, with the help of Eusebius, who had the ear of the Emperor, Athanatius was ordered to restore Arius to the Church. Athanasius refused and was summoned before Constantine, who saw him as an obstacle to peace and therefore gave him an honorable exile to Treves. But Arianism received a great blow at the sudden death of its leader during a public reception in his honor in Constantinople.

In the years following, Athanasius experienced times of peace and prosperity as well as great persecution, primarily over the Arian controversy, but also due to heathenism under Julian and other anti-Christian philosophies. He was forced into exile four different times and restored to his beloved Alexandria just as many. The refuge of Athanasius among the monks and hermits of the desert during his third and fourth periods of exile leads up to a point that needs special mention—his relations with monasticism. Athanasius was not only the father of orthodoxy in the East, but also the first bishop to take an active part in encouraging the monastic life.

An ancient Byzantine painting of the Council of Nicea. In 325 the groundwork for the Nicene Creed was laid. This creed has been the dominant statement of faith for most of Christianity for the past 1,700 years. At the bottom is the figure of Arius stopping his ears.

Shortly before his death, the influence of Athanasius reached the ear of Roman Emperor Jovian, who subsequently declared himself a Christian. He wrote to Athanasius, "Because, after all the evil and terror of thy persecutors, thou didst not crouch in fear, and hast counted as dung the perils and menaces of the sword. And because thou holdest fast the helm of the Christian faith dear to thee, even to the present day, thou strivest for the truth and continuest to show thyself a pattern to the whole people of the faithful as a model of virtue. Therefore our royal authority greets thee and wills thee to return to the teaching of salvation." Jovian goes on to request a summary from Athanasius of the true "catholic" faith. In return, the bishop sent to the emperor a declaration embodying the Nicene Creed, with some expository comments.

Athanasius died in peace in 373, at the age of seventy-seven. His character as a Christian bishop is well summed up by Gregory of Nazianzum; "Athanasius was as humble in mind as he was sublime in his life, a man of inimitable virtue, and yet so courteous that any might freely address him. He was meek, gentle, compassionate, amiable in his discourse, but much more so in his life. He was one that so governed himself that his life supplied the place of sermons. The simple remember him as a guide, the contemplative as a divine, the merry as a bridle, the miserable as a comforter, the aged as a staff, the youth as a tutor, the rich as a steward, and the poor as a benefactor. He was a patron to widows, a father to orphans, a friend to the poor, a harbor to strangers, a physician to the sick, and a brother to the brethren, one who became all things to all men, that if not all, at least some might gain the more."

"In Athanasius there was nothing observed in his battle against Arianism other than such as became a wise man to do, and a righteous man to suffer. So the result was the whole world against Athanasius, and Athanasius against it."
—Richard Hooker

Basil wrote to Athanasius words that constitute the best eulogy of the now venerable father. "When we look at our own difficulties, we are driven to despair; but when we turn our eyes to thee, and reflect that thou art left by the Lord to be the physician of our maladies, then we draw upward our minds from despondency, and emerge into hope. For what other person is fit to be our pilot in the storm, but he who from his childhood has contended in conflicts for the faith?"

The truth that "Athanasius against the world" maintained in heroic struggle and endurance is our heritage today. It is the distinguishing honor of Athanasius to have spent his life in asserting, by word and deed, the true, essential diety of Christ, the Son of God, the Word made flesh, incarnate "for us men and for our salvation."

Key writings of Athanasius: 1. *Against the Heathen (318);* 2. *On the Incarnation (318);* 3. *Four Arations Against the Arians (338)* 3. *Festal Letters (329-339);* 4. *Apology Against the Arians (347);* 5. *Defense of the Nicene Council (351);* 6. *Defense of Dionysis (356);* 7. *Apology to Constantius (357);* 8. *History of Arians for Monks (357);* 9. *Letter to Serapion on the Death of Arius (358);* 10. *On the Synods of Ariminum and Seleucib (359).*

Worth Reading: *Early Church Fathers: A Selection From the Writings of the Fathers from Clement of Rome to Athanasius,* by Henry Bettenson (1969).

Basil of Caesarea *329-379*
Cappadocian Father

The provinces of Pontus and Cappadocia, in Asia Minor, have held a place in Christian history from very early days. To Jews from these regions the gospel was preached by Peter on the day of Pentecost. For several generations afterwards, the light of the Gospel continued to shine here with varying radiance until, soon after the beginning of the fourth century, we find in Casarea, the chief city of Cappadocia, a Christian teacher of rhetoric and public pleader of high repute and considerable wealth, named Basil.

The history of the special bond between Jonathan and David is well-known to all familiar with the stories of the Old Testament. In the fourth-century Church a bond no less powerful was formed between three men from a small city in Asia minor, called Cappadocia. Through correspondence, sermons, and theological treatises, Basil stood firmly for the doctrine of the Trinity. He and his brother Gregory, who became Bishop of Nyssa, were staunch defenders of the deity of Christ and the Holy Spirit and were influential in defining the terms by which the three persons of the Trinity are one God. With Gregory of Nazianzus, they also defended the complete humanity of Jesus. One heresy of the day was that Jesus had a human body but not a human soul or mind. "The Three Cappadocians," as they were called, recognized that Jesus had to be fully human if he was to be our Savior. The importance of the role of the Cappadocians in the theological and doctrinal realm cannot be overestimated. The Church had been scandalously divided, and even riotous over theological issues, particularly Arianism. The Cappa-docians skillfully worked through key issues with deeper understanding so that a level of peace could be achieved without compromising Biblical truth. They were known as leaders in the formation of the Nicene Creed.

Basil combined a pastor's heart in caring for his church with a theologian's love for the truth. When he died in 379 his last words were "Into Thy hands, O Lord, I commit my spirit; Thou hast redeemed me, O Lord, God of truth."

Basil's birth nearly synchronizes with the transference of the chief seat of empire from Rome to Byzantium. By this time, Rome was reduced to the subordinate rank of a provincial city, awaiting the crowning outrage of the barbarian invasions. Her desperate grasp of ecclesiastical stability was, in reality, a failed attempt of regaining something of her lost imperial prestige.

Basil and Gregory grew more attached while attending the famous schools of Athens together, yet their personalities were quite opposite. Basil was calm and philosophical, of clear insight and strong will. Gregory was vivacious and enthusiastic, with a poet's sensitivity. They became known as inseparable, "of one soul."

Three members of Basil's family: (L-R) his sister, Macrina, brother Gregory and Basil, as depicted by an early Byzantine artist.

At the age of twenty-six, Basil opened a school of rhetoric in Caesarea, and his popularity grew. The splendors and attractions of success led to a vaulted spirit, and his sister, Macrina, knew it. Her gentle and humble pleadings to see the vanity of earthly things reached his heart, and he resolved to follow Christ decidedly and vigorously. Though Basil chose to lead a more ascetic life, he believed firmly that a social life is necessary for the growth of highest Christian character.

Basil was ordained Bishop of Caesarea in 370. His first acts were directed at restoring integrity and discipline among the clergy and eliminating many abuses that had crept into the Church. Novel human inventions were rife in the church, worldly wisdom reigned in clergy, houses of prayer were bereft of faithful preachers, and pews full of mourners. Though he worked diligently to bring holiness and the love of Christ back into the pastorate, he is most known for his procurement of the faith as declared by the Nicene fathers, in which Basil succeeded the great Athanasius. Basil believed in the single procession of the Holy Spirit from the Father alone, and Christ as the only begotten Son of the Father.

Two years after Basil's death, the new Emperor Theodosius called a church council at Constantinople to finally deal with the Arian heresy in favor of the Cappadocians.

Basil's love and reverence for the Word of God was remarkable, and in this he stands supreme among the Church fathers. "This," he writes, "is the characteristic of the believer, that with full assent of his mind he believes the force of those things to be true, which are spoken in the Scripture, and that he rejects nothing, and that he dares not to desire anything new."

What a Family!
The church remembers not only the work of Basil, but also his sister Macrina, his two brothers, Gregory of Nyssa and Peter of Sebaste, his grandmother Macrina, and his mother Emmelia. Quite a Cappadocian family!

His old friend, Gregory, says of Basil's writings, "When I take into my hands and read his *Hexaemeron*, I am brought into communion with the Creator. When I peruse the books he has written on the Holy Spirit, I find out God. When I read his expositions, I pierce beneath into the spirit and hear 'deep calling unto deep'; I behold light streaming into light, and thus I grasp the sublime meanings of Holy Scripture."

Basil struggled with feebleness in body for five years until in 379 he lay down for the last time. Crowds surrounded his residence, praying eagerly for his restoration to them, and willing to give their lives for his. After a few final words of advice and exhortation, he said: "Into thy hands I commend my spirit."

Key Writings of Basil: 1. *Hexaemeron, or Sermons on the Six Days of Creation;* 2. *Morals;* 3. *Against Eunomius;* 4. *Homilies on Thirteen of the Psalms;* 5. *On the Holy Spirit.*

Gregory of Nyssa *332-395*
"The Father of Fathers"

The doctrine of the Trinity had been under attack since the Council of Nicea in 325. Gregory, his brother Basil, and their friend Gregory of Nazianzum took up the battle against the Arian influences that a generation before was fought by Athanasius and other faithful men.

 regory was born into a deeply religious family, not very rich in worldly goods, to which circumstances he probably owed the pious training of his youth. His mother Emmelia was a martyr's daughter, and two of his brothers, Basil of Caesarea and Peter of Sebaste, became bishops like himself. His eldest sister, Macrina, became a model of piety, and instrumental in his spiritual sanctification.

His belief in the sanctity of his life, his theological learning, and his strenuous advocacy of the faith embodied in the Nicene clauses, have received the praises of Jerome, Socrates, Theodoret, and many other Christian writers. Indeed such was the estimation in which he was held that some did not hesitate to call him "the Father of Fathers" as well as "the Star of Nyssa."

Along with his brother Basil, and friend Gregory of Nazianzum, Gregory of Nyssa is among the most honored and revered of the Nicene fathers.

Gregory's first inclination or impulse to make a public profession of Christianity is said to have been due to a remarkable dream he had. His mother Emmelia, at her retreat at Annesi, urgently entreated him to be present and take part in a religious ceremony in honor of the Forty Christian Martyrs. He had gone unwillingly, and wearied with his journey and the length of the service, which lasted far into the night, he lay down and fell asleep in the garden. He dreamed that the Martyrs appeared to him and reproached him for his indifference. On awakening he was filled with remorse, and hastened to amend his past neglect by earnest entreaties for mercy and forgiveness. He then realized that God had the right to demand his whole life.

By the powerful persuasions of his sister Macrina, at length, after much struggle, he altered entirely his way of life, severed himself from all secular occupations, and retired to his brother's monastery in the solitudes of Pontus, a beautiful spot where his mother and sister had established a similar place for women.

Here, then, Gregory was settled for several years, and devoted himself to the study of the Scripture and the works of his master Origen. Here, too, his love of natural scenery was deepened so as to find afterwards constant and adequate expression. For in his writings we have in large measure that sentiment of delight in the beauty of nature of which are so few and far between in the whole range of Greek literature.

Shortly after Basil made him Bishop of Nyssa, he encountered opposition. The Arians accused him falsely of mismanagement and saw him arrested and deposed. He escaped and wandered for two years until the appointment of a new emperor ended the religious conflict. Gregory returned to Nyssa where he was warmly welcomed. Basil died soon afterward and Gregory took on a more important role in the defense of the Trinity.

There are two qualities in Gregory's writings not to be found in the same degree in any other Greek teacher: his far-reaching use of philosophical speculation (quite apart from allegory) in bringing out the full meaning of Church doctrines and Bible truths; and his excellence of style, which proved that patristic Greek could rise to the level of the best of its time.

No father has discussed the subject of Adam's nature more fully than Gregory in his treatise *On the Making of Man*. In a number of his writings Gregory affirms and defends the Unity of the Godhead—the three persons of the Trinity being distinct, yet one God. He also taught that it is not so much our sins that keep us out of Heaven as our unwillingness to accept God's freely offered forgiveness. In his great treatise *On the Soul and the Resurrection*, he rests a great deal on the parallel between the relation of man to his body, and that of God to the world. "The soul is as a cord drawn out of mud; God draws to Himself what is His own." He calls the human spirit "an influx of the divine in-breathing."

An early painting of the forty martyred soldiers as recalled in Gregory's dream.

On a cold, wintery day in March A.D. 320, forty Armenian soldiers refused to sacrifice to false gods as ordered by emperor Agricola. They were therefore stripped and placed on a frozen lake to die. All remained resolute to their Christian faith, exclaiming, "We are soldiers of the Lord and fear no hardship. What is death for us but an entrance into eternal life?" On this day, March 9, 320, singing hymns, they stood shivering on the pond as the sun sank.

Baffled, Agricola ordered hot baths around the pond. Surely the warm water would lure the men off the ice! But the crisp night air carried a prayer to all ears: "Lord, there are forty of us engaged in this battle; grant that forty may be crowned and not one be wanting from this sacred number."

Key Writings of Gregory: 1. *Gregory of Nyssa Against Eunomius;* 2. *On the Holy Spirit;* 3. *Against the Followers of Macedonius;* 4. *On the Holy Trinity, and of the Godhead of the Holy Spirit;* 5. *On "Not Three Gods";* 6. *On the Faith;* 7. *Ascetic and Moral Treatises;* 8. *Treatise On Virginity;* 9. *On Infants' Early Deaths;* 10. *On Pilgrimages;* 11. *Philosophical Works;* 12. *On the Making of Man;* 13. *On the Soul and the Resurrection;* 14. *Apologetic Works;* 15. *The Great Catechism;* 16. *Oratorical Works;* 17. *On the Baptism of Christ;* 18. *Letters* (18).

John Chrysostom 347-407
"Golden-mouthed"

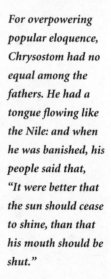

The "Schism of Antioch," as it was called, had lasted for seventeen years at the time of Chrysostom's birth, and during his boyhood it was at its height. Arianism had disputed the ecclesiastical ground with Orthodoxy and strife was running high. Bitter controversies often ended in riots and even bloodshed. The Church was yearning for such a one as Chrysostom to guide it back on track to its grand purpose.

In the humble home of the Greek widow Anthusa the seeds of greatness were being sown. John Chrysostom (Golden-mouthed), was one of the brightest ornaments of the ancient Greek churches. He was born, about the year 347, at Antioch in Syria, where he spent most of his public life. From infancy, he was taught in the things of God by his pious mother, who decided to renounce the opportunities in society and forego remarriage after her husband's death, that she might devote herself to the spiritual training and education of her only son. With a mother's care she strove to win his heart to Christ by her love and holy example.

The boyhood of the young disciple was passed in stirring times. He was only fourteen years old when Emperor Julian, known as "the Apostate," succeeded the sons of Constantine on the Imperial throne and made it his first business to restore the paganism that his great predecessor had renounced. The city where the disciples were first called "Christians" was the scene of Julian's chief attempt. Near Antioch was the famous grove of Daphne, formerly consecrated to the worship of Apollo, then the site of a Christian church and cemetery. The Emperor caused the church to be destroyed, the bodies of the buried Christians there to be exhumed, and the temple of the Sun god to be restored to its former magnificence. Serious riots ensued, the temple was destroyed by fire as soon as rebuilt, and many lost their lives. In revenge Julian closed the cathedral at Antioch and confiscated its treasures.

When John was eighteen years old, Anthusa placed him with Libanius, the most celebrated rhetorician of his time, to study the art of advocacy. Chrysostom soon became his favorite pupil. Libanius regretfully said upon his deathbed, "John would have been my successor, had not the Christians stolen him from us." For some years the young orator studied and practiced assiduously acquiring use of those weapons that he was hereafter so nobly to employ in Christian warfare. But his religious convictions already influenced him in another direction. Although strongly feeling the attractions of the world, and in particular

For overpowering popular eloquence, Chrysostom had no equal among the fathers. He had a tongue flowing like the Nile: and when he was banished, his people said that, "It were better that the sun should cease to shine, than that his mouth should be shut."

passionately fond of the theater, the influence of his mother never left him, and he decided to renounce the world for Christ. He sought the counsel of Meletius, Bishop of Antioch, a man of devout and gentle spirit. By Meletius he was more fully instructed, and baptized, after long probation, at age twenty-three. The ardent youth now found the profession of the law uncongenial. He was already adept in the pleader's art, and had won his first successes, but it seemed to him at variance with Christian integrity. The lessons of Diodorus, another of his teachers, opened his mind to the fullness of Scripture, and were invaluable in later years in leading him to a wise understanding of Biblical truth.

Through such influences, Chrysostom was attracted to a student's life and spent some time as a hermit in the montains. But his constitution was not cut out for such a life and he returned to his calling to preach the Word of God as a deacon in Antioch. He acquired great influence in the city as a thinker and teacher, and in 386 was ordained to the priesthood.

The number of Chrysostom's sermons is as remarkable as their excellence. At Antioch he preached twice every week, on Saturday and Sunday, as well as on every special holiday. His discourses were delivered from memory, while he would often

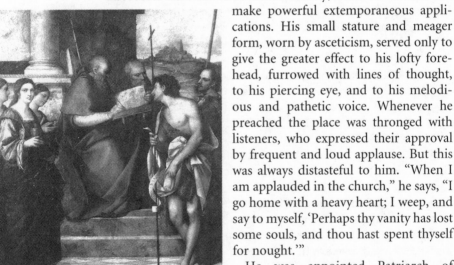

Early painting of Chrysostom as Bishop of Antioch.

make powerful extemporaneous applications. His small stature and meager form, worn by asceticism, served only to give the greater effect to his lofty forehead, furrowed with lines of thought, to his piercing eye, and to his melodious and pathetic voice. Whenever he preached the place was thronged with listeners, who expressed their approval by frequent and loud applause. But this was always distasteful to him. "When I am applauded in the church," he says, "I go home with a heavy heart; I weep, and say to myself, 'Perhaps thy vanity has lost some souls, and thou hast spent thyself for nought.'"

He was appointed Patriarch of Constantinople in 398 against his own desire. But it was not long before he realized the predominent emphasis on worldly pursuits among the clergy, the people, and the Empress Eudocia in particular. He accused the beautiful and treacherous empress as being a "second Jezebel." His preaching addressed these issues in a powerful way, as did his life, and it soon became too much for that corrupt metropolis to bear. Incurring the displeasure of Eudocia, the clergy, and many of the courtiers, he was deposed and banished after being falsely accused of insubordination to authority. In essence, he preached himself right out of the pulpit and into exile.

John was much beloved to the people of Constantinople, though, and they rose up and clamored for his return. Emperor Theodosius finally consented, and Chrysostom's return was strikingly similar to the Lord Jesus' triumphant entry into Jerusalem on Palm Sunday. He rode into the city on a humble mule to the shouts of the people who spread their garments along the path under him.

"There is not anything in the Scriptures which can be considered unimportant. There is not a single sentence of which does not deserve to be meditated on; for it is not the word of man, but of the Holy Spirit, and the least syllable of it contains a hidden treasure."
—John Chrysostom

Though he returned for a brief period at this tumultuous call of his people, he was again exiled because of his condemnation of the wicked activities of Eudocia and others. He died on the road to Pityus on September 14, 407, with his favorite expression on his lips, "God be praised for everything." He left this world cheerful and with great confidence that the work he had been called to carry out would continue by the providence of God and for His glory.

The "Golden-mouthed," though dead, still speaks in more than 600 sermons, that are still in print today in various forms. It is believed by many scholars that John Chrysostom did more to make the pulpit a powerful influence for righteousness than any other preacher in the first Christian millennium.

Key Writings of Chrysostom: 1. *On the Priesthood;* 2. *Seven Discourses on Paul.*

Worth Reading: *The Life and Times of Chrysostom,* by W. R. W. Stevens (1886); *Golden-Mouthed: The Story of John Chrysostom,* by J. N. D. Kelley (2001).

Aurelius Augustine 354-430
Bishop of Hippo

The fifth century saw the decline of one Roman Empire and the rise of another, the Roman Catholic Church. As the barbarians increasingly threatened the Empire, sacking the city of Rome, the influences of Christianity were conquering the forces of paganism. Persecution was all but eliminated, New Testament canon was confirmed, and millions poured into the faith. Yet with all this the world saw a major shift in the Christian Church from being the persecuted to becoming the persecutors. It was at this time we see the birth of a "spiritual Roman empire." But, in an effort to combat heresy and false religion, the Church declared Rome as its center and became the very thing it had labored to destroy. Augustine wrote City of God *(413-426), demonstrating that the truly grandest movement of history was the unseen conflict between sin and salvation, between the city of man and the Kingdom of God.*

reat art thou, O Lord, and greatly to be praised; great is Thy power, and Thy wisdom infinite. And Thee would man praise—man, but a particle of Thy creation; man, that bears about him his mortality, the witness of his sin, the witness that Thou resistest the proud. Yet would man praise Thee—he, but a particle of Thy creation."

O what joy it must have been for Monica, the pious and devoted mother of Augustine, to hear such words spoken by her son (in his *Confessions*) after waiting on the Lord for thirty-two years to see her son come to faith in Christ.

Augustine was born in South Africa in the age when Christianity was flooding paganism out of the Roman world. He was given an excellent education, and Monica, his mother, hoped this might be a means of his more fully reaching God. It was from her that Augustine derived his fineness of organization, his aptitude for speculation, and his strength of spiritual energy.

But Augustine ignored his mother's warnings against youthful lusts and pursued a life of self-gratification and immorality while continuing his classical education. He lived with a woman not his wife and fathered a child. Monica didn't have the words to convince her son of the truth of Christianity, but she determined never to stop praying that he would turn to God.

For the next eleven years Augustine dedicated himself as teacher of rhetoric, first at Thagaste, then Carthage (376-383), then Rome (383), and finally Milan, where he went in 384.

Milan proved to be a turning point in Augustine's life. He went there with much ambition, eager for friends and fame. Instead he met Bishop Ambrose, and was startled to find in him a reasonable mind, a keenness of thought, a powerful faith, and an integrity of character in excess of anything he had ever known. The first result of the preaching of Ambrose was the emancipation of Augustine's mind from the Manichaean

The conversion of Augustine in 387 A.D., after years of faithful prayers by his mother Monica, ushered one of the greatest in heart and mind into the army of King Jesus. His Confessions *and* City of God *are two of the most famous and impactful writings in the history of Christendom.*

Augustine with his mother, Monica, from an old print by Ary Sheffer.

misrepresentations of Christianity. He was convinced that Manichaeism was false, although as yet he could not see that Christ was the truth. And he resolved to become a spectator in the Christian church until his mind could come to a fuller knowledge and clearer conviction. During the next two years he rejected Manichaeism, discovered Neo-Platonism, came under the influence of Ambrose, and finally in 386 after much mental and spiritual anguish, he gave his life to Christ.

The impression that Ambrose made upon him is thus described by himself: "That man of God received me as a father, and showed me an episcopal kindness on my arrival. At once I was attracted by him, not because he was a teacher of the truth (which I utterly despaired of finding in the Church), but because of his kindness to myself. I gave much attention to his preaching also, for though I scorned the matter of it, I was anxious to see whether his eloquence was as remarkable as it was commonly reported to be. Gradually, however, as I said within myself, 'How eloquently he speaks,' there entered this other thought, 'How truly he speaks.'" His mother arrived in Milan from Africa and received the news of Augustine's abandonment of Manichaeism with composure, as if she had expected such an answer to her prayers.

Possessed by a deep sense of spiritual things and a wonderful intellect, Augustine left a stronger mark on the Western church than any other theologian.

Augustine, though a Christian, was not yet baptized, and as Easter was at that time a favorite season for baptism, he returned to Milan about a month previous to that festival. On Easter eve, 387, he was received into the Church by baptism, along with his son Adeodatus and his friend Alypius. Ambrose baptizing Augustine was a spectacle that could not fail to stimulate the imagination of the Church, and fancy has been pleased to commemorate the scene by attributing to it the origin of the greatest of Christian hymns, the *Te Deum*. Ecclesiastical legend tells us that Ambrose uttered the first clause and Augustine responded with the second, and so on alternately till the hymn was complete. But the most interested spectator of an event whose importance to the Church could not at that time be understood, was undoubtedly Monica. She now saw the fulfillment of her lifelong desire, and possibly in her soul was saying, "Now, lettest Thou Thy servant depart in peace." Very shortly after the saintly and intellectual woman, to whom the world owes so much, passed into her rest in the fifty-sixth year of her age after a brief illness of nine days.

In his *Confessions* Augustine spoke of his grief and weeping for the mother "now gone from my sight, who for years had wept over me, that I might live in your [God's] sight." She died a happy woman for she had seen her prayers answered, and both her husband and her son had become believers.

Augustine returned to North Africa planning to live a quiet monastic life near his native Tagaste, but he was not permitted to devote himself to the retired life. Instead, the people persisted in electing him first a priest and then, in 395, a bishop at the town of Hippo. For the next thirty-eight years Augustine ministered faithfully among the people of Hippo. His numerous letters and writings spread his influence throughout the Christian world of the late Roman Empire.

Of his preaching we have such opportunity to judge as is afforded by printed sermons. Of these we have almost four hundred. Most are short, because as a bishop he sat while his audience stood, and simple in style, because, as he said, a simple style is the one to which people can listen with the least weariness. His sermons were never abstruse, for his audience was composed of sailors, fishermen, boatbuilders, peasants, and tradesmen, with a small sprinkling of educated persons. He adopted a colloquial style, not only because the congregation frequently interrupted him with applause, and even with questions, but on principle: "I would rather," he says, "that the grammarians found fault with me than that the people should misunderstand me." Yet while he aimed at simplicity of expression, there is no theological or philosophical truth that he avoided in the face of the congregation. His felicity in illustration enabled him to explain what preachers of less vigorous intelligence would do well to leave alone. Discussions that might otherwise be wordy are relieved in his sermons by flashes of genius that irradiate the whole subject, and by appeals to those experiences in which the plain man and the cultured thinker are alike interested.

Seventeenth-century painting of Augustine by Spanish artist Murillo.

It is as a writer more than any of his other great qualities that Augustine has acquired such a commanding influence.

Among his 113 surviving works the best known are the *Confessions* (Confessiones), comprising reflections on his life and conversion, and *The City of God* (De civitate Dei). In the twenty-two books of *The City of God*, history is presented as a conflict between two opposing cities: the city of God—consisting of Christians—and the city of Satan—consisting of pagan unbelievers. His *Confessions* are the history of his heart; his *Retractions*, of his mind; while his *Letters* show us of his activity in the Church.

Shortly before Augustine wrote his classic *The City of God*, Jerome exclaimed, "The city which has taken the whole world is itself taken!" This in reference to the destruction of Rome by invaders, led by Alaric the Visigoth. Pagans declared that Christians were at last being punished by the traditional gods for ancient Rome. Augustine answered their charges with his masterpiece, *The City of God*.

The influence and strength of Augustine's love for his Savior and the people of God survived the heresies of Donatism, Manichaeism, and Pelagianism. The result was a stability and confidence in the Christian faith for present and subsequent generations.

In 430, the city of Hippo was beseiged by barbarians. Augustine remained at his post and continued to minister and write. But three months after the seige commenced, he contracted a serious fever that confined him to his bed. He passed into glory in humble and solitary communion with the God he so adored and so faithfully served.

No theologian has exercised so great an influence as Augustine. The greatest of the medieval schoolmen and the leading reformers were alike his pupils. His intellect was at once comprehensive and acute; and it was propelled by a spirit of unflagging intensity and ardor, while it wielded as its instrument a style peculiarly his own and eminently effective. He possessed the intelligent and creative eloquence that expands language to ampler meanings, and compels it to a flexibility which fits into every turn of feeling and cranny of thought. He never passes from a thought till he has fitted it with its final and best expression. Often, indeed, it is with intense labor he arrives at this, but he always does arrive at it, and with one brilliant saying that makes further discussion superfluous, he wipes out the memory of pages of sterile argument. And even the most wearisome of his pages are to some extent redeemed by the earnest personal presence that shines through them. Happily his character reflected the truth and efficacy of the doctrines he expounded. His life and his writings alike breathe an enthusiasm for God and His grace.

The City of God represents Augustine's learning, breadth of intelligence, his sympathy, theological thinking, his skill as a reasoner, eloquence, and his interest in all human and divine affairs.

Key Writings of Augustine: 1. *The Confessions of Augustine* (395); 2. *The City of God (413);* 3. *Sermons Against Arianism (413);* 4. *Retractions (426);* 5. *On the Trinity;* 6. *Faith, Hope, and Charity;* 7. *The Problem of Free Choice;* 8. *The Literal Meaning of Genesis.*

Worth Reading: *The Complete Works of Augustine,* by Gaume (1836); The earliest printed edition of Augustine's collected works was by Amerbach, 9 vols., Basel, (1506); *Life and Labors of Augustine,* by C. Bourke (1880); *Augustine of Hippo: Life and Controversies,* by Gerald Bonner (1986); *Augustine: His Thought in Context,* by T. Kermit Scott (1995).

Patrick of Ireland 386-459
Shining Light in a Dark Age

Ireland was wholly heathen in the fifth century, and ripe for Patrick who was the chosen vessel of God to Christianize the land and organize its Church. While in captivity in Ireland, he often reflected how blessed it would be to carry the glad tidings of Jesus to the land of his exile and those who held him captive. His prayer was answered in a great way.

n November 8, 432, Patrick arrived in Ireland to begin his ministry. Patrick was born in the Christian town of Bonavern, near present day Glasglow, Scotland. Although his mother taught him the Christian faith, he preferred to pursue pleasure in his early years.

At the tender age of sixteen, while playing by the sea one day, Irish pirates captured Patrick and sold him into slavery to a cruel Druid chieftan on a farm in Ireland. Alone in the fields, caring for sheep, Patrick began to remember the Word of God his mother had taught him. Reflection and changed circumstances made him regret his past of selfish pleasure-seeking, and he turned to Christ as his Savior.

We have his own words from his "Confession" detailing his conversion: "I was sixteen years old and knew not the true God and was carried away captive; but in that strange land (Ireland) the Lord opened my unbelieving eyes, and although late I called my sins to mind, and was converted with my whole heart to the Lord my God, who regarded my low estate, had pity on my youth and ignorance, and consoled me as a father consoles his children. . .Well, every day I used to look after sheep and I used to pray often during the day. The love of God and fear of him increased more and more in me, and my faith began to grow, and my spirit stirred up, so that in one day I would pray as many as a hundred times and nearly as many at night. Even when I was staying out in the woods or on the mountain, I used to rise before dawn for prayer, in snow and frost and rain, and I felt no ill effect and there was no slackness in me. As I now realize, it was because the Spirit was glowing in me."

In A.D. 432 Patrick went as a missionary to Ireland. Taken there in slavery while just a teenager, he returned to lead multitudes of Irish people to the Christian faith.

Six years after his captivity, Patrick escaped and returned to his family in Britain, yet his heart increasingly longed to return to his Irish captors and share the Gospel of Jesus Christ with them. Returning to Ireland in A.D. 432, Patrick preached the gospel to the pagan tribes in the Irish language he had learned as a slave. He spent some thirty years there and evangelized and baptized many thousands—some estimate over one hundred thousand. He lost count. More than two hundred churches were established. His ministry confronted and challenged pagan practices and soon heathen songs were replaced with hymns praising Jesus Christ as Lord.

Patrick was known as the apostle of the Irish, as Augustine was the apostle of the Saxons and Columba of the Picts.

One can only imagine the impact of Patrick's evangelism in Ireland in the generations to follow. The spiritual revival that followed clearly carried the torch of truth throughout the "Island" and beyond for centuries.

As wave after wave of German barbarians swept over the Roman Empire in the fifth and sixth centuries, Roman political structure disintegrated, and centers of learning and education disappeared. This period is often referred to as "the Dark Ages," when civilization itself seemed on the verge of vanishing. During this dismal time, it was the Irish who preserved the books and learning of the classical and Christian authors.

It was Ireland and Celtic Christianity that had never been part of the Roman Empire. Not connected with the papal system or the Roman hierarchy, Celtic Christianity developed around individual leaders and monasteries, and the Irish monks were leaders in spreading and preserving the Christian faith. The study of the Scriptures was central to the Celtic monastic schools, and the scriptorium was a key part of the monastic compound. Here the monks carefully copied the Scriptures and many of the Greek and Latin classics. Many of the earliest Latin manuscripts available today are those made by the Irish monks, and more than half of our Biblical commentaries between the years of 650 and 850 were written by Irishmen.

As we examine history, it is fair to say that thousands came to Christ because a young boy was moved by the Spirit of God to return to the land and the people that enslaved him, that they too might know the love and grace of his Savior.

Key Writings of Patrick: 1. *Confession;* 2. *Epistle Concerning Coroticus.*

Worth Reading: *How the Irish Saved Civilization,* by Thomas Cahill; *The Real St. Patrick,* by John M. Holmes.

Clovis of France *466-511*

"Savior" of Western Europe

Now that the Roman Empire was in ruins, what would prevent the destruction of its Church by the barbarians who had seized power? In the providence of an always faithful God, there arose a king from Gaul (France) who cast off the paganism he inherited, and by the mighty hand of his Maker, evangelized many nations in the name of King Jesus. Christianity has been the predominant religion of Europe ever since.

efore the events that brought about his conversion, Clovis, King of the Franks, lived and ruled like many of the pagan kings before him. Though he married a Christian woman, Clotilda, he did not at first embrace the faith she held so precious. He saw the "Christian" Roman Empire destroyed, and the death of his first-born son just days after his baptism. "What kind of God would be real, in light of these awful events?" he thought. Clovis was worldly and violent, but the God of Heaven and Earth had grander plans for this young King.

Clotilda was a very pious woman and loved and honored her husband. She shared her faith in Christ with him both in word and deed, but he remained resolute in his denial. But in the year 496, amidst a very fierce battle against the Alemanni, Clovis saw his forces in a losing effort and lifting his eyes to Heaven he cried out, "God of my Queen Clotilda, grant me victory, and I here now vow to worship none other than you." Clovis and the Franks were victorious, and true to his word he was baptized at Reims by Remigius, bishop of that city. His sister Albofleda and three thousand of his warriors embraced Christianity.

Remigius continued to instruct the warrior king in the faith. Much of what Clovis heard seemed to demonstrate the passion of genuine love he had for his Savior. In one instance, Remigius described the wrongful persecution of Christ and His death on the Cross, and the king started up angrily, exclaiming, "If I had been there with my Franks, I would have avenged His wrongs!"

The conversion of Clovis to the religion of the majority of his subjects soon brought about the union of the Gallo-Romans with their barbarian conquerors. While in all the other Germanic kingdoms founded on the ruins of the Roman Empire the difference of religion between the Christian natives and Arian conquerers was a very active cause of destruction, in the kingdom of the Franks, the contrary was true. The fundamental identity of religious beliefs and equality of political rights made national and patriotic sentiments universal and produced the most perfect harmony between the two races.

The conversion and baptism of Clovis is of primary importance in the history of the Church in that it rallied to its support the most powerful of the barbarian kingdoms and thus insured the triumph of Christianity among the Germanic tribes. Moreover, it marked the beginning of the end of Arianism and guaranteed the unity of the Church in the West.

From that point on, the Frankish kingdom was the representative and defender of Christian interests throughout the West, primarily due to the determination of King Clovis to see the influence of Christianity permeate the lives of the people in the throughout the various lands. Those historians who do not understand the problems of religious psychology have concluded

that Clovis embraced Christianity solely from political motives, but nothing is futher from the truth. On the contrary, all evidence proves that his conversion was sincere.

Master now of a vast kingdom, Clovis displayed the same talent in governing that he had displayed in conquering it. From Paris, which he had finally made his capital, he administered the various provinces through the agency of counts (comites) established in each city. These counts were selected by him from the aristocracy of both races, conformably to the principle of absolute equality between Romans and barbarians, a principle that dominated his entire policy. He caused the Salic Law (*Lex Salica*) to be reduced to written form, revised and adapted to the new social conditions under which his fellow barbarians were subsequently to live.

King Clovis punishing a rebel. Nineteenth-century engraving by Alphonse de Neuville for Great Men and Famous Women (1894).

Acknowledging the Christian Church as the foremost civilizing force, he protected it in every way possible, especially by providing for it the National Council of Orleans (511), at which the bishops of Gaul settled many questions pertaining to the relations between Church and state.

As a Christian statesman he succeeded in accomplishing what neither the genius of Theodoric the Great nor that of any contemporary barbarian king could achieve. Upon the ruins of the Roman Empire he built up a powerful social and political system that was founded on the Word of God as its standard. Its influence spread rapidly and dominated European civilization during many centuries. France, Germany, Belgium, Holland, and Switzerland, in addition to northern Spain and northern Italy were, for a time, under the civilizing regime of the Christianized Frankish Empire.

Worth Reading: *History of the Political Institutions of Ancient France* (1875); *The French Empire*, (1888); *Establishment of Christianity With the Gauls* (1889); *The Franks*, by L. Sargeant (1898).

Benedict of Nursia 480-547
Founder of the Benedictines

ST. BENE DICT+

There are many whose deeds and influence combined to shape the Church of Western Europe. Augustine, Patrick, and Clovis captivate our minds and hearts as eminent fathers of the faith. Yet there is one whose simple life and godly example remains undimmed to this day, Benedict of Nursia. Not only was he considered the father of Western monks, but he has been called the Co-Patron of Europe, along with Cyril and Methodius. Through the influence of Benedict's spiritual sons and daughters, Western civilization was nurtured and largely preserved. In fact much of Europe's Christian roots were planted directly or indirectly through the work of the Benedictines, the black monks of legend who named a religious order after Benedict.

enedict was born in Nursia, a village high in the mountains northeast of Rome. His parents sent him to Rome for classical studies but his tender conscience found the life in such an immoral city too degrading. So "giving over his books, and forsaking his father's house and wealth, with a mind only to serve God, he sought for some place where he might attain to the desire of his holy purpose." Consequently he fled to Subiaco, southeast of Rome, where he lived as a hermit for three years tended by the monk Romanus.

Benedict's life became one of prayer, silence, and much study of both holy Scripture and histories of Church fathers. As he grew in holy wisdom and stature, he was discovered by a group of monks in Vocovaro, who prevailed upon him to become their spiritual leader. His life of purity and faithfulness to the Word of God soon became too much for the lukewarm monks, so they plotted to poison him. Gregory recounts the tale of Benedict's rescue; when he blessed the pitcher of poisoned wine, it broke into many pieces.

Benedict left the wayward monks and established twelve monasteries with twelve monks each in the area south of Rome. In a thirteenth he lived with "a few, such as he thought would more profit and be better instructed by his own presence." With the establishment of these monasteries began the schools for children, and amongst the first to be brought in were Maurus and Placid.

In 529, he moved to Monte Cassino, about eighty miles southeast of Rome. There he destroyed the pagan temple dedicated to Apollo and built his premier monastery. It was there, too, that he wrote the *Rule for the Monastery of Monte Cassino*, though he envisioned that it could be used elsewhere. His *Rule* was meant to be for the governance of the domestic life of lay individuals who wanted to live in the fullest possible way the

Responding to the secularization of the Church, Benedict of Nursia established the monastery of Monte Cassino and the Benedictine Order in 529. Benedict's Rule for monks (c. 540) became a standard for monastic life and practice.

path that led to God. In other words, it was penned for those whose desire was to live in a radical imitation of Christ.

Benedict's *Rule* lays down no specific tasks for his organization, unlike later orders that specifically dedicated themselves to such charisms as preaching, teaching, combating heresies, emancipating slaves or nursing the sick. Instead, his admonitions were simply to aid a man in his search for God. For Benedict, a monastery was nothing more or less than, "a school for the Lord's service. In drawing up its regulations, we hope to set down nothing harsh, nothing burdensome. The good of all concerned, however, may prompt us to a little strictness in order to amend faults and to safeguard love. Do not be daunted immediately by fear and run away from the road that leads to salvation. It is bound to be narrow at the outset. But as we progress in this way of life and in faith, we shall run on the path of God's commandments, our hearts overflowing with the inexpressible delight of love. Never swerving from his instructions, then, but faithfully observing his teaching until death, we shall through patience share in the sufferings of Christ that we may deserve also to share in his kingdom. Amen."†

Benedict's life ended with an occasion of fitting tenderness. He had one sister, a twin, by the name of Scholastica, and she, too, had from an early age consecrated herself to God. Gregory tells us that Scholastica used to visit her brother once a year and that their meetings would take place in an outbuilding near the gates of Monte Cassino. During their final visit, as it was drawing to a close, she expressed the desire that he not leave her so soon, that they should talk until morning "of the joys of the Heavenly life." Benedict quickly declined, insisting that he could not for any reason remain for a night outside his monastery. Upon his refusal, she is said to have joined her hands together and, putting them on the table in front of her, reclined her head over them in prayer to God. When she once again raised her head, there was immediately such a violent thunderstorm that none could venture forth. To him she said, "I asked thee and you would not listen. I asked God and he heard me." And so, as was her desire, they spent the entire night together in prayer and holy conversation. She died not many days after. Brother and sister both died about the year 547.

During the next 600 years, the Benedictines erected hundreds of monasteries, bringing intellectual and spiritual enrichment to much of Europe.

Eighteenth-century painting of Benedict and his twin sister Scholastica.

"Listen carefully, my son, to the Master's instructions, and attend to them with the ear of your heart. This is advice from a father who loves you; welcome it, and faithfully put it into practice. The labor of obedience will bring you back to him from whom you had drifted through the sloth of disobedience. This message of mine is for all, and armed with the strong and noble weapons of obedience to do battle for the true king, Christ the Lord."
—The Rule of Benedict, Prologue, verses 1-3

Writings of Benedict: *The Rule of Benedict* (Originally titled *The Rule of the Monastery of Monte Cassino*).

† Text in quotes is taken from the *Dialogues*, written by Gregory the Great, on the life and works of Benedict.

Worth Reading: *The Life of Benedict* (or *Dialogues*), by Gregory the Great; *Benedict of Nursia*, by Patrick O'Donovan; *Reading Saint Benedict, Reflections on the Rule*, by Adalbert de Vogüé.

Columba *521-597*
Irish Missionary

Celtic Christianity, as it is often called, was introduced by Columba of Ireland to Northumbria. He was exiled from Ireland and landed in Scotland in 563 where he founded the monastery at Iona. From Iona his followers spread through Scotland and northern England converting thousands to the Gospel of Jesus Christ.

About sixty years after the death of Patrick, Columba was born on December 7, 521, in Donegal, Northern Ireland, to the royal family of Fergus. He became a brilliant, consecrated scholar, committing to memory most of the Scripture. God called him to be a missionary, and his miraculous ministry has caused many historians to deem him one of the eminent Church fathers.

Columba set the foundation for the greatest achievement of the Irish Church and its monks in the sixth and seventh centuries, the Christianization of North Britain.

As a young man, Columba soon took an interest in the Church, joined the monastery at Moville, and was ordained a deacon by Finnian. After studying with a bard called Gemman, Columba was ordained a priest by Etchen, the bishop of Clonfad. Columba entered the monastery of Mobhi Clarainech, but disease attacked the majority of monks and the monastery was disbanded. Columba then decided to travel north where he founded the church of Derry in 546.

In 563, at the age of forty-two, he and twelve of his followers sailed to Scotland, "wishing to go into exile for Christ," where they established a center of missionary activity at Iona. The pure gospel that was preached by Columba and his fellow workers spread over the whole of Scotland, turning it to God. It also overflowed into Ireland and over Northern Europe. His means of spreading the gospel was one wherein twelve men under a leader would go into a new area and literally build a gospel-centered town. Amongst these twelve men there were carpenters, teachers, preachers, and so on, all wonderfully versed in the Word and holy living. Each little colony was enclosed by a wall. Soon this enclosure would be surrounded by students and their families in their own homes, learning the Word and preparing to go out and serve the Lord as missionaries, leaders, and preachers. The men were free to marry, though many did not, in order to serve God without distraction. They remained free from state help, and thereby steered clear of politics. It was the practice of Columban students to never attack other religions. Instead, they taught the simple truth that they believed was weapon enough to accomplish the ends that God had in mind for them. They were blessed to be absolutely independent of Rome.

This impressive ninth-century Celtic cross from Kells Monastery, Ireland, is dedicated to two of Ireland's notable evangelists, Patrick and Columba. The site of this cross housed for many centuries another national treasure of Ireland, the Book of Kells, the illuminated gospel manuscript now in Trinity College, Dublin. Kells Monastery was foundedby Columba, one of the most important figures of the early Christian Church.

Through the Columban process of evangelism the mainland north of Glasgow and Edinburgh, as well as the western islands, was studded with monasteries, whose inmates looked after the spiritual welfare of the neighboring population, all of them dependent on the mother monastery at Iona.

In one of his missionary journeys, as he approached a walled city, Columba found the gates barred against him. He lifted his voice in prayer that God might intervene and allow him access to the people in order to preach. But as he prayed the court magicians began to harass him with loud noises. He then began to sing a psalm. As he sang, God so increased the volume of his voice that he drowned out the cries of the heathen. Suddenly the gates burst open of their own accord. He entered in and preached the gospel, winning many to the Lord.

Columba was the founder of a great Bible school on the island of Hy (off the Southwest coast of Scotland). When he went there the island was so barren and rocky that it could not bear enough food for them all to live. But Columba planted seed with one hand while he held the other high in prayer. Today the island is one of the most fertile in the world. From this Bible-centered island went forth mighty scholars with wisdom and the power of God.

His ministry contrasted sharply with that of Augustine of Canterbury, who later came to Britain. Augustine represented the Roman church, while Columba was a product of the Celtic church of Britain. Revered by both Scotland and Ireland as a great spiritual benefactor and saint, he was passed into the presence of his Savior beside the altar of a local church where he had been engaged in midnight prayer.

Worth Reading: *Life of Columba,* by Adamnan (1874); *Aelfric's Lives of Saints,* ed. Walter William Skeat (1966); *Lives of the Scottish Saints: The Lives of Saints Columba, Servanus, Margaret, and Magnus,* tr. W. M. Metcalfe (1990); *Soldiers of Christ: Saints and Saints' Lives from Late Antiquity and the Early Middle Ages,* by Thomas F. X. Noble; *Columba's Island: Iona from Past to Present,* by E. Mairi MacArthur.

Isidore of Seville 560-636
Spanish Evangelist

More than a century had passed since the fall of the Roman Empire, and its ancient institutions and classic centers of learning were disappearing. In Spain, a new civilization was beginning to evolve itself from the various racial elements that made up its population. For almost two centuries the Goths had been in full control of Spain, and their barbarous manners and contempt of learning threatened greatly to hinder the progress of Spanish civilization. Realizing that the spiritual as well as the material well-being of the nation depended on the full assimilation of foreign elements, Isidore set himself to the task of welding into a homogeneous nation the various peoples who made up the Hispano-Gothic kingdom.

sidore was the son of Severianus and Theodora. He received his elementary education in the Cathedral school of Seville, Spain. He applied himself with great diligence to his studies and in a remarkably short time mastered Latin, Greek, and Hebrew.

Whether Isidore ever embraced monastic life or not is still an open question, but though he himself may never have been affiliated with any of the religious orders, he esteemed them highly.

On the death of Leander, Isidore succeeded him as Bishop of Seville, and he was well respected for his wisdom and piety. He presided over numerous councils in Spain, but it was the fourth council in Toledo where he had the opportunity to serve his country in a mighty way. He availed himself of all the resources of religion and education. At this council, in 633, all the bishops of Spain were in attendance. Isidore, though far advanced in years, presided over its deliberations and was the originator of most of its enactments. It was at this council and through his influence that a decree was passed commanding all bishops to establish seminaries in their Cathe-dral Cities, along the lines of the school already established by Isidore at Seville. Within his own jurisdiction he had availed himself of the resources of education to counteract the growing influence of Gothic barbarism. His was the quickening spirit that animated the educational movement of which Seville was the center. The study of Greek and Hebrew as well as the liberal arts was taught. Interest in law and medicine was greatly encouraged. Through the authority of the fourth council this policy of education was made obligatory upon all the bishops of the kingdom. Long before the Arabs had awakened to an appreciation of Greek philosophy, he had introduced Aristotle to his countrymen.

Isidore was the last of the ancient Christian philosophers, as he was the last of the great Latin fathers. He was undoubtedly the most learned man of his age and exercised a far-reaching and

Isidore was undoubtedly the most learned man of his age and exercised a far-reaching and immeasurable influence on the educational life and spiritual growth of God's people in the Middle Ages.

immeasurable influence on the educational life of the Middle Ages. His contemporary and friend, Braulio, Bishop of Saragossa, regarded him as a man raised up by God to save the Spanish people from the tidal wave of barbarism that threatened to inundate the ancient civilization of Spain.

As a writer, Isidore was prolific and versatile to an extraordinary degree. His voluminous writings may be truly said to constitute the first chapter of Spanish literature. It is not, however, in the capacity of an original and independent writer, but as an exhaustive compiler of all existing knowledge, that literature is most deeply indebted to him. The most important and by far the best-known of all his writings is the *Etymologiae*, or *Origines*, as it is sometimes called. It was written shortly before his death, in the full maturity of his wonderful scholarship, at the request of Braulio. This wonderful book is a vast storehouse in which is gathered, systematized, and condensed all the learning possessed by his time. It is divided into twenty-four books and 154 authors from the past are quoted. Throughout the greater part of the Middle Ages it was the textbook most in use in educational institutions and influenced for Christianity the heart of the civilization. So highly was it regarded as a depository of classical learning and Christian power that in a great measure, it superseded the use of the individual versions of the classics themselves. Not even the Renaissance seemed to diminish the high esteem in which it was held. In fact, it was reprinted ten times between 1470 and 1529.

16th-century icon from one of Isidore's writings. As a writer, Isidore was prolific and versatile to an extraordinary degree. His voluminous writings may be truly said to constitute the first chapter of Spanish literature.

Among the specific scriptural and theological works of Isidore the following are especially worthy of note:

De ortu et obitu patrum qui in Scriptura laudibus efferuntur is a work that treats of the more notable scriptural characters. *Allegoriae quaedam Sacrae Scripturae* deals with the allegorical significance that attaches to the more conspicuous characters of Scripture. In all some two hundred and fifty personalities of the Old and New Testament are thus critiqued. *Secretorum expositiones sacramentorum, seu quaestiones in Vetus Testamentum* is a rendering of numerous Old Testament books, based on the writings of the early fathers of the Church. *Regula monachorum* is his work on the style of life prescribed for monks. Isidore furnishes abundant proof of the true Christian democracy of the religious life by providing for the admission of men of every rank and station of life. Not even slaves were debarred. "God has made no difference between the soul of the slave and that of the freed man." he said. He insisted that all are equal in the sight of God and of the Church.

Worth Reading: The first edition of the works of Isidore was published in folio by Michael Somnius (Paris, 1580); *Works of Isidore,* 7 vols., by Arevalo (1797).

Venerable Bede 672-735
Teacher of the Middle Ages

By the end of the seventh century major shifts in the constitution of religion had taken form. Theological, political, and geographical tensions caused the split of the Church into the Eastern (Greek Orthodox) and Western (Roman Catholic) churches. Islam, a new religion founded by Mohammed, who claimed to be God's prophet, conquered most of the Byzantine Empire and stretched from Spain to central Asia within on hundred years. Instead of becoming entangled in the controversies of the day, Bede dedicated himself to serving God in obscurity and using his gifts to produce some of the finest works of ecclesiastical literature known to man.

o name is more illustrious in the history of literature, science, and religious revival during the Middle Ages than that of Venerable Bede.

Bede, or Beda as he called himself, was born in Jarrow, Northumbria (Northern England). Bede is known as "the venerable," a name given to him in 835 and applied to no other major figure of history. He is also called the "Father of English History," primarily because of his   completion in 731 of supreme achievement, the invaluable *Ecclesiastical History of the English Nation.* In it he sets forth in detail the first authoritative history of Christian origins in Britain and surrounding nations from the first generation before Christ up to 729. The book speaks of the Celtic people who were converted to Christianity during the first three centuries of the Christian era. It details the invasion of the Anglo-Saxon pagans in the fifth and sixth centuries, and their subsequent conversion by Celtic missionaries from the north and west, and Roman missionaries from the south and east. His work is our chief source for the history of the British Isles during this period.

Bede's motive for recording history reveals his deepest desires. He clearly states his purpose in his writings when he says, "For if history records good things of good men, the thoughtful hearer is encouraged to imitate what is good; or if it records evil of wicked men, the good, religious reader or listener is encouraged to avoid all that is sinful and perverse, and to follow what he is in God."

At the conclusion of his classic book he gives a brief autobiographical sketch: "I was born in the territory of the Jarrow monastery, and at the age of seven I was, by the care of my relations, given to the most reverend Abbot Benedict, and afterwards to Ceolfrid, to be educated. From that time I have spent the whole of my life within that monastery, devoting all my pains to the study of the Scriptures. And amid the observance

Bede became known as "The Venerable Bede," the greatest scholar of Saxon England. **His Ecclesiastical History of the English Nation** *is the source of most information on early English history. Bede's thirty-seven works include grammar, history, hymns, and the lives of saints. He also introduced the Christian chronology (B.C. —before Christ, and A.D.— anno Domini) to Europe.*

of monastic discipline and the daily charge of singing in the Church, it has been ever my delight to learn or teach or write. In

my nineteenth year I was admitted to the diaconate and in my thirtieth to the priesthood, both by the hands of the most reverend Bishop John [John of Beverley], and at the bidding of Abbot Ceolfrid. From the time of my admission to the priesthood to my present fifty-ninth year, I have endeavored for my own use and that of my brethren, to make brief notes upon the holy Scripture, either out of the works of the venerable Fathers or in conformity with their meaning and interpretation."

Bede was a prodigious writer, the author of forty-five volumes, including commentaries, textbooks, and translations. His range was encyclopedic, embracing the whole field of contemporary knowledge. He wrote grammatical and chronological works, hymns and other verse, letters, and homilies, and compiled the first martyrology with historical notes. These are in Latin, but Bede was also the first known writer of English prose (no longer extant).

Bede is depicted in art as an old monk writing with a quill and rule.

Bede's Biblical writings were extensive and important in their time, but it is as an historian that he is most famous. His method of dating events from the Incarnation of Christ—*Anno Domini*—came into general use through the popularity of his *Ecclesiastical History*.

He was trained by the abbots Benedict Biscop and Ceolfrid, and probably accompanied the latter to Jarrow in 682. There he led a life of simplicity and devotion, finding his chief pleasure in being always occupied in learning, teaching, or writing, and zealous in the performance of his duties. His works show that he had a command of all the learning of his time. He was proficient in patristic literature, and quoted from many of the classical writers, some with disapproval. His works were so widely spread throughout Europe and so much esteemed that he won the name of "the teacher of the Middle Ages." He knew Greek and some Hebrew, and his Latin was impeccable. In most things his good sense was evident, and he was kind and generous. His love of truth and fairness, his unfeigned piety, and his devotion to the service of others made him an exceedingly attractive individual.

Bede was perhaps the best known and most influential Biblical historian, especially in England. He was a careful scholar and distinguished stylist. His works De Temporibus *and* De Temporum Ratione *established the idea of dating events anno domini (A.D.), which we still use today.*

The prayer with which he closed his *Ecclesiastical History* revealed the heart of a man who spent a great deal of time meditating on eternity: "I pray you, noble Jesus, that as you have graciously granted me joyfully to imbibe the words of Your Knowledge, so You will also of Your bounty grant me to come at length to Yourself, the fount of all wisdom, and to dwell in Your presence forever."

But the best-known story is related by his friend and co-laborer, Cuthbert, of how when illness and weakness came upon him at the end of his life, his translation of John's Gospel into the English tongue was still unfinished. Despite sleepless nights and days of weariness, he continued his task, and though he made what speed he could, he took every care in comparing the text and preserving its accuracy. "I don't want my boys," he said, "to read a lie or to work to no purpose after I am gone." His friends begged him to rest, but he insisted on working. "We never read without weeping," remarked one of them.

"I can with truth declare," writes Cuthbert of his beloved master Bede, "that I never saw with my eyes or heard with my ears anyone return thanks so unceasingly to the living God."

When it came to the last day, he called his scribe, Wilbert, to him and told him to write with all possible speed. "There is still a chapter wanting," said the boy as the day wore on. "Had you not better rest for a while?" But Bede persisted with his task. "Be quick with your writing," he answered, "for I shall not hold out much longer."

Bede is shown here in A.D. 735 at the end of his life dictating to Wilbert. "The Venerable Bede Translates John" is a painting by J. D. Penrose. He loved to spend time in the Scriptures and to meditate in his small stone hut, "alone with God."

When night fell, the boy said, "There is yet one sentence not written." "Write quickly," Bede replied. The young scribe completed his task and rejoiced, "It is finished!" "Thou hast spoken truth," Bede answered, "it is finished. Take my head in thy hands for it much delights me to sit amidst any holy place where I used to pray, that so sitting I may call upon my Father." When it was done, he said, "All is finished now." Then after sending for his fellow monks and distributing to them his few belongings, in a broken voice he sang the *Gloria Patri*. When he had named the "Holy Ghost," he breathed his last, and so departed to the heavenly kingdom.

Bede's influence was perpetuated through the school founded at York by one of his star pupils, Archbishop Egbert, and was spread throughout Europe by Alcuin, who studied there before becoming master of Charle-magne's palace school at Aachen.

Key Writings of Bede: 1. *The Ecclesiastical History of the English People* (731); 2. *Homilies on the Gospels;* 3. *The Lives of the Holy Abbots of Weremouth and Jarrow: Benedict, Ceolfrid, Easterwine, Sigfrid, Huetberht;* 4. *Commentary on the Acts of the Apostles;* 5. *Conversion of England: A Biblical Miscellany;* 6. *The Abbreviated Psalter.*

Worth Reading: *Northumbria in the Days of Bede* (1976), by Peter Hunter Blair; *Bede and His World: The Jarrow Lectures* (1994); *Bede as Early Medieval Historian* (1946), by Charles W. Jones; *Bede and Gregory the Great* (1964), by Paul Meyvaert; *Bede, His Life, Times and Works* (1935), by A. H. Thompson.

The Baptism of Charlemagne. During his reign, Charlemagne made reluctant pagans, such as the Saxons and others he conquered, receive baptism. He also imposed a tax of ten percent of all income, called a tithe, on all Christians within his kingdom to support religious life.

Charlemagne 742-814
Charles the Great

Western Europe was falling into decay when Charlemagne (Charles the Great) became king of the Franks in 768. For the most part, people had all but forgotten religion, education, and the arts. Boldly, Charlemagne conquered kingdoms and barbarian strongholds. By restoring the roots of learning, order, and religion, he preserved society, revived culture, and rejuvenated the Christian faith in Medieval Europe.

 harlemagne (Charles the Great), the greatest of Medieval kings, was born on April 2, 742, in Northern Europe. His father was the famous Frankish king Pepin the Short, and his mother was Bertha, daughter of the Count of Leon. He bore the characteristics of his people—strength of body, courage of spirit, pride of race, and a crude simplicity—which enabled him to accomplish such great revival.

After his father's death in 768, he shared the kingdom with his brother, Carloman. Charlemagne received the portion of rule previously in his father's hands, and Carloman received his uncle's reign. Yet relations between the two were strained, and Charlemagne bore his brother's unfriendliness and jealousy most patiently, and could not be provoked to be angry with him. Carloman died three years later from disease, leaving Charlemagne to reign over the entire kingdom.

His mother, Berthra, passed her old age with him in great honor. He entertained the greatest veneration for her, and there was never any disagreement between them except when he divorced the daughter of King Desiderius, whom he had married to please his mother. He cherished with the greatest fervor and devotion the principles of the Christian religion that had been instilled in him by his mother from infancy.

Charlemagne carried his religious passion into all his conquests and his reign as king. He extended his influence with firm military organization and propelled it with deliberate commitment to Christ and His Church. His vision was beyond comprehension and could will the means as well as affect the ends. His abilities were such as could lead an army, persuade an assembly, humor the nobility, and dominate the clergy.

He loved administration and organization more than war. His purpose in battle was to force some unity of government and faith upon a Western Europe torn for centuries by conflicts of power and greed. During his reign he sent out more than fifty

"By the sword and the cross," he became master of Western Europe. Through his enlightened leadership the roots of learning and order were restored to Medieval Europe.

It was during Charlemagne's reign that the first bell was cast by the monk Tancho. The emperor was so much pleased with its sweet and solemn tones, that he ordered it to be placed on his chapel as the call to prayer or worship. Hence the origin of church bells.

military expeditions. He rode as commander at the head of at least half of them. His battles were chiefly against the Lombards, Saxons, and Arabs. He moved his armies over wide reaches of country with unbelievable speed, but every move was brilliantly planned in advance. Before each campaign he told the counts, princes, and bishops throughout his realm how many men they should bring, what arms they were to carry, and even what to load in the supply wagons. He so largely increased the Frank kingdom, which was already great and strong when he received it at his father's hands, that more than double its former territory was added to it.

By 800, Charlemagne was the undisputed ruler of Western Europe. He was strong enough in body and nerves to bear a thousand responsibilities, perils, and crises, even to his sons' plotting to kill him. His vast realm covered what are now France, Switzerland, Belgium, and the Netherlands. It included half of present-day Italy and Germany, part of Austria, and parts of Spain. By thus establishing a central government over Western Europe, Charlemagne restored much of the unity of the old Christian Church and paved the way for the develop-

In the year 800, Charlemagne's empire extended across much of what is now Western Europe.

ment of modern Europe. In his desire to recapture the glory of the Roman Empire, Charlemagne set up schools throughout his empire and provided funds that allowed monks to copy the works of Greek and Roman authors. But Charlemagne's empire crumbled soon after his death, and the promise of returning the glory of Rome to Western Europe soon faded.

One of many instances worthy of recognition in the life of Charlemagne is the conquest and conversion of Witikind. The barbarian Westphalians were again ravaging the Frankish frontiers, under the command of Witikind, their most popular chief. Their cruelty was met with retaliation by the forces of Charlemagne's army. The ensuing battle left Witikind's troops nearly annihilated. Yet the spirit of the barbarians, supported by an indomitable passion for war and plunder, continued as strong as ever. Witikind continued his campaigns, even when suffering nothing but disasters. Finally, Charlemagne broke their pagan spirit (more by policy than war), and won them over to the Christian faith.

Charlemagne had deep sympathy for the peasants and believed that government should be for the benefit of the governed. When he came to the throne, various local governors, called "counts," had become lax and oppressive. To reform them, he expanded the work of investigators, called *missi dominici*. He prescribed their duties in documents called capitularies and sent them out in teams of two churchman and a noble. They rode to all parts of the realm, inspecting government, administering justice, and reawakening all citizens to their civil and religious duties. His generosity extended beyond his own realm, though. When he discovered that there were Christians living in poverty in Syria, Egypt, and Africa, at Jerusalem, Alexandria, and Carthage, he had compassion on their wants and sent money overseas to them. The reason that he zealously strove to make friends with the kings beyond seas was that he might supply some relief to the Christians living under their rule.

He was temperate in eating and drinking, abominated drunkenness, and kept in good health despite every exposure and hardship. He often hunted, or took vigorous exercise on horseback. He was a good swimmer, and liked to bathe in the warm springs of Aachen. He rarely entertained, preferring to hear music or the reading of a book while he ate. While at table, he listened to reading or music. The subjects of the readings were the stories and deeds of olden time. He was especially fond of Augustine's books, and especially of the one entitled *The City of God*.

Twice a year Charlemagne summoned the chief men of the empire to discuss its affairs. In all problems he was the final arbiter, even in Church issues, and he largely unified church and state.

Like every great man he valued time, he heard cases in the morning while dressing and putting on his shoes. Behind his poise and majesty were passion and energy, and his vital force was not consumed by his many battles. He gave himself also, with never-aging enthusiasm, to science, law, literature, and theology. It grieved him to think of any part of the Earth, or

The baptism of Witikind, in the presence of his conqueror, Charlemagne, is powerfully portrayed in this nineteenth-century photogravure, reproduced from a painting by Paul Thumann.

61

any section of knowledge, unmastered or unexplored. In some ways he was mentally ingenuous. He scorned superstition and proscribed diviners and soothsayers, but he accepted many mythical marvels, and exaggerated the power of legislation to induce goodness or intelligence. This simplicity of soul had its fair side. There was in his thought and speech a directness and honesty seldom seen in men of distinction. He could be ruthless when policy required and was especially intense in his efforts to spread Christianity. Yet he was a man of great kindness, many charities, warm friendships, and varied loves.

Fourteenth-century icon of Charlemagne crowned king of the Franks (768). Grandes Chroniques de France, Paris, France.

Of his pious character, much of his communication was about religion. He would throw out scriptural quotations at corrupt officials or worldly clerics with such intensity that any suspicion that his piety was a political ploy falls completely unjustified. Eginhard records that, "He cherished with the greatest fervor and devotion the principles of the Christian religion, which had been instilled into him from infancy. He was at great pains to improve the church reading and psalmody, for he was well skilled in both although he neither read in public nor sang."

He wept at the death of his sons and his daughter. The poem *Ad Carolum regem Theodulf* draws a pleasant picture of the Emperor at home: "On his arrival from labors his children gather about him; son Charles takes off the father's cloak, son Louis his sword; his six daughters embrace him, bring him bread, wine, apples, flowers; the bishop comes in to bless the King's food; Alcuin is near to discuss letters with him; the diminutive Eginhard runs to and fro like an ant, bringing in enormous books."

The conquest of heathen peoples was not thought complete until they were Christianized and the newly acquired territory had been provided with a well-ordered and comprehensive ecclesiastical establishment.

In his old age he foresaw, like Diocletian, that his overreaching empire needed quick defense at many points at once. He therefore divided it in 806 among his three sons—Pepin, Louis, and Charles. But Pepin died in 810, Charles in 811; only Louis remained, so absorbed in piety as to seem unfit to govern a rough and treacherous world. In 813, at a solemn ceremony, Louis was elevated from the rank of king to that of emperor, and the old monarch uttered his gratitude: "Blessed be Thou, O Lord God, Who hast granted me the grace to see with my own eyes my son seated on my throne!"

Four months later, in 814, while wintering at Aachen, he was seized with a high fever, and developed pleurisy. He tried to cure himself by taking only liquids, but after an illness of seven days he died, in the forty-seventh year of his reign and the seventy-second year of his life. He was buried under the dome of the cathedral at Aachen, dressed in his imperial robes.

Worth Reading: *The Civilization of Charlemagne,* by Jaques Boussard (1968); *The Age of Charlemagne,* by Donald Bullough (1973); *The Life of Charlemagne,* by Eginhard (1970); *Daily Life in the World of Charlemagne,* by Pierre Riche (1978).

Cyril 827-869 Methodius 826-885
"Apostles of the Slavs"

In the course of recognizing eminent Christians in ages past, it is difficult to separate the influence of these two pious brothers, who together were used by the Lord to advance His Kingdom. Their dedication as missionaries brought the gospel to many people in the Slavic lands.

These two brothers, the "Apostles of the Slavs" as they were affectionately known in history, were born of a senatorial family in 827 and 826. The father of Cyril and Methodius was a high ranking officer in the Byzantine Army, born of Greek descent. However, their mother, Mary, was of Slavic birth. Both sons were acquainted with the Slavic tongue from childhood. They both studied at the Imperial School of Constantinople, where all the children of the higher imperial officials received their advanced education.

Cyril became a professor of philosophy at the Imperial School and then librarian at the cathedral of Santa Sophia. Methodius became governor of a district that had been settled by Slavs. Weary of various official intrigues and jealousies, they renounced the secular honors of their heritage to pursue their love of Christ on the mission field and retired to the monastery on Mt. Olympus in Bythinia, Asia Minor.

In about 861, the Emperor Michel III sent them to work with the Khazars, who were Jews, northeast of the Black Sea into the region of what was later Russia. Both brothers were brilliant linguists and soon familiarized themselves with the Khazar language. Their work as missionaries bore much fruit and they saw many conversions. They came back to their monastery after a successful mission, and Methodius became abbot of an important monastery in Greece.

In about 863, Prince Rotislav, the ruler of Great Moravia (Czechoslovakia), asked the emperor for assistance from missionaries, specifying that he wanted someone "to explain to us the Christian truths in our own language." After signing the alliance with Prince Rotislav, the Emperor decided to send the two missionary brothers, Cyril and Methodius, who already proved their missionary skill and were familiar with the Slavic language and customs.

Cyril, who was one of the best linguists of his time resolved first to compose a Slavic alphabet, and then, with the help of his brother Methodius, he proceeded to translate the Church liturgy and portions of Scripture (the Epistles and Gospels) into the Slavonic language.

Today Cyril and Methodius are honored by Eastern and Western Christians alike, and the importance of their work in preaching and worshipping in the language of the people is recognized on all sides.

Since Slavonic had no written form, they invented an alphabet for it, the Glagolitic alphabet, which gave rise to the Cyrillic alphabet (named for Cyril), which is the basis for Russian and (with modifications) several related languages. The resulting alphabet had forty-three letters. It has since undergone development, chiefly simplification and the omission of letters. Thus, the modern Russian alphabet has only thirty-two letters. The Cyrillic alphabet with minor variations is used today for Russian, Ukrainian, Bulgarian, Serbian, and formerly for Rumanian.

These two heroes of the faith are considered the "Apostles of the Slavs." Even today the liturgical language of the Russians, Serbians, Ukranians, and Bulgarians is that designed by Cyril and Methodius.

During their missionary journeys, the two Christian brothers travelled through Bulgaria, Transylvania, and Hungary spreading the "Good News" of Jesus Christ to all peoples along the way.

Cyril and Methodius recognized the peculiarity of the language and customs of the people and called the land "Rhos" or "Rus." And the people began to call themselves Rusi syny (children of Rus), or Rusiny.

Having settled in this land that they called "Rus," Cyril and Methodius were not able to continue their journey to Moravia because of the Germanic invasion. So they remained among the Rusyn ancestors until the summer of 864, preaching to them the Gospel of Christ.

Thus, between 863-864, the Rusyn became Christianized by the "Apostles of the Slavs," and began to worship Almighty God. The gospel in its Slavonic form, was understood even by the simple people. Seeing the great success of their mission among the Rusyn people, Cyril and Methodius provided them with their own Bishop and necessary priests.

After Cyril's death in 869, Methodius was appointed Bishop of the Slavic peoples, but the Germanic missionaries, who from the very beginning opposed Slavic missionaries in Moravia, seized Methodius on his return from Rome, and kept him in prison for almost three years. They released him only by Popish intervention, but soon after his release the German bishops once again accused him of heresy. This time Methodius' innocence and piety was firmly recognized by Church authorities and he was further venerated.

Finally, Methodius returned to Constantinople to complete a translation of the Bible that he and Cyril had begun together. Methodius' struggle with the Germans continued throughout the balance of his life.

Worth Reading: *Cyril and Methodius,* by Michael Lacko (1963); *Cyril and Methodius of Thessalonica: The Acculturation of the Slavs,* by Anthony-Emil N. Tachiaos (2000)

King Alfred *849-901*
The Protestant Before Protestantism

The ninth century is a most interesting epoch in European history. It is quite noticeable that it began with the great reign of Charlemagne and ended with an even more glorious reign of Alfred, the patriot and Christian who is the most illustrious, intelligent, and the most pious of all medieval princes. His reign has been recognized as a key turning point in English political and ecclesiastical history.

T hough he lived more than 1,100 years ago, during one of the most dreary and calamitous periods of history, no name is so justly popular in the hearts and minds of the English people than that of Alfred the Great. His vision for his people, his personal courage, his spiritual devotion and love for his Savior, and his treatment of his enemies offer profound wisdom for peoples of every era. Winston Churchill commented when looking back over the centuries at Alfred's life in relation to the history of England that, "we are witnessing the birth of a nation."

In 871, Alfred succeeded his brother to the throne of Wessex, at a time when the entire country was suffering under the ravages of the Danish Vikings who had mercilessly attacked, raided, and plundered the coastal areas. It seemed that all of England would fall into heathen anarchy, and Christianity would be forced from the island, but God had a plan to be fulfilled by His servant Alfred. The Danes conquered the commercial town of London and began to settle in Northumbria and East Anglia. This was all Alfred needed to take the field against these brave and ruthless invaders. It was his first battle and his Saxons lost, but he was resolved to persevere against the enemy, and his skill and courage brought one victory after another in subsequent battles until the Danes were put to flight.

One fine example of Alfred's genius as a general comes during a time when the Vikings swift navy attacked various shores of England at will. Alfred knew it was vital to create a navy at a time when the Saxons knew not how to build or manage ships. He therefore befriended Frisian seaman, neighbors of the Danes, to build a fleet superior to any ever before seen. With his armament complete, Alfred fell upon the Danes and utterly destroyed them.

One man who did more than any other to fight against the spiritual decay within the English Church as well as against the Viking invaders was Alfred the Great. He established the English royalty, created the first English navy, authored English literature, and ensured the survival of Christianity in England.

With the Danes decisively beaten on the battlefield, hope was restored to the Saxon people. Soon after, King Ethelred died, and Alfred became King of Saxony.

One of the sorest griefs of Alfred's life was that as a young man when he had the leisure for learning he could find no teachers. His friend and biographer, Bishop Assur, records a story of his boyhood that so strongly characterized him as a king, leader, conqueror, and lover of literature in latter life. "One day, his mother was reading to him and his brothers a beautifully illuminated book of Saxon poetry. She held it before them and offered the challenge, 'Which ever of you first learns to read it, shall have it for his own.' Thus stimulated, Alfred dedicated himself to the task and won the prize." This, no doubt, created fresh impulses to his natural appetite for knowledge, and most likely affected his passion for the advancement of English literature.

Alfred had viewed the fight as not just a military conflict but also a spiritual war between Christians and heathen barbarians. As the victor, Alfred required the Danish leader Guthrum be baptized. How genuine Guthrum's conversion was is unknown, but Guthrum at least nominally became the first Christian Viking.

After this marvelous king had rescued his country from invasion, and gave it a stable system of laws, he was then determined to establish its literature. To improve the quality of English education, Alfred brought scholars from Europe. He personally translated many Latin works into Anglo-Saxon so the English nobility could read them. Among his many translation projects were *Aesop's Fables*, Boethius' *Consolation of Philosophy*, Augustine's *Confessions*, Bede's *Ecclesiastical History*, and Orosius' *Universal History*. Alfred also had translated Gregory the Great's *Pastoral Theology* and sent copies to every diocese in the kingdom. He himself translated the psalms of David, and he was the author of a great many original pieces, all in the plain-spoken language of the people. He wrote a book against unjust judges, another on the various fortunes of kings, and another was a manual of meditations. He collected a book of proverbs, and also another of parables and jokes.

In the various literary works to which Alfred set his hand, he appears to have provided for the edification of the clergy, for the instruction and intelligence of the more thoughtful of his people, and even for the amusement and rational delight of those who could not ascend to more thoughtful pursuits.

Here we have a sample from the royal author and poet:

> *Wise the sayings Alfred said,*
> *Christ the Lord I bid thee dread;*
> *Meekly, O mine own dear friend,*
> *Love and like Him without end;*
> *He is Lord and life and love,*
> *Blest all other bliss above,*
> *He is man, our Father true,*
> *And a meek and mild Master too,*
> *Yea, our brother; yea, our King;*
> *Wise and rich in everything,*

So that nought of His good will
Shall be ought but pleasure still
To the man who Him with fear
In the world doth worship here.

Wanting every freeborn Englishman to learn to read English, Alfred had a plan for the general education of the people and donated half of his personal income to the Church and schools. Alfred believed that a king's instruments of rule included men of prayer, men of war, and men of work. Without these three classes properly trained, the king could not effectively perform his duty. So, Alfred required his nobles to learn how to read and to know something of the civilized heritage of Christendom. He required genuine and conscientious ministers for the churches and able masters and teachers for the schools, and that all teaching must be done in the language of the common people.

Alfred paid a great deal of attention to the interest of the Church and advancement of Christianity among the people, but it appears he did not have any fondness for the tactics of the Church of Rome. His life, his works, his childlike and serious reverence for the institutes of Christianity and for the Scriptures appear side by side with the most perfect freedom from all superstitious reverence for the Church and therefore makes him look more like a Protestant, before Protestantism even came into history.

Alfred's law code began with an introduction containing a translation of the Ten Commandments into English. God's law was to be the basis of the law for Alfred's Christian nation if it wished to be blessed by God. Following the Ten Commandments, Alfred included the Law of Moses (Exodus

King Alfred visiting a monastery school. Engraving by Benziger Pinxit for Great Men and Famous Women (1894).

21:1-23:19), the Golden Rule (Matthew 7:12), and a brief account of apostolic history and the growth of Christian law among the Christian nations.

Alfred devoted himself to great and manifold works during his 30-year reign (871-901), in spite of the fact that he suffered since the age of seventeen from an unknown and incurable disease. Though he suffered greatly his entire life, this "thorn in the flesh" tended rather to strengthen him in the work of his kingly mission by deepening those feelings of sincere piety for which his whole life was so remarkable.

Alfred shows the immense role one man can play in a nation's history. He once described himself as working in a great forest, gathering timber from which others could build. The world has had other instances of kings who have been great generals and great magistrates, but no other of a sovereign who voluntarily added to his conquests on the field, and his cares in the cabinet, the task of personally forming the literature, and building up the intelligence of his people. Edmund Burke states it so well, "One cannot help being amazed that a prince who lived in such turbulent times, who commanded personally in fifty-four pitched battles, who had so disordered a province to regulate, who was not only a legislator but a judge, and who was, continually superintending his armies, his navies, the traffic of his kingdom, his revenues, and the conduct of all his officers, could have bestowed so much of his time on religious exercises and speculative knowledge, but the exertion of all his faculties and virtues seems to have given mutual strength to all of them."

Alfred was married in 868, in his twentieth year, to Elswitha, the daughter of Ethelred, Earl of Gaini, or Gainsborough. She was of the royal family of Hercia, and from all that we know of her, she was worthy of her husband. She shared with him his sorrows and adversities, his royalty and his triumphs. Alfred's love for the God-fearing and faithful queen was shown not only by his attachment to her through life, but by the rich provision he made for her in his will.

In the year 901, having fulfilled his earthly mission as the defender and civilizer of the English people, the great and good King Alfred expired on October 26, at the early age of fifty-three years, no less beloved by his contemporaries than admired by all people in ages to come. Alfred's descendants followed his example for the next seventy-five years of wise rule for their Christian land.

Local government ought to be synonymous with local Christian virtue, otherwise it becomes local tyranny, local corruption, and local iniquity.
—King Alfred

Key Writings of King Alfred: *The Whole Works of King Alfred the Great,* by the Alfred Committee (1852).

Worth Reading: *The Life of King Alfred,* by Dr. Giles; *Alfred the Great: The Truth Teller, Maker of England,* by Beatrice Adelaide Lees (1915).

King Wenceslaus 907-935
Bohemian Martyr

Ludmilla and her husband, Prince Borivoj, were baptized by Methodius, the apostle of the Slavs, and built Bohemia's first Christian church near Prague, zealously encouraging the establishment of Christianity in the area. After Borivoj died, their son Rotislav ruled, and married Drahomira (a pagan), daughter of the prince of Lusatia (now eastern Germany). Ludmilla was entrusted with the upbringing and education of her grandson Wenceslaus, and raised him as a faithful Christian. Like many saints before him, he was martyred for his commitment to truth and justice.

Many of us know the name, Wenceslaus, from the popular Christmas hymn, "Good King Wenceslaus," written in the nineteenth-century by John Mason Neale. But few know that the spirit of the hymn reflected the pious character and influence of a real-life King Wenceslaus who lived and ruled more than 1,000 years ago in Bohemia.

The nineteenth-century Christmas hymn, "Good King Wenceslaus" is an allegorical depiction of the real-life tenth century King of Bohemia who was martyred as a lover of Christ and a provider of the poor and needy.

Wenceslaus was born near Prague, in Bohemia (modern Czechoslovakia). His parents were King Rotislav and Queen Drahomira. His grandmother, Ludmila, wife of the first Bohemian duke, asked that she might educate the young prince. Along with his Slavic language he was taught to love God.

She taught him that faith has to be put into action or it is not genuine. Because of her teaching and example, Wenceslaus learned true concern for the poor and suffering.

Wenceslaus was just thirteen when his father died in 921, fighting against the Magyars. Ludmila acted as guardian and protector of the young man. Drahomira, on the other hand, tried to suppress Christianity and did all she could to persuade Wenceslaus to renounce the faith. Much of her action against Christians came about because of the influence of some evil noblemen who still clung to the traditional pagan sacrifices.

It became clear that Queen Drahomira wanted the throne for herself. She had Ludmila killed and took control of the country. Wenceslaus did not wait to come of age, but seized the throne from his wicked mother, and banished her to a neighboring country.

During his short reign, Wenceslaus encouraged German missionaries to preach in Bohemia, urging his people to convert to Christianity. At the same time, he reformed his country's judicial system and courted peace with neighboring nations.

On one occasion, when a neighboring tribe led by a certain duke raided the country, Wenceslaus suggested that he and the duke might settle the issue by single combat, thus sparing the blood of many soldiers. Just as his adversary was about to throw a javelin at him, he saw a brilliant cross shining on the forehead of Wenceslaus and threw down his weapon.

The young king sought to quiet the civil and political unrest in his land by establishing a "liberty of conscience" among the pagan nobles who saw Christianity as a threat to their position and power. "If God bores you, why forbid others to love Him?" he asked them. He successfully reduced the oppression of the peasants by the nobility for a time, but contention arose, especially after he developed friendly relations with Henry I (the Fowler) of Germany.

"Good King Wenceslaus" as depicted in Medieval art. His godly grandmother, Ludmila, on his left, is adorned with wings. His wicked mother, Drahomira, is standing to his right. The two women were representative of the influences of good and evil in his life.

He loved God above all things and with a pure heart. It was his habit to wear penitential garments under his royal robes, and spend many nights in prayer. He kept very strict fasts, and more than once made a pilgrimage, barefoot along the icy roads.

His desire for unity, together with the promotion of Christianity, gained Wenceslaus many enemies among the heathen. The nobles conspired and secured the support of Boleslaw, the brother of Wenceslaus, and together they formed a plot against him.

Wenceslaus was invited to his brother's home at Boleslava for a banquet. It was planned that he would be assasinated there, but the murderers hesitated and decided to wait until the next morning. On September 28, 935, as Wenceslaus was on his way to church, he recognized that trouble was near and said to Boleslaw, "Brother, you were a good subject to me yesterday."

"And now I intend to be a better one!" shouted Boleslaw and struck his brother in the head with his sword. The brothers struggled, but three other rebels rushed up and killed the king. As the good Wenceslaus died, he murmured, "Brother, may God forgive you."

Bohemians look at Wenceslaus as a martyr. His picture appeared on their coins and his crown was a symbol of Czech independence. "Good King Wenceslaus" is not only a beautiful hymn sung at Christmas time, but a great man who loved the Lord Jesus Christ and who walked into the annals of Christian veneration.

Worth Reading: *The Story of Bohemia, by C. Edmund Maurice (1896).*

Olga *890-969* **Vladimir** *956-1015*
Founders of Russian Christianity

The "Baptism of Rus" in 988 marks when Christianity became the official religion of Russia. Vladimir, Grand Prince of Kiev, sent trusted men to observe the world's religions. They returned saying Islam was too strict with food and drink, Roman Catholicism too formal and cold. But Orthodox Christianity was different! The beauty of the religion in Byzantium caused them to exclaim, "We thought we were in heaven!"

It has often proven true that "Behind every great man stands a great woman," and in a very true sense this was the case for Russian prince Vladimir. Credited with bringing Christianity to the Russian nation, Vladimir was following in the steps of his grandmother, Princess Olga of Kiev, who attempted the same task during her reign and poured her heart out in prayer for her grandson when he ascended to authority years later.

Olga and Vladimir were called by the Lord to powerfully lead a nation from pagan ritualism to embrace the great religion of Jesus Christ.

Olga is believed to be of Viking ancestry, and married Igor I, Prince of Kiev, at a young age. When her husband was assassinated in 954, she became regent for her son Svyatoslav, who took over for his father. But he was not the leader his father was and his costly wars had brought Russia to near ruin.

Olga replaced her son in the place of power and immediately executed her husband's murderers and ruled for the next twenty years, implementing effective fiscal, social, political, and religious reforms throughout the principality. Already a convert to Christianity, she visited Constantinople and in 957 was baptized. She returned to Russia with a saint's hunger for the souls of her people and attempted to lead them to the Christian faith. Led by her son, Svyatoslav, the pagan nobles felt threatened by Christianity and resisted her efforts. Svyatoslav himself almost converted to Islam and sought to push the Islamic faith upon the Russian people. But Olga's Christ-like influence had a hand in averting her son's efforts, and she managed to win enough support among the political leaders who were interested in seeing Russia Christianized. Olga died in 969 and her pagan son gave her a Christian burial.

In 972 Svyatoslav died, and his three sons fought for the crown. Yaropolk killed Oled, and Vladimir fled to his Viking kinsmen in Scandinavia. In 980 he returned with Viking support, killed Yaropolk, and took the throne.

Christianity had made some progress in Kiev, but Vladimir remained pagan, had seven wives, established temples, and participated in idolatrous rites, possibly involving human sacrifice. He was, however, wise enough to recognize that a common faith could give his country unity. Accordingly, he sent messengers to investigate the three great faiths of the Mideast: Islam, Judaism, and the Roman and Orthodox branches of Christianity. Vladimir thought Judaism and Islam, with their dietary restrictions, undesirable. He found Roman Catholicism "too formal and cold." But his messengers sold him with their report of the ritual they witnessed in Byzantium. Speaking of the worship they saw and the people they met they exclaimed, "We did not know whether we were in heaven or on earth. It would be impossible to find on earth any splendor greater than this... Never shall we be able to forget so great a beauty."

His heart also was made new by Christ. Vladimir's conversion seems to have been real. Under his rule the Christianization of Russia proceeded rapidly. He married Anna, sister of Byzantine emperor Basil II (976-1025), put away his former collection of pagan wives and mistresses, destroyed idols and pagan temples, built churches and monasteries and schools, brought in Greek missionaries to educate his people, and gave lavish alms to the poor. He even abandoned the death penalty. Not only did he turn away from his lust for pleasure-seeking, but he lost much of the careless cruelty to which he was previously identified. On June 5, 988, Vladimir was baptized with hundreds of other men and women of Kiev and Novgorod, and ordered the pagan idols to be thrown into the Dnieper River.

The Christianization of Russia, which was contemporaneous with the conversion of Hungary and Poland, was closely connected with Vladimir's alliance with the Byzantine emperors and his marriage with their sister, Anna.

Vladimir's subjects did not balk at this new faith and way of life as Olga's had. In time the whole Northeastern Europe and North Asia was Christianized. One man's personal tastes and political cunning had added a precious jewel to the kingdom of Christ.

Some of Vladimir's former pagan wives and their sons raised an armed rebellion against him, and he was killed near Kiev on July 15, 1015.

The Christianity that Olga tried to bring to Russia had finally taken root by the effectual call of her grandson to Jesus Christ. She and Vladimir are honored as the founders of Russian Christianity.

Worth Reading: *An Introduction to the History of Christianity,* by F. J. Foakes-Jackson (1921); *Origins of Russia,* by George Vernadsky (1959).

Anselm of Aosta *1033-1109*

"The Second Augustine"

The eleventh century produced one of the greatest thinkers and theologians of all time, Anselm of Aosta, who on the battlefields of life became a great captain. His writings exhibit the fruit of the gifts of faith and reason, and have influenced and guided the Church for over 1,000 years.

 nselm was born in the small town of Aosta, on the Italian side of the Alps. He was of noble lineage and was blessed, like Augustine, with a mother whose affection while she lived, and whose memory after she had passed away, ever acted like a charm upon her son. Ermenberga seems to have been a woman of gracious presence and of marked individuality. She was beautiful, pious, and believed that she could best serve God by devoting herself, under His guidance, to the wise management of her household. "Sanctified reason" seems to have been the guiding principle of her life. It was probably from her that Anselm received the refinement of his moral nature and his desire to bring all things into subjection to the law of God.

Anselm at an early age learned to think for himself, and before he was fifteen years old he decided that the Christian way was to be preferred over the secular life. He then applied to an abbot that he might join the monastery, but the abbot declined him, since he had not obtained his father's consent. His father became a harsh man after Ermenberga's early death and he treated his son very poorly. The desire of Anselm's heart was not to be granted at that time in Italy. But in faraway Normandy a door would open upon which he so earnestly knocked.

At age twenty-three Anselm left home and wandered in his travels as well as in his heart for nearly three years. His journey landed him at the little monastery at Bec in Normandy. Its Prior, Lanfranc, was the famous scholar and devoted Christian whose reputation spread far and wide. In 1060, Anselm became his student and grew in his faith through the godly teaching and influence of his master. Thus was the beginning of their thirty-year friendship. Anselm's peaceful life as a monk at Bec expressed the beauty of a rich and varied Christian experience and the depth and force that a gentle, trained intellect can manifest in searching the deep things of God.

Men like Anselm stand out preeminently in whatever work they are engaged. In the secular realm he was a famous scholar. In the peaceful existence of the monastery he became an

Anselm's lot was cast in troublous times, but manfully he fought against evil in cloister and in court, against corrupt monks, and against the worst king who ever wore the crown of England. He conquered them all because he was first conquered by Christ.

exemplary leader. His friend, fellow monk, and biographer, Eadmer, records of Anselm, "whoever wished to live a wholly religious life found much to imitate in Anselm."

In 1063 Lanfranc became Abbot of Caen, and Anselm succeeded him as Prior of Bec. It was at this time that he began to exert to the full his splendid mental powers in the study of the fascinating problems of theology. Some of the greatest theologians, Augustine, Aquinas, and Calvin, to name a few, have also been men of a profound spiritual nature. Doing the will of God, taught by His Spirit, they have penetrated and experienced the depths of Christian truth. When Anselm was Prior of Bec, he was relieved from the ordinary round of the convent duties and spent a great deal of time in prayer and meditation and in earnest pursuit of Divine truth. In this pursuit he reached such understanding that "he saw through and unravelled the most abstruse problems, and until his day, unsolved—concerning the Divine nature and the Christian faith, and by clear trains of reasoning showed that his conclusions were sound in themselves, and in accordance with the catholic belief. For he had so steadfast a belief in the holy Scriptures that, with unshakeable firmness of mind, he believed that there was nothing in them that passed in any degree beyond the solid pathway of truth. On this account, with the greatest zeal, he directed all his efforts to this end, that up to the full measure of his faith he might penetrate, by the eye of reason, the things which in the Scriptures he found here and there hidden in much darkness," says Eadmer.

Anselm also possessed a remarkable ability of reading character. This is a gift often manifested by those who study Scripture deeply and reverently. He was also always ready to hear of the difficulties and sorrows of those about him. He spent many days and nights in this sacrificial labor of love.

His honesty and simplicity made the diplomatic clergy very uncomfortable. He possessed an unfeigned humility and was kind of heart and charitable in judgment. He was zealous in good works and patient under trial and adversity. He was skillful in winning and training the young and achieved remarkable success as a teacher. In the history of theology he stands as the father of orthodox scholasticism, and has been called "the second Augustine." His mind was keen and logical, and his writings display devotion, originality, and a masterly grasp of intellect.

It was as Prior of Bec that Anselm began to write the treatises on the doctrine of God that gave him a prominent place in the foremost rank of theologians—*Monologium* and *Proslogium*. His *Monologiun* is the first statement on record that addresses the "ontological argument for the existence of God." In other words, it is an attempt to show what reason can teach about God and to prove that what faith perceives by the teaching of Scripture is reasonable and logical. The ideas of goodness, holiness, and so

Even Luther and the Reformation have been able to add but little to Anselm's treatises on the Atonement, and have found in it little that needs to be taken away.

His belief in God centered on the basis of faith and logical reasoning. Anselm's argument on the existence of God is as follows:

1. God is defined as the being in which none greater is possible.

2. It is true that the notion of God exists in your understanding.

3. And that God exists in reality. (God is a possible being.)

4. If God only exists in the mind, and may have existed, then God might have been greater than He is.

5. Then, God might have been greater than He is (if He existed in reality.)

6. Therefore, God is a being which a greater is possible.

7. This is not possible, for God is a being in which a greater is impossible.

8. Therefore God exists in reality as well as the mind.

on, in the heart and mind can only be accounted for by the existence of a Being who perfectly and completely possesses these qualities, and who is greater than all things, and independent of all things. In his *Proslogium* the concept is further refined. Here in his own words: "The human mind possesses the idea of the most perfect Being conceivable. But such a Being is necessarily existent, because a being who may or may not exist is not the most perfect we can conceive of. But a necessarily existent Being is one that cannot be conceived of as nonexistent, and therefore is an actually existent Being. Necessary existence implies actual existence. In conceiving, therefore, of a Being who is more perfect than all others, the mind inevitably conceives of a real and not an imaginary being." In Anselm's view the idea of God is unique, and hence an argument can be constructed out of it such as cannot be constructed out of the idea of an other being.

In 1087 William the Conqueror died, causing the power of Normandy and England to be split between his two sons. Normandy went to Robert and England to William Rufus. Unfortunately for England and Anselm, William did not have the same reverence for spiritual things that his father had. His selfishness and inflexible will caused him to diregard wise counsel, especially when it came to the appointment of Anslem to Archbishop of Canterbury. Anslem preferred the quiet life of a monk over the position anyway, and pleaded not to be considered. But in 1093, the king fell gravely sick and in fear made the proclamation of Anslem's appointment, even against the prior's will. The king recovered and though he did not revoke the appointment, his relationship with Anselm was filled with dissention.

In 1098, Anselm spent his summer in the solitude of the mountain village, Schiavia, rejoicing in the peace and rest all about him. Here Anselm lived over again the quiet life of Bec, dedicating himself once more to the studies that had been so dear to him. Here he finished a work he had long had in mind, his most famous and greatest treatise, *Cur Deus Homo?* (Why did God become man?) This book has powerfully influenced Christian thought from the time it was written until the present hour. For the first time in the history of the Christian church, it gave a clear, scientific, scriptural view of the atonement of Christ. Written in response to Jewish claims that the Incarnation impugned the honor and dignity of God, it's become an epoch in theology. Even Luther and the Reformation added but little to the theory of Anselm and have found in it but little that needs to be taken away. The book is very short, taking up only twenty-three pages in the old Latin folio of Anselm's works, but it is hardly too much to say that even now it is the best possible corrective, next to the careful study of Scripture itself, for the loose, unscientific views of the atonement so commonly held in our day.

In 1099, Anselm appealed to Pope Urban that he might be

"He who, because I refuse to renounce obedience to the chief Pontiff of the Roman Church, would thence prove that I violate the sworn faith which I owe the Sovereign, let him show himself, and he will find me ready to give him an answer as I ought, and where I ought."—Anselm

released from his position of Primacy, but to no avail. Instead he was summoned to Rome for the Lateran Council, where he disagreed with the pope's position on a number of issues.

Later that year, Jerusalem was captured by the Crusaders, Pope Urban died, and King William was experiencing the worst reign England had ever known. Riot, bloodshed, and disregard for law and justice was rampant. His total opposition to anything godly came to a sudden end in 1100, when on a journey in the New Forest, an errant arrow, shot by an unknown hand, struck the wicked king between his armor and pierced his heart. Violently he lived, thus violently he died.

Henry assumed the throne and redressed the wrongs of his older brother William. He promised to God and all the people to put down the injustices of his brother's reign and to restore good law. When contention arose between the king and the pope, Anselm was called to a vital position of arbitration, and found himself between two masters. Yet Anslem remained wholly upright and resolved the dispute brilliantly, restoring both sides to a position of authority and honor.

The close of Anselm's life was one of peaceful resignation to the will of God, though his mind was still quite occupied with deep theological questions. In particular he was wrestling with the question of the origin of the soul. He became so weak he had to be carried around in a chair. On April 21, 1109, at the age of 76, the great theologian and Archbishop gave up his spirit into the hands of his Creator and slept in peace.

Like Augustine, Anselm possessed a great love of God and His people. His power over men of all types, from William Rufus to the pope, from Henry to Eadmer, testifies strongly to his affectionate nature and to his steadfast integrity.

In all the manifold relations he sustained during his long and faithful life as: child, pupil, monk, abbot, visible head of the Church in Britain, opponent of the King, and adviser of the pope. He was "great indeed in goodness, and worthy to be had in honor of all," says Eadmer.

The primary sources for Anselm's life are the *Historia Novorum* and *Vita Anselmi* written Eadmer. His *Meditations* and his *Letters* reveal to the reader much of his great loving heart. The best edition of Anselm's works is by G. Gerberon, a monk of the Congregation of Bt. Maur, Paris, 1675 (Reprinted in 1744, with corrections and additions).

Key Writings of Anselm: 1. *Book of Meditations and Prayers;* 2. *Monologium;* 3. *Proslogium;* 4. *Cur deus homo.*

Worth Reading: *Historia Novorum; Vita Anselmi,* both by Eadmer; *The Life of St. Anselm,* by R. W. Church (1870); *Life and Times of St. Anselm,* by M. Rule, 2 vols. (1883); *Anselm and His Work,* by A. C. Welch (1896); *History of Norman Conquest,* by E. A. Freedman (1901).

"If God wills that I should remain longer among you, at least until I have solved the question concerning the origin of the soul, which I am turning over in my mind, I would receive it gratefully, the more so because I fear that no one will solve it after my death."

—Anselm, on his deathbed in 1109.

Bernard of Clairvaux *1090-1153*

"Greatest Churchman of the Twelfth Century"

In the early twelfth century, there were few individuals who so completely embodied the thought and piety of Christianity as Bernard of Clairvaux. It was the love of Christ and the desire for union with the divine that animated Bernard. His writings speak of "the deepest desires of the holy soul," of uniting with Jesus through our common humanity. This likened him to Augustine more than any other Church father, and secured for him a prominent place on the list of eminent Christians.

ernard of Clairvaux (Bernardus Clarœvallis) was one of the most influential and prominent Christians of the twelfth century and of the entire Middle Ages. He breathed new life into the Church of his day while influencing ecclesiastical and political affairs, especially that of monasticism and the royalty. He also contributed greatly toward awakening an inner piety in the nobility as well as in the common circles. He was gifted in inspiring the masses by his powerful preaching, and he also understood how to lead individual souls into communion with Christ, by his quiet, pious example and loving instruction. It was said in his time that the Church had not seen a preacher like him since Gregory the Great. That this is no exaggeration is proven in Bernard's writings, which in depth of thought and beauty of exposition have few equals. Praised by Luther and Calvin, Bernard's name has retained a good reputation among many Protestants, though some things he represented were rejected by the Reformers.

In A.D. 1115 Bernard founded the monastery at Clairvaux. He and the monastery became a major center of spiritual and political influence.

Bernard was born in Fontaines, France. He was the third son of the knight Tecelin and his wife Aleth, a very pious woman, whose godly influence was used by the Lord to shape his future. At the age of nine he was sent to school at Chatillon-sur-Seine where he studied language and literature, poetry and the sacred Scriptures. At this time, the tumult surrounding the First Crusade had scarcely abated when the boys of the Middle Ages, of which Bernard was one, showed themselves familiar with the sword and shining armor.

At nineteen Bernard left school and returned to his father's castle near Dijon. Ten years had brought many changes in the outstandingly brilliant student. He was grown up and exceedingly attractive, vigorous, and joyously alive. Temptations of impurity and worldliness often seized the handsome youth, but he escaped sin by fighting the evil foe and gaining a most important victory over self. Alert to subdue his sinful nature, Bernard showed a measure of the heroism of which he was made. The next great trial that came upon him was the loss of his wonderful mother, which came as a terrible shock to all the family. Bernard cherished Aleth with a deep, abiding love and her absence seemed to temporarily rob him of all joy and happiness. He was twenty and living in an atmosphere of war when he received the call of Heaven to be a soldier of Jesus Christ. It happened one day while he was on his way to visit his brothers, who were in the battle area on the side of the Duke of Burgundy. As he rode along, deep in thought, the vanity of the world with its lusts, passed before his mind. Suddenly a voice sounded in the depths of his heart, "Come to Me all you that labor and are heavy laden, and I will give you rest; take My yoke upon you, and you shall find rest for your souls." The living words of Christ struck home and a heavenly longing took possession of Bernard. Thrilled as never before, he stopped and dismounted before the door of the next church on the road. Trembling with fear and anticipation he entered and prostrated himself before the altar. Bernard prayed as never before, raising his tear-filled eyes to Heaven, and pouring out his heart like water before the face of the Lord. His answer came when a peace fell upon his soul, and he knew that he was a new creation in Jesus Christ. At that moment, he recalled his pious mother's prayers for his soul and consecrated his whole existence to God, joyfully accepting the yoke of Him who is meek and humble of heart. Bernard made an heroic decision that day to bury his vision for a career of knighthood and become a child and servant of God.

> "..the reason for loving God is God Himself; and the measure of love due to Him is immeasurable..."
> —Bernard of Clairvaux, On Loving God.

He convinced some of his brothers, relatives, and friends to follow him as he was in Christ, and after spending a number of months together they entered the "new monastery" at Cîteaux. In 1115, a daughter monastery was founded at Clairvaux and Bernard became abbot. He gave all his energies to the foundation of the monastery and spent his time in ascetic practices. Bernard became the spiritual adviser not only of his monks, but of many who sought his advice. All who came left Clairvaux impressed by the spirit of solemnity and peace. His sermons also began to exercise a powerful influence and Bernard soon became not only the most influential and famous personality of the entire order, but one of the most prominent men of the Church in France.

Before long Bernard found himself at war with the false teachers of the age. One of these was Peter Abelard, a Breton, and a brilliant theological teacher of the twelfth century—though sadly, vanity, ill-temper, and reckless language marred his genius. As early as 1115, while Bernard prayed at Cîteaux, Abelard's school in Paris had become famous, attended by thousands of pupils. Abelard's career was spoiled by a passionate affair with a young girl, yet he still managed to persuade followers to eagerly sit at his feet. Abelard's contemporary brand of relativism taught that all truths should be challenged, that a thing could be true in theology and false in philosophy, and that one could believe something even if it is proven untrue. Such bold teachings, together with a brazen flaunting of authority, got him into trouble with the austere heroic abbots of that day. Bernard, whose piety was offended, attacked the adventurous thinker and a duel ensued which made plain two conflicting currents of thought—the new rationalism vs. traditional authority. In a letter to Pope Innocent II Bernard declared: "Peter Abelard is trying to make void the merit of Christian faith, when he deems himself able by human reason to comprehend God altogether...The man is great in his own eyes." At the Council of Sens in 1140, the Abbot of Clairvaux confronted Abelard who was charged with heresy.

The Abbot of Clairvaux already an acknowledged theologian and a wise counselor, was equally famous for his humility, meekness, and kindness. It was said that he truly feared no man, yet reverenced all men. If the occasion demanded, Bernard was ready to speak to pope, king, or commoner with equal freedom.

The ecclesiastical and political affairs of France soon made a new claim upon Bernard's attention. Young King Louis VII, made reckless use of his royal authority causing friction between him and the pope. After a while Bernard was asked to mediate. He faithfully performed this difficult task, setting the king aright. He enjoyed the confidence of the king to the end of his life, but his relations to the pope appear to have been troubled to the end.

Bernard's entire life was dedicated to the resolution he made as a youth—to work out the salvation of his soul, and dedicate himself to the service of God.

In the last years of his life, Bernard experienced many things that caused him great sadness. He was deeply affected by the death of several friends with whom he shared an intimate bond of fellowship. At the same time, his relations with Church leaders were often troubled, and the frailty and the pains of his body increased. But through all this, his mental vitality remained active and his last work, *De consideratione*, displays freshness and unimpaired force of mind and spirit.

Bernard's entire life was dedicated to the resolution he made as a young man—to consecrate himself to the service of God. Bernard's quiet hours, in spite of the many pressing claims on him, were devoted to study, primarily of the holy Scriptures. His knowledge of the Bible was remarkable. Not only did he often quote Bible passages, but all his orations were impregnated with Biblical references, allusions, and phrases. As he was nourished by the Word of God he also mastered how to bring "the pure milk" near to others. All the qualities of a great shepherd were powerfully united in Bernard.

Religious geniality was the most distinguishing quality in the whole disposition of Bernard. To it is due the impression which he made upon his era, and the importance which he obtained in the history of the Church. In his approach to the Christian life, Bernard is related not as much to Luther, as to Augustine. Bernard was most greatly impressed by the feeling of total indebtedness to the grace of God. He firmly stood on the truth

*The popular hymn
sung in many
Protestant churches
today, "O Sacred Head
Now Wounded," is the
English translation of
one of Bernard's hymns.*

that on God rests the beginning and end of our salvation, and that we are to trust only in his grace, not in meritorious works. From the forgiveness of sin proceeds the Christian life, and faith is the means by which we lay hold of the grace of God. Man can never obtain salvation by resting his hope upon his own righteousness, for all our works remain imperfect. On the other hand Bernard did not deny that man can and should have merits, but that good works are only possible through the continual working of the grace of God. He believed they are gifts of God, which have rewards in this life and in the world to come, but without becoming a cause of self-glory. Before God there is no legal claim.

To serve God wholeheartedly required a struggle against nature, and in this struggle Bernard was deeply earnest. When he speaks of becoming one with Christ in God, his thought is clothed with biblical expressions. The fact that Bernard does not intend to go beyond the meaning of these words can be seen by reading his explanations, where the union with God to which the humble soul attains, is most keenly distinguished from a consubstantiality, as it exists between Father and Son in the Trinity.

Notwithstanding Bernard's many-faceted activity, he was and remained above all things a monk, and would not exchange his monasticism either for the chair of Ambrose or for the primacy of Reims. Though he preferred the life of a monk, he acknowledged that true Christianity is possible while living in the world.

The works of Bernard include a large collection of letters, sermons, a number of treatises (dogmatic and polemic, ascetic and mystical) on monasticism, and on church government. He also wrote a biography of Malachy, the Irish archbishop. Many influential writings and hymns are also ascribed to him. The most important are the letters which constitute one of the most valuable collections of Church history. A number of the books in his *De consideratione* contain a critique of the Church affairs of his time and they lay down a program for papal conduct which a contemporary pope would have found difficult to follow.

Bernard was devoted to poetry from his youth and his work is known for its beautiful form and composition, and distinguished by its tender and living feeling of holy love. The popular hymn, "O Sacred Head Now Wounded" is the English translation of one of his hymns.

Key Writings of Bernard: The *Bibiliographia Bernardina*, by L. Janauschek, lists more than 2,000 of his writings. 1. *De consideratione* (1153); 2. *Thesaurus hymnologicus*, 5 vols., revised H. A. Daniel, 1841-56 (Bernard's hymns)

Worth Reading: 1. *Works of Bernard*, J. M. Hortsius (1687) 2. *Bernard of Clairvaux, the Times, the Man and his Work*, New York, R. S. Storrs (1892); *Vita prima*, biography written by William of Thierry during Bernard's lifetime; *Bernard as a Hymnist*, by R. C. Trench.

Peter Waldo *1140-1217*

Founder of the Waldenses

The Waldenses proclaimed the Bible as the sole rule of life and faith. They rejected the papacy, purgatory, indulgences, mass, and other mere forms of religion in favor of gospel simplicity. They believed that worship, Bible reading, prayer, and preaching can be conducted by all Christians as moved by the Holy Spirit. Their distinctive pre-Reformation doctrines survived centuries and still influence the true Church of Christ in the present day.

n 1160 there was at Lyons in France a wealthy citizen named Peter Waldo. He amassed his gain by wicked usury and he was content to store up worldly riches in any way possible. One evening, while entertaining friends at his home, one of them was attacked by a sudden seizure and died. The incident shook Waldo and awakened in him thoughts of death and of life beyond the grave.

In his search for answers he began to regularly attend church services, but the readings were in Latin, and he understood only enough to kindle a deeper, burning desire for truth. Impatient of delay and inflamed with the holy desire of reaching the springs of salvation, he engaged two priests to come to his house to translate the Gospels into the vernacular. The two priests between them put together portions of Holy Scripture, along with various quotations from early Church fathers and arranged them under different headings, and placed the whole of their work in the hands of Waldo. Excited over his new acquisition, he read, meditated on, and made careful study of all they had written. The words had a powerful impact on his mind and heart, and many were impressed upon his memory. He fed on them and found some comfort, but not that full peace which he longed for. The words of Jesus regarding the foolishness of vainly pursuing earthly riches, and the folly of those who put all their hopes on them, painfully affected him. Again and again he read and re-read the parable which begins, *"Take heed and beware of covetousness, for the abundance of a man's life consisteth not in those things which he possesseth"* (Luke 12:15).

At another time he saw himself depicted as the foolish rich man who was busy laying up treasures on Earth, and becomes truly poor, not being rich towards God. His conviction was great and the Holy Spirit moved mightily in his soul to trust fully in Christ alone for salvation. His past sins weighed heavily upon his heart and he gave all that he had to the poor in his community as restitution for his former business practices.

In one sense, he was a protestant more than 200 years before John Huss. His followers, the Waldenses, began a reformation to which the latter Reformation of the sixteenth-century would strikingly resemble.

Waldo's resolution drove him to the Church for answers to the burning questions regarding what he read in God's Word. He inquired of the bishop concerning the Scriptures which state that Christ is the only way of salvation. And he pressed the bishop on matters of death and Heaven. The bishop had little to say that quenched his thirst, but could only point him back to the authority of the Church, and to tradition as an answer. At the conclusion of their meetings, Waldo was saddened by what he had heard from the bishop and became more resolved to deny himself and follow Christ.

Some Waldensian precepts for living in the world:
1. We must not love the world.
2. We must, if possible, live at peace with men.
3. We must shun evil company.
4. We must not avenge ourselves.
5. We must love our enemies.
6. We must possess our souls in patience.
7. We must not be unequally yoked with unbelievers.

Waldo's quest for the simple and serene life was not easy, since he had been such a wealthy man. One of his most difficult tasks was breaking the news to his wife and two daughters. After many tears were shed, they released him to continue his quest for God.

His vow of charity was carried out in the most practical matters. His regular distribution of food and provisions to the poor proclaiming "No man can serve two masters..." greatly moved the masses and many were drawn to follow him. He expounded the holy Scriptures to all in his path, and his generosity spoke wonders about his genuine faith in Christ. Some praised God with him, others thought him mad. His reply to them was, "My friends and fellow citizens, I am not out of my mind as some of you think. I have avenged myself on these my enemies, who kept me in such slavery, that I cared more for money than for God, and served more willingly the creature rather than the Creator. I know many blame me for doing this so publicly, but I did so both for my sake and for yours. For my own, that afterwards, if any one sees me in the possession of money, he may say with truth that I am out of my mind, but also for your sake, that you may learn to fix your hopes on God, and not on riches."

When Waldo had finished the distribution of his property, he found the poor standing by his side. Many were not content with mere existence, but desired to really live as Christians. Waldo's conduct and passion was admirable, and the people were encouraged to abandon worldly pursuits to read and study the gospel diligently in the "new version." While they meditated on its precepts and applied them to themselves and to others, an amazing thing happened: they began to see in a clear light their own sins and the vices that prevailed around them. In brokenness they began to confess their sins to God and one another. They then rose up to make known the wonderful Word of Life to others. Their preaching consisted in repeating the precepts of Christ and in inviting their hearers to join them in the life which they had chosen. This was the origin of the community and the missionary work of the first Waldenses. This had been the mission of Jesus himself, and they knew that since their great Master had been crucified, that they as His followers could not hope to escape hatred and persecution.

Waldenses rejoiced in their new found faith, but with it they also saw the errors of the established Church. The prelates in power did not approve of them and rejected their appeal to establish a new religious order. The larger and more vocal the Waldenses became the more opposition they felt at the hands of Rome. They were ostracized, persecuted, and had property confiscated, while some were even murdered for the faith. Waldo had made a vow to follow Christ. He would not give Him up in order to obey the precepts of the pope, and he fervently renewed his cry, "It is better to obey God than man."

The Waldenses would have liked nothing better than to leave the privilege of preaching in the hands of the priests, provided that they were allowed to retain the right of free speech.

Everywhere the Waldensian preachers left traces behind them, while their brethren of Milan with equal zeal scattered the gospel seed in Lombardy, Austria, and Germany. Meanwhile the wrath of the clergy vented itself in threats and in attacks made upon them; sometimes with the great thunderbolts of anathemas, as at the Council of Verona; and sometimes with the little hailstones of lesser synods. Their enemies hunted them down, letting loose upon them the whole pack of the "agents of the Inquisition." Many of the Waldensians were imprisoned, some put to death, and others remained closely hidden in the houses of their faithful friends in the cities. At last a whole multitude of fugitives found a refuge in the Cottian Alps. They pitched their tents in the three valleys of Pragelato, Angrogna, and Chisone. From there a new swarm penetrated to Calabria. The Waldensian dispersion was so wide that it overspread the limits generally assigned to it, from the Rhine to the Raab, and from the Ionian Sea to the Baltic. An inquisitor who followed them with eagle's eyes had to confess about the end of the twelfth century that there was hardly a country which they had not reached. But the dispersion was not only great in extent, it was still greater in its heroisms, its struggles, its martyrdoms, and its beneficial marks on the history of Christianity. On the eve of the Reformation their fire was still emitting many sparks. For the time the mission of the Waldenses had accomplished its purpose.

Meanwhile, high up in their sure refuge in the Alps, their little light continued to shine steadily. In the midst of the darkness around them, nourished by their love for Christ, it kept its brightness aglow.

Such was the community of the followers of Waldo. They were called "Poor men of Lyons," says Stephen Bourbon, "because they began there by making a profession of Poverty. Referring to themselves they call themselves poor in spirit, because the Lord says, 'Blessed are the poor in spirit.' Their enemies gave them, as a term of reproach, the name of 'Waldenses.'

Some Waldensian precepts for personal holiness in believers:
1. *They not serve the lusts of the flesh.*
2. *They shall govern well their thoughts.*
3. *They shall mortify their members.*
4. *They shall shun idleness.*
5. *They shall practice works of mercy.*
6. *They shall live in faith and morality.*
7. *They shall fight against lusts.*
8. *They shall speak to one another of the will of God.*
9. *They shall diligently examine their consciences.*
10. *They shall purify, improve, and compose the spirit and mind.*

The name remains still a sign of victory and a title of honor."

Though our knowledge of Waldo's personal history is scanty, enough has been related to explain why he was rightly recognized as one of the four "Reformers before the Reformation," along with Wycliffe, Huss, and Savonarola. Neither Waldo, nor the representatives of England, Bohemia, and Italy which surround him made an absolute break with Rome, as Luther did. It was Rome who excommunicated, persecuted, and in the case of two, martyred them.

Reinerius, a Dominican friar and cruel inquisitor against the Waldenses, purposed to defame them because they frequently read the holy Scriptures, confessed that "when the Waldenses wished to display their learning, they adduced many things relating to purity, humility, and other virtues, showing that sin must be shunned, and quoting thereto the words of Christ and His apostles."

Yet they deserve all honor as Protestants and were truly forerunners of Luther, because they all alike grasped the great principle of the supreme authority of Holy Scripture, salvation by grace through faith, and the right of the people to be instructed in the truths of the Bible. Waldo's leading principle was this: What Christ commanded must be done, and if the decrees of popes or councils should be found to contradict God's Word and Christ's precepts, they must give way. Christ's law must be supreme. Waldo could not have anticipated all the results which would follow from his bold adherence to this principle.

Waldo, the imperfectly educated layman and merchant, would not consciously begin to form a theological system, or at once see how widely in doctrine the Church of Rome had departed from the scriptural faith. But he had entered on the way which could have no other result—a final and complete rupture from Rome. How far he himself went on this way we cannot tell, but we know that above all he was committed to the supreme authority of the Scripture. He clung to the Christ of Scripture as the author of his salvation and the guide of his life. In His cause he braved all the terrors of persecution and death, and for His sake Waldo became an ardent missionary, spreading His word among the people. This great leader of the people known as Waldenses, left behind him in his followers those who faithfully carried on what he had begun. This community of believers still remain as living witnesses to the extent of Peter Walo's influence and of the power of his faithful example.

Worth Reading: *History Of The Waldenses, From The Earliest Period To The Present Time,* by American Sunday School Union (1829); *History of the Waldenses,* by Blair Adams (1832); *The Waldenses or Protestant Valleys of Piedmont,* by William Beattie (1838); *History of the Ancient Christians Inhabiting the Valleys of the Alps I. the Waldenses, II. the Albigenes, III. the Vaudois,* by Paul Perrin (1846); *The Waldenses: Sketches of the Evangelical Christians of the Valleys of Piedmont* (1853); *Cross and the Crown,* by James D. McCabe (1873); *History of the Waldenses,* by J. A. Wylie; *In His Name, a Story of the Waldenses, Seven Hundred Years Ago,* by Edward E. Hale (1873); *The Waldenses: Their Rise, Stuggles, Persecutions and Triumphs,* by Guy Teofilo (1920); *A Brief Sketch of the Waldenses,* by C. H. Strong (1983).

Clare of Assisi *1194-1253*
Beautiful Daughter of God

Like pious men and women of all ages, Clare cultivated God's presence. To her, contemplation was living in His presence, regardless of her outward duties. She fixed her mind on Christ, meditating upon him as both man and God: "Jesus is the splendor of glory, the fight of the eternal fight, the mirror without tarnish." As her heart grew in Christ her contemplative vision and dedicated humility stretched the souls of all she touched that they too might embrace the object of her affection, Jesus the Lord!

It was the year 1212. Clare, daughter of Favorino Scifi, Count of Sasso-Rosso, of the noble family Offreduccios in Italy, was a beautiful eighteen-year-old woman with the promises before her of all the world had to offer. While most young women her age were preparing to leave home as happy brides, Clare was content to make herself truly beautiful for her beloved Lord and Savior, Jesus Christ.

In fact, one Palm Sunday morning, Clare had attended church dressed like a princess. To all around her she seemed somewhat preoccupied. When the other girls went forward to accept their palm leaves, she remained seated. The bishop had to bring a leaf down to the contemplative girl.

Young men looked on and wondered while the poor girls envied. Clare's beauty, wealth, and virtue had made her a prize to be pursued, but she rejected all who called on her in favor of the one great "Suitor." Like Francis, whom she heard preach that Palm Sunday, she planned to renounce her wealth with a desire to whole-heartedly serve Christ. Knowing that she would never be able to return to a life of pleasure and ease, she vowed one night to leave home and follow her Shepherd.

It was a late March evening and her shadowy figure labored to clear the debris from the rarely-used gate of her mansion home. This "door of death" (as it was often called because it was used by the family solely to bear the dead out to their final resting place) barely creaked open enough for her to pass by and out into the meadow where she met the Franciscan brothers who agreed to assist her in her escape. It was to Francis that the young woman was going, and he welcomed her arrival.

Six years earlier Giovanni di Pietro Bernardone, commonly called Francis, the son of a wealthy merchant had renounced his parent's wealth in favor of serving God through a simpler life of poverty and devotion. He began by begging for stones to repair a ruined church. As the work of restoration progressed, he meditated on Scripture, washed lepers' sores, sought to follow Christ completely, and began to preach repentance and faith. His changed life attracted other rich young men who renounced their wealth and gathered around him, forming a brotherhood at a

From her earliest years Clare seems to have been endowed with the rarest virtues. As a child she was most devoted to prayer and to practices of mortification and devotion, and as she became a young girl her distaste for the world and her yearning for a more spiritual life increased.

85

small church of Assisi called the Portiuncula.

Her escape and rejection angered her parents who were committed to her return. They tracked her down to the Benedictine convent of San Paolo in Basti, where Francis had moved her. Clare's father and uncle, with the assistance of a small army of men, stormed the doors and entered the sanctuary. Clare was found clinging to the altar and silently refused to budge. She was no longer wearing the jeweled clothes and graceful shoes of her former life, but the open sandals and coarse cloth of the convent.

When the angry men and Clare's weeping mother urged and begged for her to return with them, she removed her head covering, and they saw that it was shorn of its lovely blond tresses. This was too much for her parents and they all finally left, brokenhearted and helpless in the face of her firm resolution.

Francis moved Clare to another location. Two weeks after Clare's escape, her sister Agnes joined her. Her mother and father had tried to force Agnes into marriage in an attempt to prevent her from going the way of her sister, but they failed.

Other women soon joined Clare. Francis placed her in charge of these "Poor Clares" as they were called, and gave her the chapel of San Damiano, which he had restored with his own hands. Francis suggested that Clare serve as the Superior. But she refused the position until she turned twenty-one. Although Clare did not want this responsibility, she would bear it for forty years. The "Poor Clares" devoted themselves to prayer, nursing the sick, and to works of mercy for the poor and needy. Despite their way of life, or perhaps because of it, the followers of Clare were often the most beautiful young girls from the best families of Assisi. Eventually, Clare had the consolation, not only of seeing her younger sister Beatrix, her mother Ortolana, and her faithful aunt Bianca follow Agnes into the order, but also of witnessing the foundation of many "monasteries of Clares" far and wide throughout Europe.

Francis was a poet of the soul, and not a man of administration. Because of this, even in his lifetime, direction over the Franciscans was taken from him. In his uncertainty, Francis consulted Clare at times over many issues of faith and practice. He knew that he could count on her for prayerful advice. It was she who encouraged him in the work of evangelization, when he debated whether the brothers should live lives solely of contemplation or to travel about preaching. "Go ye into all the world and preach the gospel," was her scriptural counsel.

Clare viewed joy as an attitude which must be adopted regardless of the vicissitudes of life. Physical pain itself became a chance to express joy. Clare, who was often near death said, "I tremble with joy, and I do not fear that anyone may rob me of such happiness."

Worth Reading: *Francis and Clare: The Complete Works (The Classics of Western Spirituality)*, by Regis J. Armstrong.

While many people chose to live for the world and deny religion, Clare chose to do the opposite. She recognized the essential emptiness of mere things before she was eighteen years old.

Thomas Aquinas *1225-1274*
Theologian and Philosopher

Thomas Aquinas lived at a critical juncture of western culture when the arrival of the Aristotelian corpus in Latin translation reopened the question of the relation between faith and reason. Thomas' teaching combined with his great faith in Christ was highly regarded by the teachers, philosophers, and theologians of his day. His greatest writing Summa Theologica *is still one of the classics of Christian truth.*

homas Aquinas sat huddled in the corner of the cold prison cell of the family castle tower, wondering if his family would ever accept his choice to become a Dominican priest instead of one of the more prestigious Benedictines. His parents had kidnapped him seventeen months earlier from this order in an attempt to persuade him to reconsider. His resolve was unshakable, and they felt compelled to resort to more desperate measures. Thomas' brothers then arranged for a high-class prostitute to visit him in his cell, hoping he might break his vows. "With pain in his loins," he wrote later, he rejected her advances and cast her from his presence with a brand which he snatched from the fire. Because his brothers feared the threats of Innocent IV and Frederick II, Thomas was set at liberty, being lowered in a basket into the arms of the waiting Dominicans. With this victory he gained strength of spirit and became a noted theologian and philosopher of the Middle Ages.

Thomas Aquinas' extensive theological writings, along with his simple and profound style of presenting the gospel, makes him one of the most frequently quoted fathers of the Church.

Thomas Aquinas was born Thomas d'Aquino, the son of a baron, in his family's castle at Roccasecca, in the vicinity of Naples in southern Italy. At the age of five, Thomas parents placed him in the Benedictine monastery at Monte Cassino. His uncle had been abbot of the monastery, and his family had similar ambitions for Thomas. Diligent in study, he was early recognized as being meditative and devoted to prayer, and his advisor was surprised at hearing the child ask frequently: "What is God?"

In 1236, as a teenager, Thomas enrolled in the University of Naples. There he met members of the new Dominican Order and was moved by their Aristotilian teaching and their monastic life. He was appointed to be trained under the famous Albertus Magnus, and within a short time men were more anxious to hear Thomas than they had been to hear Albert, whom Thomas eventually surpassed in power of exposition and passion, if not in universality of knowledge. His teaching attracted the attention both of the professors and of the students. His duties consisted principally in explaining the *Sentences* of Peter Lombard, and his commentaries on that textbook of theology furnished the materials and the plan for his chief work, the *Summa theologica*.

Thomas was always teaching and writing. He lived on Earth with one passion: an ardent zeal for the explanation and defense of Christian truth. So devoted was he to his sacred task that with tears he begged to be excused from accepting the Archbishopric of Naples, to which he was appointed by Clement IV in 1265. Had he accepted this appointment, his *Summa theologica* would most likely not have been written.

Detail of "Apotheosis of St. Thomas Aquinas" by Francisco de Zurbarán (1598-1664).

December 6, 1273, after a physical and mental breakdown from years of exhaustion and overwork, Aquinas set down his pen and would write no more. While going north to attend the Council of Lyon, Thomas injured his head and fell ill. The Cistercian monks of Fossa Nuova pressed him to accept their hospitality in his time of need, and he was conveyed to their monastery. Upon entering, he whispered to his companion, *"This is my rest for ever and ever. Here will I dwell, for I have chosen it"* (Psalm 132:14). As the end drew near he poured out his heart in love for his Savior: "I receive Thee, the price of my redemption, for whose love I have watched, studied, and labored. Thee have I preached, Thee have I taught. Never have I said anything against Thee. If anything was not well said, that is to be attributed to my ignorance." He died in the Cistercian abbey of Fossa Nuova on March 7, 1274.

Although Thomas lived less than fifty years, he composed more than sixty works, some of them brief, and some quite lengthy. Though some of his beliefs and writings were not accepted by the Protestant Reformation, they have remained powerful influences in the Church for more than 700 years.

Key Writings of Aquinas: 1. *On Being and Essence* (1242-43); 2. *On the Principles of Nature* (1252-56); 3. *On Truth* (1256-59); 4. *On Potency* (1259-63); 5. *Of God and His Creatures* (1260); 6. *On the Divine Names* (1261); 7. *On Evil* (1263-68); 8. *Summa Theologica* (1265-72); 9. *Commentary on Aristotle's De memoria et reminiscencia* (after 1269); 10. *On the Eternity of the World* (1270); 11. *On Separate Substances* (1271).

John Wycliffe *1324-1384*
"Morning Star" of the Reformation

In the sixteenth century drastic reform burst forth from within the Church at the hands of courageous and godly men such as Luther, Zwingli, and Calvin, but it was two centuries earlier that John Wycliffe opposed the spread of ecclesiastical errors in the stated Church and received the title of the "first English Reformer."

 he "Black Plague" had swept across England and Europe wiping out one-third of the population with devastating alacrity. The "100 Years War" between England and France sapped valuable energy and resources. Wage controls locked the poor into a menial existence and led to the violent Peasant's Revolt in England in 1381. Meanwhile, the Church was filled with illiterate and corrupt clergy who seized every opportunity to oppress the weak and advance their own lust for power, prestige, and worldly gain. Such was the world into which John Wycliffe was born.

Now imagine that those who lived at this time were not permitted to read the Bible. The Scriptures were not allowed in the hands of anyone but the Church officials. It was they alone who could determine its language and meaning, and they alone dictated to the people how to live "according to God's directives."

John Wycliffe was educated at Oxford and received his doctorate in Theology. While attending school and studying Latin (the language in which the Bibles of his day was written) his passion for the truth found in the Word of God grew. As his knowledge and faith matured he came to detest the errors and abuses so evident in the Roman Church. Though he was officially part of it, he wanted nothing to do with it. His heart, mind, and energies were earnestly devoted to the immense task to which God had called him—the translation of the Scriptures from Latin into English.

John Wycliffe believed that in order for the truth be known regarding the abuses of the Church, men and women needed to read the Scriptures for themselves. He was convinced that churches were sadly populated primarily by ignorant and suppressed parishioners, and that the Church leaders did all they could to maintain superiority. He criticized not only the organization of the medieval Church, but its theology as well. He believed it was imperative that the Church return to the Scriptures, and its ministers should live lives of simplicity and holiness, preach the pure gospel, and shepherd their flock.

The Lord had given Wycliffe keen insight into the abuses of

Church officials feared to see the Bible in the hands of "commoners," but John Wycliffe believed the Word of God should be open to all people. His translation of the Scriptures from Latin to English was a milestone in Biblical enlightenment and Church growth.

the Church of his day and his heart was greatly burdened. He had no greater passion than getting the Bible and its liberating truth into the language, then prayerfully into the hearts of the people. He knew the Scriptures would change lives and release people from blindly following Church dogma. As he put it, "God's words will give men new life more than any other words that are for pleasure. O marvelous power of the Divine Seed which overpowers strong men in arms, softens hard hearts, and renews and changes into divine men, those men who had been brutalized by sins, and departed infinitely far from God. Obviously such miraculous power could never be worked by the work of a priest, if the Spirit of Life and the Eternal Word did not, above all things else, work with it."

The Church was already irritated with Wycliffe for supporting the Parliament over and against the pope in disputes regarding ecclesiastical rights and authority. But once the word spread of his resolve to publish the Bible in English and distribute it to the "common" people, the Church authorities attacked him with vehemence. Wycliffe was stripped of his position in the Church and bands of priests were formed in order to harass him and threaten any who sought to aid him.

Though old and exhausted, Wycliffe remained undaunted in his pursuit, and his dream became a reality in 1382 when he successfully translated the New Testament into the English language. His faithful friend, Nicholas Hereford, translated a sizable portion of the Old Testament, and with the help of a few others, the whole Bible was completed. Many transcribers then took up the task of duplicating this great work for it's ultimate destination—the firesides of "common" families.

"The Dawn of the Reformation." With his English translation of the Bible, Wycliffe exposed his adversaries' false doctrines. By sending forth his "Poor Priests," he acquired much influence for good. (Below) Artist Y. A. Yeames depicts Wycliffe sending out the Lollards from Lutterworth, carrying copies of his English Bible.

Though papal persecution remained steady, it was no match for the resolve of Wycliffe and his followers. Wycliffe gave himself unceasingly to preaching and shepherding of souls. Since it was his desire to do away with the existing hierarchy in the Church, on the ground that it had no warrant in Scripture, he put in its place a community commonly known as "Poor Priests" or "Lollards." They traveled throughout the land distributing the precious new English Bible. These men lived simple lives, were bound by no vows, and had received no formal consecration. These priests were itinerant preachers who spread abroad among the people the teachings of Christ. Two-by-two they went barefoot, clad in long dark red robes and carrying a staff in hand. This staff was a symbolic reference to their pastoral calling. They passed from place to place preaching the sovereignty of God. These "Lollards" had reached wide circles in England and faithfully preached "God's law, without which no one could be justified."

The title page to Wycliffe's 1525 edition of his Dialogues.

Wycliffe's death in 1384 did nothing to hinder the work he had begun and inspired. In fact, thirty-one years later, the grave of the great Reformer was opened by order of the Council of Constance, Wycliffe's remains were torn from their resting place. The Roman Church attempted to silence his followers by digging up his body and burning his bones in public ridicule, but it only served to inspire his followers even more. In addition, the Church seized as many copies of the English Bible as they could and burned them in public displays. They also persecuted the Lollards in their effort to inhibit biblical learning, but the power and truth of the Word of God had reached the hearts and minds of so many people, that the Papists found themselves, as it were, fighting against God.

From generation to generation copies of the proscribed volume were handed down as heirlooms in many English homes. Soon hand-to-hand circulation of the Bible was superseded by the invention of the printing press by Gutenberg, and through the untiring labors of Tyndale and Coverdale.

Key Writings of Wycliffe: 1. *The New Testament, Translated from the Latin Vulgate* (1378); 2. *Last Age of the Church*; 3. *On Christ and His Adversary Antichrist*; 4. *Summa Theologiae*; 5. *Dialogues*; 6. *Trialogues*; 7. *De civili dominio*; 8. *The Wicket, or Learned and Godly Treatise of the Sacrament*; 9. *Treatises Against the Begging Friars*; 10. *An Apology for Lollard Doctrines.*

Worth Reading: *Church History of Great Britain*, by Thomas Fuller; *Life of John Wycliffe, with a Sketch of the British Church and the Reformation* (1865)

The martyrdom of John Huss

John Huss *1369-1415*
Reformer Before the Reformation

The ashes of Wycliffe had hardly found rest in the Swift River when the Lord raised up John Huss, to carry the torch lit by the great reformer and Bible translator. Following in the footsteps of his hero, Huss advanced the cause of Christian truth, amidst the corruption of the established Church, and became an early martyr of the Reformation. Like his predecessor, Huss was "faithful unto death."

 s a young student at the University of Prague, John Huss experienced a foreshadowing of the suffering he would be called to endure for the sake of his Savior and King. One winter's evening when reading by his fireside, John's heart was stirred as he read the *Life of Lawrence*. His imagination was kindled at the narrative of the martyr's sufferings, and he thrust his own hand into the flames. He then told his fellow students, "I was only trying what part of the tortures of this holy man I might be capable of enduring."

John Huss was born into a poor family in a small rural town near Bohemia. Though their resources were scarce, his parents spared little to secure a fine education for their beloved son. He attended the University of Prague where he received various degrees in the arts, but his training in divinity came through the generosity of one of his professors whose extensive theological library was liberally made available to Huss. John took full advantage of the opportunity and pursued reading many theological works that had a tremendous influence on him.

When a British student first showed John the propositions of Wycliffe, he was alarmed and begged his friend to throw such dangerous writings into the river. Yet the scandalous license and corruption of the clergy was making an indelible mark on young Huss' impressionable soul. Meanwhile, his daily study of the holy Scriptures, and his exchanges with the learned Jerome of Prague, gradually opened his eyes. After devoting himself to the study of Wycliffe's writings, John's opinions gave way to reason and his heart overflowed with fervent approbation. Regarding John's studies, his fellow collegians reproachfully remarked to him that, "by a decree of the Council of Constance, Wycliffe had been sent to hell." Huss earnestly replied, "I only wish that my soul may reach the place where that excellent Briton now dwells."

Within a few years Huss was a sought after public theological and philosophical lecturer. In 1402, he was ordained a

In the remarkable providence of God, the work of John Wycliffe made its way from England to Bohemia and into the mind and heart of John Huss. This humble priest would stand against the formidable forces of the corrupt clergy and become an undaunted pioneer of the Reformation of the sixteenth-century.

Bohemian preacher in the Bethlehem Chapel at Prague, where he acquired a great love for the people, and they for him.

As the mind of the reformer became more thoroughly illuminated by the Holy Spirit, he assumed a more independent front, and through his preaching and writing attacked the highest clergy, denouncing their scandalous lives, and the gross corruptions of the Church they represented. All classes of people crowded to hear him, including the queen. His fame spread throughout the empire and attracted both friends and foes to Bohemia.

Bethlehem Chapel itself was a tangible illustration of Huss' teachings. On its walls were paintings contrasting the behavior of the popes with that of our Lord Jesus Christ. For example, the pope rode a horse while Christ walked barefoot. Jesus washed the disciples' feet while the pope had his feet kissed. Czech nobles had built and maintained the chapel as a place for worship. A place to redress the lack of preaching in parish churches and for promoting biblical instruction in the language of the people. Protected by the nobility, preacher after preacher managed to survive both the established Church's suspicion as well as its eagerness to dismantle the institution.

The great success of Huss in his native country was due mainly to his unsurpassed pastoral activity, which far excelled that of the famous old preachers of Bohemia. But even here Huss was the docile pupil of Wycliffe. Huss himself put the highest value on the sermon and knew how to awaken the enthusiasm of the masses.

The *sola-scriptura* writings of John Wycliffe found their way deep into Bohemia, mainly through the efforts of God's faithful servant, Jerome. John Huss then painstakingly copied Wycliffe's books for his own use. Like Wycliffe, Huss emphasized personal piety and purity of life. He stressed the role of the Bible as sole authority in the Church, and as a result, he elevated biblical preaching to an important status in the worship services.

Under Archbishop Sbinko of Hasenburg, Huss enjoyed a great reputation. In 1405, however, as he was active as a synodical preacher, his severe attacks upon the clergy, through papal pressure the bishop was compelled to depose him. This was the start of problems for Huss and his followers. Wycliffites (as they were called) were labeled as instigators of all ecclesiastical disturbances in Bohemia. As a result the pope issued his "papal bull" (order) of December 20, 1409, which empowered the archbishop to proceed against Wycliffism. All books of Wycliffe were to be given up and his doctrines revoked, while free preaching was prohibited. The collected books and valuable manuscripts were then publically burned by the hand of the archbishop himself.

In 1412, a dispute arose concerning the growing practice of "indulgences" in the Roman church. Preachers of indulgences urged people to crowd the churches and give their offerings as a means to have their sins forgiven. This prompted Huss to deliver his objection in his *Quaestio magistri Johannis Huss ... de indulgentiis.* It was taken literally from the last chapter of Wycliffe's book, *De ecclesia,* and his treatise, *De absolutione a pena et culpa.* No pope or bishop, according to Wycliffe and Huss, has a right to take up the sword in the name of the Church, and he should pray for his enemies and bless those that curse him. Man obtains forgiveness of sins by genuine repentance and faith in Christ, not by money given.

Opposition to Huss's influence grew fierce, and three men from the lower class who had openly contradicted the orders of the pope were beheaded. They became the first martyrs of the Hussites. Huss was asked if he was finally prepared to admit obedience to the pope, to which he replied, "Yes, as long as they agree with the doctrines of Christ [as they are set forth in the Bible], but when I see the contrary I will not obey them, even if you burn my body." It was Wycliffe's teaching that if the pope, clergy, or any other men "contraried" Christ they were to be resisted and counted as enemies of Christ.

Huss was then accused of heresy and summoned by the Council of Constance in Switzerland, to defend his opinions before the clergy of nations. The poor excommunicated priest made his departure for Constance with a simple trust in God and a courage supplied by the Holy Spirit. On this journey Huss was warmly welcomed by all the townspeople, and led with triumph through the streets of several communities that lay along the way.

On reaching Constance, the companions of Huss waited on the pope, announcing his arrival under a "safe-conduct" of the emperor, and asking further assurance of his personal safety. "Had he killed my own brother," replied the pope, "not a hair of his head should be touched during his stay here."

Before appearing before the Council of Constance, Huss published his most notable work, *De ecclesia* or *Concerning the Church*. In his writing, he challenged the claim of the pope as the ultimate authority. He said, "They were not the Church. The Church had once existed without them. The foundation of the Church is Christ, not Peter." This same position was take more that 1,000 years earlier by Augustine, as recorded in his *Retractions*.

Within a month of his arrival in Constance Huss was arrested and thrown into a dungeon in a Dominican monastery near a city sewer. There he experienced rough conditions and starvation. He complained, but was aware of the danger and soon realized his fate had been predetermined. "I confide altogether in my Savior," he wrote at that time. "I trust that he will accord me his Holy Spirit, to fortify me in His truth, so that I may face with courage, temptations, prison, and if necessary, a cruel death."

Huss, whose body was weak by long imprisonment protested his innocence and refused to renounce his alleged errors unless he could be shown otherwise from Scripture. He said, "I would not, for a chapel full of gold, recede from the truth."

When the cruel treatment of Huss became known in Bohemia, it excited universal indignation. In the generous mind of Jerome of Prague, sympathy for his friend overpowered all

What Huss says in his sermons on the corruption of the Church, clergy, and monks, on the duties of secular powers, he has taken almost literally from Wycliffe. His three great sermons, De sufficientia legis Christi, De fidei suae elucidatione, and De pace, with which he thought to convert the whole council at Constance, are exact reproductions of Wycliffe's sermons.

sense of danger, and he immediately set out for Constance. He was arrested en route and brought to Constance on a cart loaded with chains, where he was presented to a conclave of priests assembled at the convent of the Franciscans. Delivered by them to the cruel Archbishop of Riga, he was thrown, heavily ironed, into the dark dungeon of a tower in the cemetery of St. Paul. His chains were nailed to a lofty beam, preventing him from sitting, while his arms were fastened with irons behind his neck, so as to force his head down. In this dreadful dungeon Jerome was confined for a whole year. The severity of his treatment being relaxed only when his life threatened to fall a sacrifice to such rigor. Jerome solicited the privilege of sharing the same dungeon with his comrade, John Huss, but his entreaties fell on deaf ears.

In the following days, Huss appeared three times before the Council to defend the charges against him, but scarcely any show of justice was attempted. Whenever the reformer would speak, his voice was drowned by the shouts of "recantation or death" from his accusers. His day of execution was then fixed.

Huss put the highest value on the sermon and knew how to awaken the enthusiasm of the masses. His sermons were often inflammatory with regards to their content. He introduced his quarrels with his spiritual superiors, criticized many contemporaneous events, or appealed to his congregation as witness or judge. It was this bearing which multiplied his followers, and thus he became the true apostle of his English master.

On his 42nd birthday, John Huss was led from prison in chains before a pompous assembly, and forced outside to witness the "high mass" followed by the burning of his books, to which he simply smiled. Huss was then led away to the stake under a strong guard of armed men.

At the place of execution Huss knelt down, spread out his hands, and prayed aloud, "Lord, into thy hands I commend my spirit. I am willing patiently and publically to endure this dreadful, shameful and cruel death for the sake of thy Gospel and the preaching of thy Word." At this his persecutors placed a crown on his head with images of devils.

He was tied to the stake with a wet ropes and a chain around his neck and feet. An old peasant, thinking of doing good, placed a stick on the wood pile, but Huss only smiled and said compassionately, "O holy innocence!"

Through it all, even to the last moment of his life, he demonstrated astonishing peace and an undaunted spirit. The Duke of Bavaria pleaded for him to recant, but Huss replied in a loud voice, "I have ever taught according to God's Word, and will still hold fast the truth, which this very hour I shall seal with my death!" Astonished, the duke hid his face in his hands, and fled the scene in tears. As fire was set to the pile, the martyr began singing, *Christ, thou Son of the living God, have mercy upon me.* Thus the great reformer gave up his spirit and entered into the presence of his beloved Savior.

Key Writings of Huss: *De ecclesia (Concerning the Church)*

Worth Reading: *Life and Times of John Huss,* by E. H. Gillett (1870); *John Huss,* by A. H. Wratislaw (1882); *John Wycliffe and his English Precursors,* (1884); *The Dawn of the Reformation,* by H. B. Workman (1902); *The Age of Huss,* (1902).

Johann Gutenberg *1400-1468*
Inventor of the Printing Press

Books were extremely valuable possessions to those who lived during the Middle Ages. Few owned them and they would often cost as much as a large farm. Libraries were found primarily in monasteries and churches. All books to this point in history were manuscripts (written by man's hand), and were produced only after long hours of painstaking work—until Johann Gutenberg's invention changed forever the course of literature and communication among men.

But it is just a simple press you are asking from me, Master Hans," said the skillful craftsman of wood and metal, Conrad Saspach, after being asked by Johann Gutenberg to create a full-size version from a smaller model. "Yes," replied Gutenberg, with a grave and enthusiastic tone, "it is a press, certainly, but a press from which shall soon flow in inexhaustible streams the most abundant and most marvelous liquor that has ever flowed to relieve the thirst of man! Through it God will spread his Word. A spring of pure truth shall flow from it! Like a new star, it shall scatter the darkness of ignorance, and cause a light heretofore unknown to shine among men." This marked the birth of the first printing press.

Johann Gutenberg was born in the wealthy city of Maintz, off the shores of the Rhine. His father, Friel Gensfleisch, married Else von Gutenberg, who gave her name to her second son, John.

Through reading books, young Johann developed an insatiable appetite for knowledge.

During his teen years he and his family were forced into exile twice due to the political infighting between the various classes of nobility in Germany. Once peace was restored, young Gutenberg was allowed to satisfy his literary, religious, and artistic tastes by traveling from town to town studying monuments, and visiting men who were renowned for science, art, or the trades. Gutenberg traveled alone, on foot, carrying a knapsack containing books and clothes, like a mere student visiting schools, or a journeyman looking for a master. He ventured through Italy, Switzerland, Germany, and Holland. Like a man who lets his imagination wander at the caprice of his footsteps, he carried everywhere with him a fixed idea, and unyielding will, led by determination and a strong faith. His guiding star was the vision of spreading the Word of God to all people.

It was Johann's faith in Christ which was motivating him

Gutenberg loved to read, but became impatient with the time-consuming process of book-making by hand. His genius, faith and passion for the spread of the gospel propelled the events that introduced movable type and the first printing press to the world.

Gutenberg and his faithful apprecntices reviewing an early printed page in their workroom. Engraving by E. Hillimacher for Great Men and Famous Women (1895).

to seek the soil wherein to sow a single seed, of which the fruit hereafter was to be a thousand various grains. It is the glory of printing that it was given to the world by religion, not by industry. Religious enthusiasm was alone worthy to give birth to this fantastic instrument of truth.

Gutenberg's motivation and passion came to reality when, one day his friend Lawrence Koster, from Haarlam, handed him a piece of green wood that had letters carved on it, wrapped in a piece of parchment. Apparently the sap from the wood had hardened into the relief shape of the letters on the parchment. At the sight of this meager plank of wood, it was as if lightening from heaven flashed before the eyes of Gutenberg. Staring at this now small treasure, he imagined it smeared with something other than sap, and with more letters. Many more letters.

Like a man who possesses a rare treasure, and knows neither rest nor sleep until he has hidden it safely, Gutenberg left Haarlem, hastened up the Rhine until he reached Strasburg and shut himself up in his workroom. He fashioned his own tools, tried, broke, planned, rejected, returned to his plans over and over again. Finally he ended by secretly executing a successful proof upon a piece of parchment with movable wooden types. He bored through the side with a small hole, strung together and kept close by a thread, each with a letter of the alphabet cut in relief on one side. This first printer's alphabet was crude, but wonderful!

Gutenberg perceived the immense bearing of his invention on society, industry, and especially religion. He acutely felt his limitations since he was just one man, with limited resources.

Gutenberg was concerned about his work being discovered and possibly pirated. In order to keep his efforts hidden, he employed himself in the more noble crafts of jewelry and clock-making as his public vocation, but secretly worked countless hours on his mechanics of printing.

Upon word that his anonymity was being compromised, he moved his workshop into the ruins of an old deserted monastery where none but the homeless lingered. There he passed sleepless nights, wearing himself out in pursuit of his invention. There he engraved his movable types in wood, and projected casting them in metal. He studied hard to find the means of enclosing them in forms, whether of wood or of iron, to make the types into words, phrases, and lines, and to leave spaces on the paper. There he invented colored mediums, oily and yet able to dry, to reproduce the characters, brushes and dabbers that spread the ink on the letters, boards to hold them, and screws and weights to compress them. Months and years were spent, as well as his own fortune, in these persevering experiments, which alternated between success and disappointment. Until, at last, he developed a model press which combined all the elements for his vision of a printing press. He enthusiastically had the first press built in full-size by his friend Conrad Saspach.

The Gutenberg Bible (1455) was the first book ever published with moveable type. Less than 200 were originally printed and only about 50 have survived. Depicted here in black and white is the decorative and colorful first page of Genesis.

As soon as he had the "new treasure" in his possession, he began to print. His strong faith in Christ and earlier desire to see the Scriptures in the hands of all people leaves no doubt as to the nature of his first endeavor. The uncompromisingly faithful first pages included the Holy Bible and a Psalter (the first book to ever bear a date: 1457). Under the guiding hands of this pious inventor, praise and prayer were the first voices to come from the printing press.

At first, the Roman Church opposed the printing press, as it infringed upon the established scribal profession. But the awesome power that the printing press possessed could not be quenched for long. It was embraced by the Church a few years after its introduction. A section of a dedication written to Pope Paul II on behalf of the printing press reads: "Among the number of blessings which we ought to praise God is this invention, which enables the poorest to procure libraries at a low price. Is it not a great glory that volumes that used to cost one hundred pieces of gold, are now to be bought for four, or even less, and that the fruits of genius... multiply over all the earth!"

The popularity of the press grew so rapidly that Gutenberg could not sustain the demand in his small workshop, and therefore felt the need to engage in partnerships with successful business men. Unfortunately, they were not as scrupulous as the inventor, and they managed to take over his invention and his name for their own gain. He lost all hope of attaining wealth and fame in his day, and some even attempted to steal the honor of invention from him shortly after his death. Through all his trials, Gutenberg managed to maintain the secrets of his invention as well as his integrity. To all who knew him, he was an honest and faithful Christian man.

Today, the original Gutenberg Bible is considered one of the finest pieces of art left to mankind. In 1978, a two-volume edition sold for over two million dollars, the highest price ever paid for a rare book.

Gutenberg's invention of the printing press should be classified with the greatest events in the history of the world. It incited a revolution in the development of culture, equaled by hardly any other incident in the Christian era. Disseminating the treasures of the world's intellect was a necessary condition for the rapid development of information in modern times. Happening as it did just at the time when science was becoming more secularized and its cultivation no longer resigned almost entirely to the monks, it may be said that the age was pregnant with this invention. Not only is Gutenberg's labor inseparable from the progress of modern science and literature, but it has also been an indispensable factor in the education of the people. Culture and knowledge, until then considered aristocratic privileges peculiar to certain classes, were popularized by Gutenberg's invention, enabling the masses to discover for themselves great literature and the Word of God. No doubt, this one invention launched the Middle Ages out of darkness and into the marvelous light of the Renaissance and the Reformation.

Worth Reading: *Gutenberg and the Art of Printing;* by Emily Pearson (1871); *Johann Gutenberg, The Inventor of Printing,* by Victor Scholder (1963); *Gutenberg Bible: God and Various Inspired Authors,* (1968); *A Short History of the Printed Word,* by Warren Chappel (1970); *Johann Gutenberg and His Bible,* by Janet Ing (1988); *Fine Print,* by Johann Johansen Burch (1991); *Gutenberg: How One Man Changed the World With Words,* by John Man (2002).

Savonarola *1452-1498*
Early Reformer and Italian Martyr

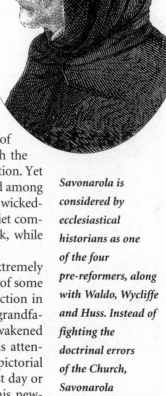

Savonarola lived in a time that was in many ways like our own. It was an age of great discoveries, extraordinary artistic and communications achievements, the emergence of new views of the world, great self-consciousness, and pride in human achievement. It was also an age of restlessness in the world of faith and religion that was bound to erupt sooner or later.

There within the walls of the once sacred Dominican monastery in Bologna sat a young monk, Girolamo Savonarola, fervently engaged in earnest meditation, the study of the holy Scriptures and prayer to the God of Heaven and Earth. He entered the monastery filled with the anguish of a heart broken over his miserable, sinful condition. Yet the healing balm and like-mindedness he expected to find among the brothers was sadly a place of much immorality and wickedness. Young Girolamo therefore dedicated himself to quiet communion with Christ and knowledge of the Sacred Book, while applying the truth to his life and conscience.

Born of Italian nobility, Girolamo Savonarola was extremely intelligent and at an early age gravitated to the writings of some of the most learned men in history. He received instruction in philosophy, logic, and medicine from his father and grandfather. But it was his reading of Plato and Dante that awakened a yearning for grander pursuits. Religion engrossed his attention. His sense of his own sinfulness as well as the pictorial illustrations of hell in *Dante's Purgatory,* left him no rest day or night. The cares of the world seemed to fade amidst his newfound convictions. In 1475, he decided to join the Dominican monastery.

There he limited himself to four hours of rest each day and employed the remainder of his time in preaching and study, as well as holding long conversations over spiritual matters with his brethren. When he left the monastery he found himself in the heart of renewal and reform in Italy.

The center of the Renaissance of the fifteenth century was Florence, Italy, where we find the timeless beauty and grandeur of art from such masters as Michelangelo, Da Vinci, and Raphael, among others. But lesser known in the history of this place is the faithful voice of Savonarola, who with fervent devotion and power of exposition preached Christ amidst the moral decay, irreligious lifestyles, and extra-biblical beliefs and practices of the clergy, particularly that of the Medici family.

Savonarola is considered by ecclesiastical historians as one of the four pre-reformers, along with Waldo, Wycliffe and Huss. Instead of fighting the doctrinal errors of the Church, Savonarola concerned himself more with the practical implications of religion in the lives of the people.

"We must regenerate the Church," said Savonarola, "God remits the sins of men, and justifies them by his mercy. There are as many compassions in heaven as there are justified men upon earth; for none are saved by their own works. No man can boast of himself; and if, in the presence of God, we could ask all these justified sinners—Have you been saved by your own strength? All would reply as with one voice, 'Not unto us, O Lord! not unto us; but to thy name be the glory!'—Therefore, O God, do I seek thy mercy, and I bring not unto thee my own righteousness; but when by thy grace thou justifies one, then thy righteousness belongs unto me; for grace is the righteousness of God.—O God, save me by thy righteousness, that is to say, in thy Son, who alone among men was found without sin!" †

Savonarola was burnt at the stake in the Piazza della Signoria in Florence.

Savonarola, like all Christian Reformers, gave special emphasis to the authority of the Bible. He commented: "I preach the regeneration of the church, taking the Scriptures as my sole guide."

The pope finally condemned Savonarola and excommunicated him from the Church. Savonarola unsuccessfully tried to bring together a convention of European leaders to remove the decadent Borgia from the papacy. The Florentine crowd turned on Savonarola. He was imprisoned and severely tortured on the rack. On one day alone he was drawn up by ropes fourteen times and then suddenly dropped.

In the face of death, Savonarola prayed, "O Lord, a thousand times have you wiped out my iniquity. I do not rely on my own justification, but on thy mercy." In between his tortures, he wrote meditations on Psalms 32 and 51, which Martin Luther later published, calling them "a piece of evangelical testing and Christian piety."

Savonarola was burned at the stake on May 23, 1498. As the bishop stripped him of his priestly garb, he said, "I separate thee from the church militant and from the church triumphant." Savonarola replied, "That is beyond your power, for thou hast no such power." Savonarola met martyrdom with courage and faith, exclaiming, "Should I not willingly die for His sake who willingly died for me, a sinful man?"

Key Writings of Savonarola: 1. *Compendium revelationum* (1495); 2. *Dialogus de veritate et prophetica* (1497); 3. *Triumph of the Cross* (1497).

† J. H. Merle D'Aubigne's History of the Reformation. Vol. 1, pp. 96-97

Worth Reading: *Spiritual and Ascetic Letters of Savonarola*, by B. W. Randolph (1907).

Albert Dürer 1471-1528
Reformer and Evangelist in Art

The end of the fifteenth century was a time full of much unrest and faithlessness. Just as the darkest hour comes before the dawn, the period immediately before the fullness of the Reformation was one of gloom and fear. There was no unity of spirit in the Church, but the deepest darkness was found in the hearts of men. This is where the pen and brush of Albert Dürer made its profoundest impact, and this pious artist emerged as an evangelist and reformer.

 hough he was not a preacher or great theologian, nor a writer of classic books on Christian truth, Albert Dürer is worthy of standing beside Luther and Calvin as a noble and strong Reformer. While others expounded the gospel in soul-piercing sermons or convicting writings, Dürer told the story of the Cross in pictures, not unlike the greatest masters of the Renaissance—and in some ways even more rich and powerful. His artwork was not by appointment of a wealthy king or by papal decree, but through a humble and contrite heart in love with his Savior. Albert was driven to proclaim, through his art, the matchless story of salvation and eternal life to all the world.

Albert Dürer is undoubtedly the greatest German artist of the Renaissance, but he is most well-known for his faith in Christ and his resolve to see his Savior honored and proclaimed through his life and his work.

Albert (Albrecht) was born the oldest son, and the third of eighteen children, to a goldsmith in Nuremberg, Germany. His father, Albert Dürer the elder, worked hard in his precious metals business to support his large family, but he faced severe trials and suffered the loss of many of his children. Only three of his eighteen children survived to adulthood. Yet, he was an honest man who trusted in God and handled his trials with fortitude and courage. Albert wrote that his father was rightfully praised from all who knew him. His son writes, "My father lived an honorable Christian life. He was a man patient of spirit, mild and peaceable to all, and very thankful toward God…He was a man of few words and was a God-fearing man…This man, my dear father, was very careful of his children to bring them up to love and honor God."

The younger Albert was an apprentice in his father's goldsmith shop, but his heart's desire was to be an artist. His father was too discerning to forbid his son, and so in the fall of 1486, he sent Albert for three years to the studio of his famous neighbor, Michael Wolgemuth, who at that time was in the height of his reputation and productive energy. A portrait of the old man, by his new apprentice, survived to this day. Under his training, Albert's history of apprenticeship is both expressive and full of suggestion. "During that time God gave me diligence, so that I learned much, but I had to suffer a great deal from the journey-men." The sensitive and conscientious spirit of Dürer winced at the rough lads who also shared apprenticeship in the master's workshop.

Dürer spent the next few years traveling from town to town with other artists developing his craft. In Mainz, where just thirty-five years earlier Johann Gutenberg had invented the printing press, Albert became familiar with Erhard Reuwich, the first artist who also was a publisher. Reuwich's book *Travels in the Holy Land* was full of sketches depicting the architecture, costumes and landscape of the Holy Land.

In 1494, he returned to Nurenberg and married the beautiful Agnes Frey. They spent the first eleven years together in Nuremberg where he devoted himself to his art. In addition to his painting, Dürer was also engaged in the art of woodcut illustrations and copperplate engravings. During these years his abilities grew rapidly, and he executed many superb works of art.

In 1505, he journeyed to Venice, intending to study among some of the great Renaissance masters. For the first time he became acquainted with classical art and began to study theories of proportion and perspective.

His commitment to the reform of the Church is clearly indicated by his writings as well as his works of art. He possessed a great affection for and intimacy with Luther and Melancthon, the latter of whom we have a portrait from his hand. When Friedrich of Saxony sent Dürer one of Luther's books in 1520, Dürer wrote to him and thanked him: "I pray to His Electoral grace, and beg humbly that you will protect the praiseworthy Dr. Martin Luther for the sake of Christian truth. It matters more than all the riches and power of this world, for with time everything passes away; only the truth is eternal. And if God helps me to come to Dr. Martin Luther, then I will carefully draw his portrait and engrave it in copper for a lasting remembrance of this Christian man who has helped me out

One of Dürer's best known works is Melancolia, which presents the melody of Psalm 90. It has the dirges of man's mortality, but is also a prayer for the beauty of the Lord to rest on us, and bless the work of our hands. (1514)

of great distress. And I beg your worthiness to send me as my payment anything new that Dr. Martin may write in German."

Durer returned to The Netherlands in 1521, and there he spent the remaining years of his life in pursuit of his art, particularly engraving, painting, and the sciences of perspective. He devoted almost all of his work to various aspects of the life of Christ, the Resurrection, and the Apocalypse. In 1526, Dürer presented to the Nuremberg City Council *The Four Holy Men.* Below the painting Dürer wrote, "All worldly rulers in these dangerous times should give heed that they receive not human misguidance for the Word of God, for God will have nothing added to His Word nor taken away from it. Hear therefore these four excellent men, Peter, John, Paul, and Mark and heed their warning."

Dürer's The Four Riders of the Apocalypse (1496-1498), is one is a series of engravings of The Apocalypse of St. John. (Rev 6:1-6)

By this time the Reformation had grown into a great reality. It was consistent with the high spirit and intellectual character of Nuremberg that it was the first free city to join the new movement; and it was no less characteristic of the artist, that he was among the earliest to show his sympathy with and admiration for Luther. Nothing better expresses Dürer's spiritual character than his entry in his *Netherland Journal* when he heard of Luther's captivity, and feared his death: "So this man, enlightened by the Holy Ghost to be the continuer of the true faith, has disappeared. Have they murdered him? I do not know. If he has suffered, it is for the Christian truth against the unchristian papacy, which works against the freedom of Christ, exacting from us our blood and sweat, therewith to nourish itself in idleness, while the people famish. It is very sad and heavy to me that God allows so much false teaching and blindness in men we call Fathers, and permits the excellent worth of religion to be falsified and removed. God of Heaven, have pity on us! O Heavenly Father, pour into our hearts by Thy Son the light that will guide us, and show us the true leader, that we may leave the false guides with a clear conscience, and serve Thee with the joy of our hearts."

But among the Reformers, Dürer's special friend was Melancthon. Like himself, gentle and liberal, yet serious and scholarly in regard to his Christian profession. Their affection for one another grew, especially in the last years of Dürer's life as we see in the now famous words of Melancthon; "His art, great as it was, was his least merit."

Jerome in His Study (1504), is a classic work of Dürer.

Such were some of the friends with whom Dürer passed his last years. They could not have been years without much deep solace and enjoyment. His own health was indeed failing, but his spiritual character seems to have, in proportion, developed and deepened. These were the years when he was writing books. Thankfully, the Church still possess some of the most precious fruits of Dürer's long and silent thought. Nobly does he speak of the art he loved. "Never imagine to, thyself thou canst make anything better than God has made it....No man can ever execute a beautiful picture relying on his own imagination, unless he has stored his mind from a study of divine work in nature. ... The mysterious treasure laid up in the heart is made known by the man's work—for the mind and heart must be in union with the life and power of God, and then the artist's hand will form that thing of beauty which is indeed a joy forever."

Dürer died suddenly in 1528, to the shock and grief of many in the arts, as well as his beloved brethren in the Church. But his art still lives and breathes today and tells of his extraordinary faith and love for Christ, and his desire for the spreading of Christian truth and beauty.

Key Works of Durer: 1. *The Adoration of the Trinity;* 2. *Melancolia;* 3. *The Four Riders of the Apocalypse;* 4. *The Four Apostles;* 5. *Jerome in His Study;* 6. *The Knight, Death, and the Devil;* 7. *Adam and Eve;* 8. *The Dance of Death;* 9. *Feast of the Rose Gardens;* 10. *The Crucifixion;* 11. *Samson Killing the Lion;* 12. *The Last Supper;* 13. *The Trinity.*

Worth Reading: 1. *Durer: His Life and Works,* by Moriz Thausing, 2 vols. (1882); *The Works of Durer Reproduced in Over Four Hundred Illustrations* (1908); *The Writings of Albrecht Durer,* by W. M. Conway (1958); *The World of Durer,* by Francis Russell (1967); *The Drawing of Albert Durer,* by Heinrich Wolfflin (1970); *The Hidden Durer,* by Peter Streider (1978); *Albrecht Durer: A Biography,* by Anne Hutchinson (1992).

Martin Luther *1483-1546*

Leader of the Reformation

He had crossed the bounds which divide insubordination from rebellion, and his banners of truth were openly unfurled, while his spirit pressed forward on the march to Rome. This champion of the gospel entered with an inexhaustible degree of courage in the pursuit of truth, and he proceeded with fearless confidence to expose the error of false doctrines and ecclesiastical superstition.

ctober 31, 1517, rings loudly as the day, more than any other, that set in motion the Protestant Reformation. Many significant events occurred before and many after, but on this day a peasant monk stood against the "establishment" and changed forever the landscape of the Church of Christ. On this day in 1517, Martin Luther nailed his *Ninety-five Theses* on the door of the Wittenberg church in opposition to the erroneous and dangerous practice of indulgences in the Church. The long unuttered protest of the conscience of truth against Rome found expression in the words of this bold monk of Wittenberg. The sound of the hammer that day would resound across Europe and eventually reach the entire civilized world with the truth of the Gospel of Christ.

Martin Luther was born in Eisleben, Germany, but the family soon after moved to Mansfeld where the future Reformer received his earliest impression of life. He was sent off to school and received a fine eduction, but the discipline was harsh and he was turned off to the things of religion, in whose name his "instruction" was given. When speaking of the preachers to whom he listened in his youth, he once said that "they preached the fire of hell rather than the tidings of great joy, and transformed the Savior into a terrible judge, who would condemn men according to their deserts."

When Martin was fourteen years of age he was sent to Magdeburg to attend school. Afterwards he went to Eisenach for the same purpose, for Hans Luther's circumstances had improved, and he was resolved that his son should be a scholar. But the boy's life in Eisenach was one of hardship. He often sang on the streets begging bread for the love of God. His sweet singing attracted the notice of a benevolent matron, named Ursula, the wife of Conrad Cotta, and she received him under her roof. Luther remembered with gratitude the kindness of this lady. He affectionately called her "the pious Shunamite," and he never

The world has rarely witnessed a chartacter and resolve as remarkable as that of Martin Luther. He was created by Providence to light the torch of the greatest revolution in the history of Christendom.

Young Martin Luther being introduced to the home of Frau Cotta.

Luther wrote more than 1,100 sermons, commentaries and tracts during his lifetime. Among the most notable are his commentaries on Romans, Galatians, and the Psalms. He is also the author of the famous hymn, "A Mighty Fortress is Our God."

forgot her love against the backdrop of his hard experiences as a poor scholar in Eisenach. "Do not despise" he once said, "the boys who try to earn bread by chanting before your door, 'Bread for the love of God.' I have done the same." His admission into the household of the Cottas, who were one of the first families in Eisenach, was the one bright episode in Luther's boyhood, and they demonstrated for him the precious love of God.

In 1501, Luther attended college with the intention of becoming a lawyer, but the sudden death of a dear friend awakened his soul to spiritual matters and he resolved himself to enter an Augustinian monastery.

In the second year of his monastic life, at the age of twenty, he accidentally found in the library a Latin Bible. He was surprised to find that it contained much more than what was read to the people. Little did he then imagine what a great revolution this treasure was to produce, first in himself, and then in the Church. It was by the reading of the Bible that a change was wrought in him. Eventually by God's grace, Luther would overturn the strongholds of superstition and idolatry, subvert the heathen divinity of the schools, and re-establish the Christianity of the apostolic age.

Luther was received with great satisfaction by the Augustines. They were pleased to see a distinguished member of the 'University' join their order, but they were determined to make him know that he was now a monk, and must not expect to be treated as a privileged person. He had to sweep rooms and perform other menial services, and he was sent through the streets with a sack on his back to beg for the monastery. Luther bore all these indignities with meekness and even with gladness. They were part of the discipline which would prepare him for greater usefulness. But he remained a stranger to the peace of soul which he had expected to find within the cloister walls. It was a cruel disappointment to his soul. He had turned his back upon the pleasures and honors of the world and had taken his place among the monks, and he still found himself a sinful man.

When he left the monastery he became a doctor of theology at the University of Wittenberg, where he became a renowned expounder of the Scriptures. During this time, Luther wrestled with understanding the Bible and came to embrace the truths of justification by faith. He made his way painfully into the light, and had experienced the power of the Spirit and the Word in bringing comfort to his doubting heart. "As they listened to him," says one student, "men felt that after a dark night a new light had arisen on Scripture doctrine. He pointed out the difference between Law and Gospel, and drew the hearts of men to the Son of God."

At first Luther was at first very unwilling to preach, but after being persuaded by his peers, he preached continually in the churches of Wittenberg. The people flocked to hear him, for he was one of the most interesting, as well as a powerful preacher.

The very first to be called Protestants were the Electors of Saxony and Brandenberg, the two Dukes of Lunenberg, the Landgrave of Hesse, and the prince of Anhalt, together with the followers in the thirteen imperial towns, among which were Strasberg, Nuremberg, and Constance.

He boldly preached against the popular practice of indulgences, and he told his hearers that Christ simply exhorted in the gospel to repent, to bear the cross, and to do good works. The reform he sought in the Church was the reform he had experienced in his own soul. Luther then took a bold step on All Saints Day, October 31, 1517. The people who went to service found a document affixed to the door of the Castle Church in Wittenberg which contained ninety-five theses or propositions against indulgences. It had been placed there by Luther, and ran quickly through all Christendom, some said, as if angels themselves had been the messengers.

Realizing a severe blow had been struck against the traffic of indulgences, Church officials attempted to silence Luther and they demanded his retraction of the *Theses*. Luther adamantly refused and the pope sent word for his excommunication as a heretic. At the same time, Luther issued his famous *Appeal to his Imperial Majesty and the Christian Nobles of the German Nation Concerning the Reformation of Christianity*. In it he appealed to the consciences of laymen and priests as to their responsibilities as Christian men as proscribed in God's Word.

The disturbances in the Church reached the ears of the young German Emperor, Charles, who desired a quick resolution, while the Pope demanded that more action be brought upon the heretical monk. Luther's popularity with the people and the princes protected him, but eventually the Emperor summoned him to appear before the Imperial Diet to be held at Worms.

As Luther entered the city, the people thronged to catch a

glimpse of the bold monk who had defied Rome. One captain of the guard who sympathized with Luther placed his hand on his shoulder and said, "Poor monk! You are to hazard a more perilous march this day than I or any other Captain ever did on the field. But if your cause is right, and you are sure of it, go on in God's name and be of good comfort, God will not forsake you."

When the hour arrived, Luther entered the Assembly and was asked if he was willing to retract his words or his writings. He replied that he would retract nothing but what could be shown to contradict Scripture. "To councils or to the pope I cannot defer, for they have often erred. My conscience is a prisoner to God's Word." As the Pope sat in the chair of St. Peter, he was looked upon as the earthly representative of the Lord of Heaven, and to disobey him was to disobey Christ. The claim of the Emperor to absolute obedience was scarcely less sacred. He was the representative of the Holy Roman Empire, and it was to him Christ had committed the sword, that he might command the obedience of men to the decrees of Holy Church. But a new world of thought was opening to mankind through the knowledge of holy Scripture and the revival of letters, the study of theology, discovery in science, and ideas of equality and freedom, were already struggling for expression in the hearts of men. But how were they to find expression so long as two awful voices kept repeating, "Thou shalt not think except as the Pope decrees, nor act except as the Emperor commands?" Luther by refusing to obey those voices opened the great drama of modern history. It was the apparent victory of the weak over the strong, but with Luther there was great strength. Luther's strength was in his faith in the living God. This was not only the source of his own personal

Luther before the Council of Worms, illstrated for Great Men and Famous Women, by E. Delperee

courage, it was the secret of his great power as a religious leader. He broke the spell of the potent names of pope and emperor by invoking a higher name. It was his positive religious convictions not merely his scorn of error and folly that enabled him to overcome Rome. There had been many before him who rightfully denounced the errors and abuses of the Church of Rome. Many men listened to Luther's forerunners with pleasure and with approval, yet most often such appeals could not induce them to leave the shelter of a Church which, with all its faults, seemed the safest refuge Earth had to offer for sinful men. Luther succeeded in the wake of his faithful predecessors, because "the fullness of time had come." All the reformers told sinful men they could find rest in the joyful confidence of God's love freely given in Christ.

Luther's wife, Catharine von Bora.

To the surprise of many, Luther married in June of 1525, at the age of forty-two. His wife, Catharine von Bora had been a nun, but like her husband, had renounced her monastic vows. Biblical principles as well as a growing affection influenced them both toward each other in their blossoming relationship. Luther and Catharine were blessed with five children and often reminded themselves that children are a gift from the Lord, "for of such is the kingdom of God."

Also in 1525, Frederic the Wise died, and was succeeded by his brother, John, who publically avowed the principles of the Reformation. Other princes then followed his example. From that time forward the burden which Luther had carried alone was born by others, and the popes' edicts and decrees against them became of little effect. The brunt of the battle with Rome and the Emperor was born by the princes. In his attempt to exert his influence against the Reformers, the Emperor passed his Edict of Spires in 1529, that prohibited freedom of doctrine and worship. Those favorable to the Reformation drew up a *Protest* against this decree, and presented it. Hence the name, Protestants, was used for the first time.

Luther's dear and long-time friend, Melancthon, championed the cause at the Diet of Augsburg, and sought to resolve peacefully with the Church of Rome, to which Luther was genuinely amused. Their negotiations did not end satisfactorily, but the Protestants were granted peace in 1532.

Shortly before his death Luther wrote, "I am of good courage about our cause, because I am certain that it is the cause of God and Christ."

Key Writings of Luther: 1. *Luther's 95 Theses* (1517); 2. *A Treatise on Good Works* (1520); 3. *Concerning Christian Liberty* (1520); 4. *Select Sermons* (1526); 5. *Small Catechism* (1529); 6. *Large Catechism* (1530); 7. *On Translating* (1530); 8. *Galatians* (1535); 9. *Disputation On the Divinity and Humanity of Christ* (1540).

Worth Reading: *History and Life of Martin Luther,* by Philip Melancthon (1549); *Pictures From the Life of Martin Luther,* by Dr. A. Wildenhahn (1882); *A Mighty Fortress is Our God,* by Jim Cromarty (2001); *Luther and His Katie,* by Dolina MacCuish (2001).

Hugh Latimer, Archbishop Cranmer, and Nicholas Ridley, who were all martyred in 1555. Notice the hand of Cranmer in the fire, representing the actual event of his death when he placed his right hand into the flames first, since it was by this hand that he reluctantly signed a recantation of his faith six months earlier.

Hugh Latimer 1485-1555
"Apostle" of the English Reformation

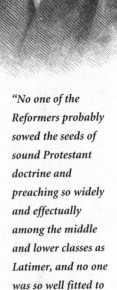

There were two great forces at work in the early part of sixteenth-century England. The revival of learning and the Reformation of religion. Scholars of the day were devoting themselves to the classical writings of Greece and Rome, while men of earnest spiritual natures were longing for truth and reality in religion.

 atimer was born at Thurcaston, a little village at the foot of the Charnwood hills, a few miles from the town of Leicester. Latimer seems to have been a sickly child, but gave early promise of mental ability. "Even at the age of four, or thereabouts," says old John Foxe, "he had such a ready, prompt, and sharp wit, that his parents purposed to train him up in the knowledge of good literature."

At the common schools of his county little Hugh made such good progress, that at the age of fourteen his father decided to send him to the University. Accordingly, somewhere about the year 1506, he became a Cambridge student.

After receiving his B. A. degree, he proceeded in due course to the higher degree of M.A. in 1514, and after much deliberation made the choice of the study of Divinity, and was ordained at Lincoln. In 1522 his ability as a preacher was recognized, and he was appointed by the University as one of the twelve Cambridge preachers licensed to officiate in any part of England.

While at Cambridge, Latimer helped form a society of Scripture students, and when Luther's books began to be known and circulated in England, copies were eagerly read by this little band. Whatever Latimer did, he did heartily. Slow and timid in embracing a new opinion, he never hesitated to act once his mind was made up, . "He was not satisfied with his own conversion only;" says Foxe, "but, like a true disciple of the blessed Samaritan, pitied the misery of others. He became both a public preacher and a private instructor to the rest of his brethren within the University within two years, spending his time partly in the Latin tongue amongst the learned, and partly amongst the simple people in his own language."

Though Latimer was still, at this point, a priest of Rome, he spoke out boldly on two significant matters: 1. The all-sufficiency of Christ's atonement, and 2. That the current ideas of holiness were thoroughly unscriptural, and that "voluntary works," "creeping to the Cross on Good Friday," decorating images, and other Romish practices, were no substitutes whatsoever for doing justly, loving mercy, and walking humbly with God.

"No one of the Reformers probably sowed the seeds of sound Protestant doctrine and preaching so widely and effectually among the middle and lower classes as Latimer, and no one was so well fitted to do it."

—J. C. Ryle

The clergy felt that he was the most dangerous opponent they had in the kingdom, and sought in every way to entangle him into compromising confessions, which might lead him at last to the stake. But the protecting care of God seemed to have been always around him, and he was as keen and shrewd as he was brave and faithful.

In March 1533, he was invited to preach by several of the Bristol parish clergy. The effect of these sermons was such that all Bristol was in an uproar. Latimer had, as usual, attacked the popular abuses of the Church's doctrines which tended to superstition and immorality, and was denounced as a heretic by those who had a vested interest in such abuses. Disturbances arose, which attracted the attention of the government, and a commission was sent down to Bristol to investigate. Several of the most disloyal of the "offenders" were committed to prison. Latimer was permitted to answer for himself, and was not only vindicated, but received the new primate's license to preach anywhere in the province of Canterbury. Thus his adversaries were ashamed and confounded.

Chief among English preachers was Hugh Latimer. His earnestness, boldness, acuteness, his knowledge of Scripture, his shrewd humor and tact, his racy English, all make Latimer one of the great preachers of history. But to those who made a trade of religion, and other unjust authorities he was labeled "a seditious fellow."

Meanwhile events of the gravest importance for England had been taking place, such as Queen Catharine's divorce, Henry's marriage with Anne Boleyn, and the final rupture between the crown and the pope. The "old order" was rapidly passing away and was giving sway to the "new." It was the men of the "new learning" who were coming to the front and occupying spheres of wider activity and responsibility. Chief among these was Latimer. He was called from his retirement, and associated with Cranmer and Cromwell in the work of the Reformation.

The ascension of young Edward to the throne of his father Henry in 1547 brought days of hope and promise to the friends of the truth in England. The Reformation had struggled on painfully, almost hopelessly, against the overwhelming ignorance and superstition of the country. But the strong hand that had so long kept back the Reformers was at last cold in death, and the work of English Protestantism rapidly advanced. The young king was wholly on their side. "Brought up with noble counselors," says Latimer, "and excellent and well-learned schoolmasters, was there ever a king so noble, so godly?"

Though silent for eight years, Latimer was now free to engage the fiery course which earned him the name of the 'Apostle of England.' He preached in the Court, in the city, and in the country, and his sermons shook the whole land. Wherever he went crowded audiences hung upon his lips. But this season of peace and prosperity was too short. Sixteen-year-old King Edward was suddenly cut down in death and after a brief struggle, his wicked sister Mary succeeded him to the throne of England.

Latimer believed that the preaching of the gospel would cost him his life, and he quietly waited for the summons which he felt sure would not be long delayed. Only two months after

Edward's death, came the summons from the queen's court. He was ordered to appear before the Council at Westminster, to which he at once obeyed. As he passed through Smithfield, where so many had suffered martyrdom before, he "merrily" remarked that "the place had long groaned for him."

On the 13th of September, Latimer stood before the Council where he received nothing but scornful jeers. He was committed to the Tower and remained a prisoner all through the autumn and cold winter of 1553, until his release the following spring. Ridley was already there, and Cranmer was consigned to the same prison the day after Latimer. "God be thanked," says Latimer, "it was to our great joy and comfort." For nearly two months, from the beginning of February to the end of March 1554, they thus continued, and "we did together read," says Latimer, "the New Testament with great deliberation and study."

During his short episcopate Latimer had the satisfaction of seeing the Bible printed in English, and allowed by Royal License "to be sold or read by every person without danger of any act, proclamation, or ordinance heretofore granted to the contrary."

In March 1554, after six months in prison, Latimer, Cranmer, and Ridley were brought down to Oxford, to dispute the Church's doctrine of transubstantiation. After the first two debated, Latimer was summoned to speak, but his age and long imprisonment weakened him so much that he was unfit to dispute and offered instead a statement of his opinions in writing. This was refused with reviling, and from eight till eleven o'clock he was challenged, interrogated, and interrupted in an attempt to have him recant. Weak as he was, nothing shook his resolute adherence to the truth. "The Queen's grace is merciful," said the Prolocutor at last, "if ye will turn." Latimer answered: "You shall have no hope in me to turn. I pray for the Queen daily, even from the bottom of my heart, that she may turn from this your false religion."

Latimer pleading his case before the bishops and canonists.

The three prisoners were formally condemned for heresy, and sent back into separate confinement. Fear temporarily seized Cranmer who signed a recantation and was set free, only to withdraw it a few months later. In September, the Pope commissioned a fresh trial of the two heretics which came down to either accept the recantations of Ridley and Latimer, or to confirm the former sentence and deliver them to death. But these two stalwarts of faith were not men to flinch from the flames. They were condemned and led forth to die.

It was a sunny October morning when Ridley and Latimer reached the place of execution in Oxford. Ridley ran to him and embraced him, saying: "Be of good heart, brother, for God will either assuage the fury of the flame or else strengthen us to abide

Latimer and Ridley ushered into glory at the stake.

"We shall this day light such a candle, by God's grace, in England, as I trust shall never be put out."

—Bishop Latimer's last words before he was martyred at the stake.

it." Then they kneeled down both of them, and prayed earnestly.

After listening to a brief and foolish sermon from a Dr. Smith, an apostate from Protestantism, they were commanded to make ready the execution. Ridley and Latimer were stripped of possessions and fastened to the stake. Their faces shone as ones ready for Heaven in victory instead of defeat.

After Ridley's soul-stirring prayer, Latimer lifted up his eyes, and with a most amiable and comfortable countenance, said: "God is faithful who suffereth us not to be tempted above that which we are able." Then he added the memorable words: "Be of good comfort, Master Ridley, and play the man; we shall this day light such a candle, by God's grace, in England, as I trust shall never be put out."

Latimer died first. He received the flames as they surrounded him. He had stroked his face with his hands, and bathed them a little in the fire, and gave up his spirit in death.

But Ridley lingered and suffered far more pain. The fire about him was not well made. Yet in all his torment he rejoiced to call upon God, "Lord, have mercy upon me." His brother-in-law, who meant it in mercy, heaped upon him more fuel, which only kept down the fire. At last, someone pulling off the wood from above, made a way for the fire to escape. The red tongues of flame shot up fiercely. Then the gunpowder finally did its work. He stirred no more, falling down dead at Latimer's feet.

And so we leave them going up to Heaven, like Elijah, in a chariot of gold. To Hugh Latimer, that old and blessed servant of God, for whose labors, travails, fruitful life, and death, this generation has cause to give thanks to Almighty God.

Key Writings of Latimer: 1. *Sermons and Remains*, (1548); also edited by G. E. Corrie for the Parker Society, 2 vols., (1844)

Worth Reading: *The Bishop, the Pastor and the Preacher of the Reformation*, by W. Gilpin (1755); *Bishops and Clergy of Other Days*, by J. C. Ryle (1854); *Select Sermons and Letters* in *British Reformers*, vol. 4 (1830); *Leaders of the Reformation*, by W. Beck (1861); J. J. Ellis (1890); *English Church in the 16th Century*, J. Gardiner (1903).

John Knox *1505-1572*
Reformer of Scotland

Under Knox's leadership, Scottish families were transformed. Countless men led worship in their own homes; the singing of psalms in daily life became widespread; and the Bible was read in every Scottish town.

By the time of his death, the "impossible" was the ordinary. The Roman Church, which began the struggle with all earthly power on its side, was defeated. In its place was a Protestant Kirk, the Presbyterian Church, ruled not by a hierarchy, but by local elders and deacons.

I n 1547, after John Knox had been preaching but a few months in St. Andrews, the castle was captured and surrendered to the French fleet. Knox and his companions were flung into the foreigner's galleys. While there for nineteen weary months he was chained to a bench and forced to pull a heavy oar under the lash. Through the bitter cold of two winters, and the heat of the intervening summer, Knox had opportunity to count the cost of the choice he so recently made. Knox's resolution alone would not have sustained him during this season of hardship, but Knox knew he had a divine call, and therefore the promise of God for his public work as well as for his private life. His faith never wavered. When the master of the galley *Notre Dame* insisted that the chained prisoner must kiss a carved image of the Virgin, whose name the vessel bore, he flung the intrusive "idol" from his presence, exclaiming, "She is light enough, let her learn to swim!" Again he went to the oar, and after many long days found himself emaciated and weak. His fellow-captive, James Balfour, pointed out to him in the dim distance, off the coast of Fife, the steeple of St. Andrews Church, the place where he was called to preach his first sermon. "Yes," Knox said, "I know it well; and I am full persuaded, how weak soever I fully now appear, that I shall not depart this life till that my tongue shall again glorify His godly Name in that place." But years were to pass before that could be fulfilled; years of banishment and hard labor.

In his youth, Knox witnessed the power struggle between the Scottish Parliament, partial to the Roman Church, and the waves of Reformation truth spreading like wildfire across the land. Parliament, seeking to quell the influence of Luther's works, sent King James' cousin, Patrick Hamilton, to Wittenberg where, much to the dismay of Parliament, he embraced biblical truths and proclaimed he had found "the long-buried truth of God." The wicked Cardinal Beauton therefore seized Hamilton and burned him at

John Knox has become recognized as the most prominent figure of the Scottish Reformation. He was influenced by the teaching of George Wishart, and worked for the abolishment of the mass and establishment of a reformed church in Scotland. Many of Knox's great accomplishments were through his writings, in particular his **History of the Reformation.**

Mary, Queen of Scots (l) and Queen Elizabeth (r). When Mary sought refuge in England, Queen Elizabeth imprisoned her. In 1586, after many attempted escapes, Mary was exposed in a plot to assassinate Queen Elizabeth and gain the crown of both England and Scotland. Mary was tried, sentenced to death, and then beheaded in February 1587.

the stake before the ancient college of St. Andrews.

Like many Reformers of this era, Knox came to embrace Reformation truths while in seminary. At the age of twenty-five he was ordained a priest, but a fellow scholar, Theodore Beza, says Knox "began to study with such proficiency that it was thought he would one day become a better teacher than his master, Majors. But after reading the works of Jerome and Augustine, he realized the errors in the conventional teaching."

In 1545, Knox's conflict deepened when his pious friend, George Wishart, was captured by Cardinal Beaton and assassinated on the stake outside the castle of St. Andrews. This heinous act enraged Wishart's followers and they stormed the castle and killed the Cardinal. Knox and others rejoiced, but it was not by the sword that Scotland would be reformed.

After his rescue from the French galleys, Knox married Marjory Bowles. They settled in England where he resumed preaching the gospel. In 1554, King Edward died and Mary Tudor (Bloody Mary) ascended the throne. Knox escaped to Geneva and shared precious fellowship with John Calvin. But in 1559, God moved upon Knox's heart and he returned to his beloved homeland, never to leave her shores again.

He dedicated himself to promoting the Reformation in Scotland. The Protestant lords united and called themselves, the "Godly Band." As the earliest Covenanters of Scotland, they selected John Knox as their mouthpiece. Once again, Knox entered the pulpit of St. Andrew, as he had vowed while chained in the galleys, and he preached the Word of God as never before. He passionately persuaded the brethren to profess the gospel, regardless of the antagonistic and idolatrous authorities in power. The people of God enthusiastically responded. The flame he kindled spread from town to town, and city to city, and all of Scotland was ignited with "The Religion." Knox was called to a pastorate in Edinburgh, but chose rather to preach throughout Scotland. "The long thirst of my heart, is satisfied in abundance."

The French forces wielded by the Queen-Regent sought to suppress the new flames of Scotland's spiritual awakening.

Knox, in turn, requested the assistance of England, now under Queen Elizabeth. She consented. The English lost a key battle at Stirling, but the indomitable Knox kindled hope once more, and the English forces prevailed. The Queen-Regent died and left Scotland in the hands of the Protestants. John Knox and the party of Reformers, called "the Congregation," drew up a petition proposing the abolition of Popish doctrine, the restoration of biblical worship and Church discipline, and the appropriating of revenue for the support of the ministry, the promotion of education, and the relief of the poor. This document, called *The Confession of Faith Professed and Believed by the Protestants within the Realm of Scotland* (The Confession), was presented to the Scottish parliament and was ratified on August 17, 1560. The doctrines, worship, and government of the Roman Church were overthrown and Protestantism was established as the national religion.

Mary, Queen of Scots, the attractive widow of Francis II, arrived in Scotland in August 1561. She was thoroughly predisposed against Knox, while he and the other Reformers looked upon her with suspicion as well.

Knox met with Queen Mary no less than five times. His presentation of the gospel to her was candid and direct, much like John the Baptist in King Herod's court. Mary was charming and somewhat successful in leading Knox to believe in her sincerity toward him and his beliefs. Meanwhile, the great Reformer continued to expound God's Word from the pulpit with resounding clarity, influence, and power, but Mary and the Roman clergy became intolerant of his "accusations."

In 1562, her true colors were revealed when she had a privy council pronouncing Knox guilty of treason. At his trial Mary acted as a prosecutor, but was thoroughly frustrated when the council found him innocent of all charges, and actually commended him for his judicious defense.

Mary's numerous marriage scandals drove her from the throne, while Knox himself had to flee to St. Andrews for safety after enemies tried to assassinate him. As he grew old, his political influence declined. The day before John Knox died, at age sixty-seven, he urged his friends to live for Christ. He had been wrestling with God in prayer and exclaimed, "I have been in heaven!" As Knox lay dying on his bed he asked his wife to read aloud the seventeenth chapter of John's Gospel saying, "Go read where I cast my first anchor." When he could no longer speak, he held up two fingers to show he still had faith, and shortly afterward he left this world for his eternal home.

The work of John Knox was the outgrowth of individual faith that is so often found in a heroic and aggressive soul. The fire that had been originally kindled in this man's spirit, became a burning and shining light when Scotland needed it most.

Key Writings of Knox: 1. *A Treatise on Prayer* (1553); 2. *The First Blast of the Trumpet Against the Monstrous Regiment of Women* (1555); 3. *Some Questions Concerning Baptism* (1556); 4. *History of the Reformation in Scotland* (1559); 5. *Treatise on Predestination* (1560).

Worth Reading: *The Life of Knox,* by Thomas M'Crie (1812)

The system of doctrine founded on the idea of God which has been explicated by Calvinism, strikingly remarks W. Hastie (Theology as a Science, Glasgow, 1899, pp. 97-98), "is the only system in which the whole order of the world is brought into a rational unity with the doctrine of grace....It is only with such a universal conception of God, established in a living way, that we can face, with hope of complete conquest, all the spiritual dangers and terrors of our time."

John Calvin *1509-1564*

Champion of the Reformation

Many theologians were raised up by Divine Providence in the sixteenth century to expound the great doctrines of the Christian faith. They defended them against the corruptions by which human error within the stated Church had for centuries overlaid them. John Calvin was raised up by the Lord as the foremost thinker in biblical understanding, and mightily gifted with oratory and literary skill and power.

The light of Heaven had begun to shine in the young scholar's heart. John Calvin associated with the Lutherans of Paris, and expounded in their assemblies the Word of God, which was to them so new and so precious. Yet he was being called to proclaim these words of truth from a more prominent position, and over a wider range. Calvin enjoyed close fellowship with Nicolas Cop, a distinguished physician, who was rector of the University of Paris. In 1533, Cop was expected to deliver a public discourse to prelates and professors. Calvin and Cop saw this as a great opportunity for the utterance of sentiments very near to their hearts, and accordingly prepared the discourse, which advocated Church reform and a return to scriptural standards. The bold message created surprise and indignation in the minds of its hearers. Calvin was suspected of being the author of this manifesto, and an extensive search was made for him by the Roman authorities.

Some of his comrades came running into his chamber, and urged him to flee that instant. Scarcely had they spoken when loud knocking was heard at the outer gate. Then the heavy tramp of the officers was heard in the corridor. In another moment Calvin would be on his way to prison to come out of it at the stake. That would have been a devastating blow to the Protestant Reformation, and most likely would have changed the whole future of Christendom. Thankfully, God interposed at this grand moment of peril.

While some of his friends

Calvin preaching at St. Peter's Church in Geneva.

detained the officers at the door, others seized the sheets on his bed, and twisted them into a rope. Calvin then caught hold of them and let himself down into the street of the Bernardins. Barely escaping from the hands of the enemy he fled from the city to the cottage of a vine-dresser. There he changed his clothes and dressed as a laborer, with a garden hoe upon his shoulder.

Luther and Calvin

Although the two greatest of the Reformers, Luther and Calvin, were much alike in their theological emphases, they gave rise to two separate Protestant traditions. Lutheranism and the Lutheran Church spread through Germany and the Scandinavian countries, and from both these European sources to America. Calvinism, or the Reformed faith as it came to be known, spread from Switzerland into the Rhine valley and became the theological impulse of the Huguenots of France, the Protestants of Holland, the Puritans of England and New England, and the Presbyterians of Scotland and of America. Thus it may be said of Calvin, the middleman between Luther who started it and Wesley, the last of the great Reformers, that though dead he still speaks in the living tradition which builds the past and ever looks toward the new day. This was a special ingredient of the Calvinistic formula. To affirm that the Church must be reformed did not mean that it had already arrived, but that it must ever be in the process of being reformed.

He ventured forward to find a place where he could serve his beloved Savior without his life being in danger. Early in his career, Calvin was brought face to face with the dangers involved in a bold fidelity to scriptural truth. From this time forward Calvin was regarded as a leading champion of the Reformation.

John Calvin was born in Noyon, France, of Gerard Caulvin and Jeanne Le Franc, who purposed to secure for him the advantages of education and religion. When only twelve years old, John received the chaplaincy in the cathedral of Noyon, which gave him a regular income. It was expected that he would become a priest, but at age twenty he resolved to study law at the request of his father.

But the hand of Providence rested powerfully on John's heart. His mind, enlightened by the Word and the Spirit of God, was dissatisfied with a religion consisting largely in outward observances. He had found no real rest for his conscience in following the customary religious practices. He came to find this rest in the Gospel of Christ alone, especially as a revelation of divine mercy to himself personally. His conversion in 1533 was rapid and thorough. Calvin wrote, "God by a sudden conversion subdued and brought my mind to a teachable frame. Having thus received some taste and knowledge of true godliness, I was immediately inflamed with so intense a desire to make progress therein. Although I did not altogether leave off other studies, I yet pursued them with less ardor. I was quite surprised to find that before a year had elapsed, all who had any desire after purer doctrine were continually coming to me to learn, although I myself was as yet but a mere novice."

In 1534, the first work which proceeded from Calvin's pen after his conversion was in opposition to those who taught that the soul, after death, sleeps until the judgment. In the same year in which this treatise appeared, Calvin revised Olivetan's translation of the Bible into French. This was powerfully used in spreading the pure Word of God among those who spoke his native tongue.

It was in the year 1536 that Calvin published his brilliant masterpiece, *Institutes of the Christian Religion.* The *Institutes* constitute a cyclopedia of scriptural theology, which cannot be said, even now, to have been superseded. Amazingly, Calvin was only twenty-six years of age when he began this impressive work. In the first edition of this work he laid down doctrines which he retained to the close of his life.

Shortly after the introduction of his *Institutes,* he sought a place where he might spend more time pursuing his literary ambitions, but his journey took an unexpected, yet providential diversion. In order to avoid the war in eastern France, he entered Switzerland. Intending to stay in Geneva for only a day, the great evangelist, William Farel, persuaded Calvin to settle in Geneva for "the cause." Calvin was ordained a minister and preached with fervor the truths of the gospel. The young theologian induced Farel to write a *Confession of Faith* for the Genevan Church, while he himself composed a catechism of Christian doctrine.

Under the wise counsel of these two pious men measures were taken to promote education among the youth of Geneva, marriage customs were reformed, psalmody was encouraged, and vice was restrained. False teachers and troublers of the Church were put down by the force of Calvin's irresistible apologetics. The Geneva experiment, a new one in the world's history, attracted attention, and at the end of 1537, visitors came great distances to see Farel and Calvin, and to observe for themselves the working of the "theocracy."

While his comrade, John Calvin, pursued reform with his pen, William Farel (above), the driving force in Geneva, preferred to evangelize amidst the multitudes.

All did not go well in Geneva though. The Roman prelates, seeing that Geneva was a source of great inspiration among the Protestants, sent disguised messengers into the community with orders to infiltrate and disperse this growing religious movement. Their plans were recognized by the Reformers and the spies were turned away. In another instance, three leaders—Farel, Vinet, and Froment—were nearly poisoned, but the hand of Providence interceded for their safety. The most disturbing incident that remains a questionable mark on the otherwise incredible events of Geneva, was the execution of Michael Servetus, by decree of the Geneva attorney general. Many have accused Calvin of being party to such an horrendous act, but he had no power to condemn or pardon.

Servetus was a Spaniard who was partial to the Reformation, but his ideas went beyond the Scriptures and he fell victim to Pantheism,

John Calvin and Michael Servetus debating before the Council of Geneva.

which supposes created things to actually be part of God. He also published a work in which *he expressly denied the deity of Christ,* and referred to the triune God in terms of contempt and ridicule. He proclaimed himself the founder of a new religious system, which would supersede Catholicism and Protestantism alike! Calvin's popularity caught Servetus' attention and envy, and the heretic wrote to Calvin stating that his theology was only half-reformed. Upon his arrival in Geneva contention arose immediately, but Calvin remained a gentleman. When the two were requested to appear before the Council and present their views, a sharp debate ensued, and the following extract shows

Calvin vs. Arminius

There are two major opposing views within Protestantism that developed since the sixteenth century: Calvinism and Arminianism. The two men never met since Arminius lived a generation after Calvin.

In 1610, after Arminius' death, his followers drew up their "Five Articles of Remonstrance," that rejected the traditional teachings of Calvinism. In 1619, the Synod of Dort responded with the "The Five Points of Calvinism," drawn from the tenets of Calvin's writings.

Though the controversy is doctrinal in its basis, it is often flamed by extremes practiced on both sides. Arminians accuse Calvinists of fatalism or Hyper-Calvinism, and Calvinists claim Arminians practice Pelagiansm and deny the Sovereignty of God.

The five points of Calvinism are summarized as:

1. Total Depravity: Fallen man is totally unable to save himself.

2. Unconditional Election: God's electing purpose is not conditioned by anything in man.

3. Limited Atonement: Christ's death was sufficient to save all men, but effective only for the elect.

4. Irresistible Grace: The gift of faith, sovereignly given by God's Holy Spirit, cannot be resisted by God's elect.

5. Perseverance of the Saints: Those who are regenerated and justified will (or must) persevere in the faith.

how far one can stray when he departs from the truth:

"What!" said Calvin, "if one were to strike this pavement with his foot, and say that he was trampling upon your God, would'st thou not be horrified at having subjected the majesty of God to such opprobrium?" Servetus replied, "I have no doubt that this bench, this cupboard, and all that can be shown me are the substance of God." When it was objected that according to him even the devil would be substantially God, he replied laughing: "Do you doubt it? All things are part and parcel of God." Servetus' views were justly condemned as heretical by the Council. At this point Calvin's responsibility in the fate of Servetus ended and he was condemned to death for blasphemies, heresies, and mostly for disturbing Christendom. Calvin and Farel pleaded for a more humane death for him, but to no avail. Servetus was bound to the stake, with his book hung round his neck. On October, 27, 1553, this unhappy victim perished amidst the flames.

Among the distinguished foreigners who were drawn to Geneva by the fame of Calvin, and of his great work in that city, not the least illustrious was the Scottish Reformer, John Knox. The language of Knox's eulogium of Geneva has often been quoted. The Scot pronounces Geneva "the most perfect school of Christ that ever was in the earth since the days of the Apostles." Calvin's profound influence upon Knox placed his feet on the path to becoming the Reformer of Scotland.

Calvin and his colleagues were banished from Geneva for refusing to administer the Lord's Supper to a godless multitude. But they returned triumphantly a few years later where they then spent the remainder of their days in service to God and His people.

The Reformation was based upon a return to the supreme authority of Scripture. It was natural, therefore, that the exposition of the books of the Bible would be one of the foremost tasks undertaken by Calvin. His mind was not only learned, but wonderfully industrious. He was endowed with clear insight and sound judgment, and he knew how to apply Scripture to the necessities of the human mind and life. His commentaries, especially those on the Epistles of Paul and on the Psalms, retain to this day a position all their own.

The honor of Calvin consisted, not in suggesting ingenious theories or speculations, but in his general accuracy in   interpreting God's Word, and in detecting and pointing out the connection of biblical doctrines, which instead of being autonomous, were shown to occupy their respective places in forming a complete and perfect system of divine truth. The errors against which he frequently wrote, arose from the elevation of human works and supposed merits into a position which divine grace and mercy alone can biblically occupy. Calvin did not deny the place and importance of good works, but opposed the tenants of the system of Romanism which taught that salvation was secured by the efforts, gifts, services, and self-sacrifice of sinful men. In contradiction, the main principle of Calvin's theology is as stated in Romans 6:23, *"For the wages of sin is death, but the gift of God is eternal life in Christ Jesus our Lord."* For to Calvin, the thought of God's sovereign mercy was so predominant it colored the whole of his doctrinal system. In several controversies Calvin maintained the sovereignty of God against the advocates of the Roman creed and practices, and in those controversies he was signally victorious. Space does not permit a thorough examination of all his views, but it must be kept in mind that Calvin's predestination was not fatalism. He strongly upheld the doctrine of justification by faith, and ever believed and taught that the free forgiveness of sins and pardon by the Divine Ruler are the assured portion of every child of Adam who earnestly repents and sincerely receives the Lord Jesus Christ.

In 1545, John Calvin wrote the hymn, "I Greet Thee Who My Sure Redeemer Art," which is still a popular hymn sung in today's churches.

Calvin's labors appear all the more prodigious when we remember the frailty of his physical frame, and how his delicate health was often interrupted by illness and severe suffering. Calvin worked in-cessantly. In answer to a remonstrance upon his too laborious habits he said, "Would you that the Lord should find me idle when He comes?"

Amidst his great sufferings and feebleness he found sweet consolation in the holy Scriptures and in communion with Christ. In his will, Calvin records his deep gratitude for his enlightenment and salvation, and for the privilege granted him in proclaiming and extending the gospel. Calvin left this world in peace, anticipating his true home with Christ.

With many tears, Farel stands before the death bed of Calvin.

Key Writings of Calvin: 1. *Institutes of Christian Religion* (1536); 2. *The Necessity of Reforming the Church* (1544); 3. *Short Treatise on the Holy Spirit* (1541); 4. *An Inventory of Relics* (1543); 5. *Calvin's Commentary of the Holy Scriptures.*

Worth Reading: *The Life of Calvin,* by Theodore Beza (1564); *Calvin, His Life and Times,* by Thomas Lawson (1895).

Anne Askew was martyred at the tender age of twenty-five, after refusing to recant her Christian beliefs.

Anne Askew *1520-1546*
Daughter of the Reformation

It could be said that of all the interesting and moving topics surrounding the history of the Church since the time of Christ, there is none more profitable to the souls of men than that which speaks to the character, sufferings, and triumphs in death of those who have distinguished themselves as champions of the truth, even in the face of powerful opposition. The stories of these martyrs remain in our hearts as beacons in a dark world that we too might not lose heart. They rejoiced in the hour of death and counted it worthy to suffer for the cause of King Jesus and the benefit of the generation of faithful men and women that would follow.

 here lived in England, during the reign of Henry VIII, a knight of an ancient and honorable family, Sir William Askew by name. He resided at Kelsay, his ancestral home, and was the father of several daughters and a son. His second daughter, Anne, was attractive in form and faith, and loved the Lord since her youth. Sir William was determined that Anne should be married to the son of a friend, Thomas Kyme, to whom her dead sister had originally been promised. Anne Askew was not only a beautiful and high spirited woman, but she was also well educated for a woman of her time, and was possessed of unusual mental gifts. She was a very pious woman, and having become a wife, she endeavored faithfully to discharge her duty to her husband. They lived together in peace for some time, and she bore him two children. The marriage was unhappy, in part because of religious disagreements.

In 1545, as the English Bible was reaching the homes of the common people, Anne acquired a copy and read it with avidity. Her heart was opened to the truths of the holy gospel and she abandoned her formal religion for the life-changing faith in a personal Lord and Savior Jesus Christ. She rejoiced in her newfound freedom, but her actions drew the attention of the priests, who sent warning to her husband about her "sedition." She confessed to him that she was no longer a Romanist, but a follower of the doctrines of the Reformation. At this, and pressure from the Church, Kyme threw his wife out of the home, although he acknowledged that she was the most devout woman he had ever known.

Anne found sanctuary with some friends who were sympathetic to her plight and secretly concurred with her beliefs. Though she lived a life of piety and devotion, she was falsely accused of heresy and arrested. In 1545, she was examined by Church leaders regarding her beliefs, in which she disagreed with their doctrine of transubstantiation. Her answers were full of wisdom and truth and she often caught them in their own questions, which only served to enrage them more. The wicked Lord Bonner was determined to see her burned for heresy. He had her brought before him and finding that he could not draw anything from her which would incriminate her, taunted her

Anne Askew was martyred for her faithfulness to the Gospel of Jesus Christ ten years before the famous Latimer, Ridley, and Cranmer, who also suffered and died on the stake. Her fine example of resolute faith and gentle piety gave courage to an entire generation of English Christians.

with the cowardly insinuation that her life was not as pure as the Scriptures required. Looking him full in the face, she answered calmly: "I would, my lord, that all men knew my conversation and living in all points; for I am so sure of myself this hour, that there is none able to prove any dishonesty in me. If you know any that can do it, I pray you bring them forth." He could not and eventually had her released.

The Lord Chancellor of England at this time was Thomas Wriothesley, one of the cruelest leaders that ever held power in England. He was intimately associated with Bishop Gardiner in all the measures brought forward to throttle the Reformation. He now undertook the prosecution of this beautiful woman whose innocence and pure womanliness had no power to touch his cruel heart. He caused her to be brought before the council and subjected her to an examination which lasted for five hours. He asked her what was her opinion of the bread in the eucharist.

"That the sacramental bread was left us to be received with thanksgiving in remembrance of Christ's death, the only remedy of our soul's recovery, and that thereby we also receive the whole benefits and fruits of His most glorious passion."

"I believe," she replied, "that as oft as I, in a Christian congregation, receive the bread in remembrance of Christ's death, and with thanksgiving, according to His holy institution, I receive therewith the fruits also of His most glorious passion." Mr. Paget, one of the council, now asked her, more kindly than the others had done: "How can you avoid the very words of Christ, 'Take, eat, this is my body which is broken for you?'"

"Christ's meaning in that passage," she replied, "is similar to the meaning of those other places of Scripture, 'I am the door,' 'I am the vine.' 'Behold the Lamb of God,' 'That rock was Christ,' and other such references to Himself. You are not in these texts to take Christ for the material thing which He is signified by, for then you will make Him a very door, a vine, a lamb, a stone, quite contrary to the Holy Ghost's meaning. All these indeed do signify Christ, even as the bread signifies His body in that place."

She was sent back to Newgate and the next day became very ill. Believing that she was dying, she requested leave to receive a visit from the good Hugh Latimer (who afterwards proved so faithful a witness for Christ), that he might comfort her with his godly counsel, but her request was refused by her persecutors. It was now very plain to her that her enemies were resolved upon her death. She was a brave woman, as all her history proves, and turned for support and comfort to Christ, and found strength to bear all her trials with Christian fortitude and meekness.

On Monday, June 28th, she was taken to Guildball to be examined again by the council. She was taunted with being a heretic, but she denied the imputation, and declared that she had done nothing for which she deserved death by the law of God. When they asked her if she denied the Sacrament of the eucharist to be Christ's body and blood, she answered, without hesitation: "God is a spirit," she replied, "and not a wafer-cake, and He is to be worshiped in spirit and in truth (John 4:24), and not by the impious superstitious homage paid to a wafer, converted, by Popish jugglery, into a God."

By the law of England, Anne Askew was entitled to an open trial by jury, but the Roman Catholic influence was strong enough in the council to deprive her of this right. The Lord Chancellor Wriothesley and Bishop Gardiner exerted themselves to induce the council to condemn her, and were successful in their efforts. On the 28th of June, Anne was condemned by the council and sentenced to be burned at the stake.

In July, Lord Wriothesley ordered her to endure the torture of being stretched on the rack. The levers were turned, causing her the most severe pain, but she murmured not a word. Wriothesley was angered at his lack of success with Anne, and ordered the torture to be increased, but the officer of the rack was moved by the pious woman he saw before his eyes, and refused to obey. In his rage, Wriothesley grabbed the levers himself and was merciless as he applied the torture. Her body was stretched until her joints were pulled asunder, and her bones almost broken.

As soon as she was released from the rack, she swooned from the awful agony. The brutal chancellor kept her sitting for two hours on the bare floor, while he urged her to renounce her faith. After this, she says, in her touching narrative of her sufferings, "I was brought to a house, and laid in a bed, with as weary and painful bones as ever had patient Job. I thank my Lord God

Her persecutors asked her, "Do you not think that private masses help departed souls?" "It is great idolatry," she answered, "to believe more in these than in the death which Christ died for us."

A seventeenth-century engraving of the martyrdom of Anne Askew in 1546.

The order and manner of the burning of *Anne Askew, John Lacels,* John Adams, Nicholas Belenian, with certaine of the Councell fitting in Smithfield.

therefore." Her words do not convey a fair idea of her condition. The torture had deprived her of the use of her limbs, which had been pulled apart, and her sufferings were intense.

Throughout her entire persecution Anne Askew had preserved the patient sweetness of her demeanor. All the cruelties of her enemies had been powerless to change this, or to wring from her one unchristian complaint or unwomanly word. She was only twenty-five years old, and life was very sweet to her, but not so sweet as to make it worth the sacrifice of her conscience. She did not desire martyrdom, but she did not shrink from it, and she bore all her sufferings with a firmness and gentleness never surpassed in the annals of Christian heroism. Not once did she revile her enemies, but like her blessed Master she prayed for her murderers, that they might be saved from the just punishment of their wicked crimes.

> " I believe all those Scriptures to be true which He hath confirmed with His most precious blood. Yea, and, as St. Paul saith, those Scriptures are sufficient for our learning and salvation that Christ hath left here with us; so that I believe we need no unwritten verities with which to rule His Church."
> —Anne Askew

The day of her execution arrived, and Anne Askew, being unable to walk or stand, as a result of her torture upon the rack, was brought in a chair to the stake, where she was fastened to the post by an iron chain passed about her waist. Three other victims of Rome were brought out to die with her. They were, John Lascels, a former member of the king's household and Anne's old tutor, Nicholas Belenean, a priest of Shropshire, and John Adams, a tailor. Anne was fastened to a separate stake, and the others to the remaining two. They constantly spoke to each other words of comfort and encouragement, and it was evident to all that the men became more resolute as they witnessed the courage of the beautiful woman who was to die with them. As for Anne, her face was calm and peaceful. "She had an angel's countenance, and a smiling face," says one who witnessed her death.

When the preparations were completed, Bishop Shaxton mounted the pulpit and began to preach to the martyrs. His words were in vain, however. Anne, in spite of her sufferings, listened attentively throughout his discourse. When he spoke the truth she audibly expressed agreement, but when he said anything contrary to Scripture, she exclaimed; "There he misseth, and speaketh without the book."

The young martyrs were offered one last chance at pardon, which was refused. The wood was immediately kindled, and the martyrs were instantly enveloped in the flames and smoke. Powder had been placed around their feet for the purpose of quicky ending their sufferings, which exploded, killing them all instantly.

Anne Askew died as one of the noblest and purest witnesses of the truth of the Christian Church. She gave her life gladly for Christ, and she has her great reward in Heaven.

Worth Reading: *Passages in the Life of the Fair Gospeler, Mistress Anne Askew,* by Nicholas Moldwarp (1866); *Anne Askew: Brave Daughter of the English Reformation,* Christian Family Publications (1999).

Joan Mathurin *1539-1560*

Heroic Vaudois Martyr

Scarcely numbering more than 20,000 at any one time in history, the Vaudois people lived in the small Piedmont valleys on the Italian side of the Alps. They became converts to the faith preached by Paul, and were known for the simplicity and purity of their lives. For centuries the Vaudois were pressured to participate in the Mass and other Romish practices to which they vehemently opposed. Their piety and resoluteness angered the pope and in 1497 he proclaimed a crusade to eliminate the Vaudois. The cruelties suffered by these stalwart men and women of God is inexpressible. After more than 800 years of persecution, the Vaudois finally received peace. In 1848, King Charles issued a Decree of Freedom for all the people of the Valleys.

The town of Carignan stands on the left bank of the River Po, south of Turin, and beyond the actual limits of the Vaudois Valleys. During the sixteenth century a number of Vaudois had been tempted by the prospect of profitable employment to settle in another valley despite the edict which confined them to their own area. For some time the Piedmontese authorities allowed these persons to remain unmolested, but eventually the Romish priests, finding that the Vaudois were assembling secretly for prayer, determined to exterminate them. The persecution began in 1560. Without giving them any warning, the priests caused them to be seized and imprisoned as heretics. They were not allowed any examination or opportunity of defending themselves. They were seized and condemned on suspicion, and were burned within three days after their arrest. They could save their lives by one means only—denying their religion and going to Mass.

"I fear Him who is able to cast both body and soul into a more terrible fire than your billets!" replied Joan to her captors.

The first person thus seized in Carignan was a French refugee named Mathurin. He had come from the Vaudois Valleys of France and had married a woman of the Vaudois Valleys of Piedmont. He was a plain and simple working man, who cared little for the great matters going on around him. His only desire was to earn an honest living to support his family and to worship God in peace. He was detected in the act of conducting family prayer in his own house, and for this "terrible crime" was sentenced to be burned alive. The commissioners urged him to abjure his religion and save his life, but he refused.

"We give you three days to reflect," they said, "but after that time you will be burned alive if you do not come to Mass."

The family of Mathurin was plunged into great grief by his arrest and sentencing. His wife, Joan Mathurin, went at once to the commissioners, and asked to be allowed to see her husband.

"We will grant your request," they replied, "provided that you do not harden him in his errors."

"I promise," she replied, "that I will not speak to him except for his good."

The commissioners interpreting this promise as an intimation that she meant to persuade him to recant, escorted the wife to the dungeon where her husband was confined. Mathurin was overjoyed at seeing her. The commissioners remained to witness the interview, curious to see if a man could withstand the tender pleadings of a young and beautiful wife to whom he was bound by the deepest affection. But they had entirely misunderstood the promise of the Vaudois wife. She devotedly loved her husband, and the prospect of his death filled her heart with anguish. She was a worthy daughter of the martyrs, however, and her greatest fear had been that her husband would prove weak in the hour of trial, and that the thought of leaving her would tempt him to forsake the path of duty. She had come to urge him to be firm, to do his duty to his God and his Church, and if necessary, she was willing to die with him.

"Accordingly," says Gilles, by whom the martyrdom is related, "she exhorted him, in the presence of the commissioners, as earnestly as possible, steadfastly to persevere in his religion, without putting the death of the body, which is of brief duration, in the balance against the eternal salvation of his soul."

The commissioners were furious when they heard her words, and bitterly reproached her for having deceived them. She paid no heed to them, however, and holding her husband's hand in her own, she went on gently, but firmly: "Let not the assaults of the wicked one make you abandon the profession of your hope in Jesus Christ."

"Exhort him to obey us, or you shall both be hanged," cried the commissioners.

Again unheeding them, she said to her husband, "And let not the love of this world's possessions make you lose the inheritance of Heaven."

"Heretical she-devil," cried one of the magistrates, "if you do not change your tone, you shall be burned tomorrow."

Turning full upon her persecutor, and looking him calmly in the face, the brave Christian woman asked him:

"Would I have come to persuade him to die rather than to abjure, if I could myself seek to escape death by apostasy?"

Soon after the introduction of Christianity into Italy by the apostles, the people of the valleys became converts to the Christian faith. They accepted and taught he doctrines of the apostles, and practiced the simple rites and usages as the early Church faithfuls.

"You should fear at any rate the torments of the stake," said the magistrate abashed by her manner and words.

"I fear Him who is able to cast both body and soul into a more terrible fire than your billets!"

"This will be the destruction of you both," said one of the magistrates.

The face of the Vaudois wife lighted up with a sudden and overwhelming joy, and turning to her husband, who clung to her hand with all his strength, she said to him tenderly, "Blessed be God, because having united us in life, He will not separate us in death."

One of the commissioners, a cruel and fanatical man, here broke into a savage laugh, and exclaimed mockingly:

"Instead of one, we shall have two to burn."

"I will be your companion to the end," said the heroic woman, quietly, speaking to her husband rather than to the commissioners.

"We shall meet again in Heaven," Joan said meekly to her husband.

"Will you come to Mass and have yourself pardon?" asked the magistrates once more.

"I would rather go to the stake, and have eternal life," was her answer.

"If you do not abjure," said one, sternly, "Mathurin shall be burned tomorrow, and you three days after."

"We shall meet again in Heaven," she said meekly.

"Think of the delay that is still granted you," said the magistrate, who had at first appeared to have pity on her.

"The length of it is of no consequence, for my resolution is for life," she answered.

"Rather, it is for death," he said sadly.

"The death of the body is but the life of the soul," was her response.

One of the most violent of the magistrates, he who had exulted over the prospect of burning two, now exclaimed brutally, "Have you nothing else to say, you damned obstinate wretch?"

"Nothing," she answered, meekly; "except that I beseech you not to put off my execution for three days, but to let me die with my husband."

The magistrates consulted together for a few moments, and then one of them said to her, "Be it so. You will both be burned at the same stake tomorrow."

With this they departed. The heavy door of the dungeon clanged behind them, and the husband and wife were left alone. But they were not alone, for God was with them to bring them solace and comfort. Upon his initial arrest, Mathurin had made up his mind to die rather than abjure. God then sent the heroism of his noble wife to confirm and strengthen him in this resolution. Above all, the pious couple was very grateful to pass their last hours on Earth together. They spent their last night in tender communion with one another in prayer. The brave wife had her reward on Earth, for she saw her husband growing stronger and even thankful for the fate which was to unite them for all eternity. Her presence made the gloomy cell seem full of warmth and light to him, and her beloved face shone upon him through the darkness as the face of an angel. Never had either one been so dear to the other. Never had their love been so full, so pure and so free from earthly taint as on this eve of martyrdom.

The next day, on March 2, 1560, a stake was set up in the public square of Carignan, and around it was heaped a pile of wood ready for lighting. A crowd of townspeople had gathered around the pile, and prominent among them were the priests and monks of the Church which had brought about this terrible deed. It was late in the afternoon when the deep tones of the cathedral bell announced the approach of the condemned. A few minutes later a detachment of armed men at arms entered the square, and halted at the stake. Then came a band of monks chanting the requiem for the dead, and after them came Joan Mathurin and her husband, hand in hand, erect, calm, and even smiling. A murmur of pity ran through the throng, but was quickly suppressed as the priests turned abruptly to discover who had dared to pity the victims of the "Holy Church." The martyrs paid no heed to the chanting or exhortations of the priests. They spoke to each other only to exhort to still greater firmness, and they did not wail when the executioner came to lead them to the stake. Hand in hand they mounted the pile, and submitted themselves to be chained to the fatal post. When the executioner fired the pile, the flames flared up wildly, hiding the martyrs from view. Through the glare of the flames and gloom of the smoke could be heard the calm, patient voice of Joan Mathurin bidding her husband to be of good cheer, for the gates of Heaven were opening on her sight. Then there was silence, broken only by the roar of the flames.

The sun went down and the soft twilight emerged. The crowd remained silent and somber around the spot of this martyrdom. The monks had ceased their miserere, and the peals of the great cathedral bell had died away. The flames still hissed and leaped around the devoted pair. Not a cry nor a groan of pain had escaped their lips. Locked in each other's arms they had yielded to the devouring element. When the moon arose, only a heap of smoldering embers and a mass of blackened bones remained to show the spot from which the Vaudois wife and her husband had passed hand in hand into the Kingdom of God.

The Vaudois people acknowledged the holy Scriptures as their sole fule of faith, and rejected all that was not taught in the books of the Old and New Testament. From the days of Constantine to the present time, they have never wavered in their faith, and have never altered in any important particular their religious observances.

Worth Reading: *The Cross and the Crown* (1875), by James D. McCabe; *The Waldenses or Protestant Valleys of Piedmont, and the Ban De La Roche,* by William Beattie (1838); *The Israel of the Alps: A Complete History of the Waldenses of Piermont and Their Colonies,* by Alexis Muston (1866).

Samuel Rutherford *1600-1661*
Scottish Presbyterian Revivalist and Author

Samuel Rutherford was most likely the greatest theologian of the "Scottish Reformation" during the seventeenth century. His "Letters" have become a religious classic and have warmed the hearts of many suffering and sorrowful Christians. The power of his preaching and the gentleness of his presence, amidst severe persecution and exile, have warmed many cold hearts and exposed the errors of godless clergy.

Rutherford was a non-conformist Presbyterian who would not be silenced by the designs of godless men. He preached with vigor. Repentance and faith in Christ alone became the hallmark of his ministry, and influenced an entire nation to deeper piety and holy living.

For more than a year Samuel Rutherford had dedicated himself to the care of his ailing wife, whom he affectionately referred to as "the desire of his eyes." She became seriously ill just a few years after their marriage. To him, this was his calling, and he performed it with tenderness and compassion; never complaining of his lot nor casting a glare at the Almighty. The children of their youth were also stricken with the disease, and at length they all departed this cold world for glory beyond the grave. The suffering and sorrow he endured at the death of his family developed in him a strength of character while deepening his communion with Christ. Rutherford was being prepared for great usefulness as a powerful instrument in the hand of Almighty God. He would defy tyranny and boldly stand in the face of all manner of persecution and ungodliness.

Samuel was born in Nisbet, Scotland. He later wrote of it as "the place to which he owed his first breathing," and declared it to be "his soul's desire that it might blossom as the rose." His father was a respectable farmer of moderate means. He was able to give to Samuel and two other sons a decent education. Samuel's natural mental abilities were discovered at a young age and he attended University of Edinburgh in 1617.

Rutherford soon afterwards entered on the study of theology with his face steadfastly and willingly set to the office of the Christian ministry. "O Lord! I love Thee. Thou hast transfixed my heart with the arrow of Thy Word, and I have loved Thee." When Rutherford had finished his curriculum of theological studies in 1627, the ecclesiastical condition of Scotland was greatly discouraging to him. There had been a marked and growing departure from the reformed system which the genius and devotion of Knox in the former century had set up. Many of the doctrines of the Reformation were frowned upon and denounced by the men in power, and those who continued to preach faithfully were treated as outcasts. The General Assembly of the Church was prohibited from meeting, except by royal permission and the various districts of Scotland were placed under prelates. These men were nominees of King Charles, and granted the power to supersede the presbyteries.

Yet, Rutherford was not deterred from his passion to minister and preach the Word of God. Under the advice of Gordon of Kenmure, the people of the rural parish of Anwoth invited him to become their pastor. What a center of influence in the cause of pure and earliest religion did that little hamlet become when Rutherford and his young wife entered the old manse. Rutherford and Anwoth! For more than two hundred years the name of the saintly man has made the place sacred. The man and the place are intertwined in the thoughts of the Church, just as we associate Boston with Ettrick, and Baxter with Kidderminster, Doddridge with Northampton, and Newton and Cowper with Olney.

"Every man by nature is a freeman born; by nature no man cometh out of the womb under any civil subjection to king, prince, or judge."
—Samuel Rutherford

The farmers and peasants packed the seats of the church whenever Rutherford ascended the pulpit. They were content to listen for hours as he melted their hearts and challenged their minds to earnestly pursue Christ. The brethren were often "raised above themselves" by the almost seraphic strains of his adoration and prayer." His sermons always breathed Christ as the incarnate, suffering, dying, risen, glorified, and reigning King of kings and Lord of lords.

There is evidence in his letters that the people of his Anwoth parish were the burden of his frevant prayers. "There I wrestled with the angel and prevailed. Woods, trees, meadows, and hills are my witnesses that I drew on a fair meeting betwixt Christ and Anwoth." The latter portion of each day was devoted by the young minister to the miscellaneous duties of an earnest pastor. He invested much of himself in visiting the sick, the sorrowful, and the dying. And he catechized, and encouraged godly living in the families of his congregation.

The Westminster Assembly began their famous meetings in 1643, and Rutherford was one of the five Scottish commissioners invited to attend the proceedings. Although the Scots were not allowed to vote, they had an influence far exceeding their number. Rutherford is thought to have been a major influence on the Shorter Catechism.

He was sensitive and alive to his position as one of Christ's under-shepherds, appointed to take the oversight of souls. He therefore endeavored to know each individual member of his flock personally. If any were afflicted, he was afflicted; and if any rejoiced, he rejoiced.

Many Christians far remote from Anwoth flocked to Rutherford's pulpit hungering for the manna of heavenly truth and abundant love. Wherever Rutherford preached, he had a similar experience. The words of his earliest biographer declared that, "the whole country were indeed knit to him, and accounted by themselves as his particular flock."

To secure for himself a quiet place for retirement and a greater security against interruption, there was a hallowed spot about mid-way between his manse and his church, to which it was his frequent practice to retire for prolonged devotion and prayer, and which has become well known as "Rutherford's Walk."

Rutherford was resolute in his theological and ecclesiastical principles. He held up high the banner of the Reformation with no faint heart or feeble hand. His powerful preaching and cogent writings bear testimony of his efforts to foster deeper holiness in the lives of the people of Scotland.

He received much indignation after he published his *Apology for the Exercise of Divine Grace.* But "the truth was," says a late historian, "the argument of that book did cut the sinews of Arminianism, and galled the Episcopal clergy to the very quick; and so Bishop Sydserff could endure him no longer."

Sydserf therefore summoned him to appear before the central High Commission Court at Edinburgh in July of 1636, charging him, not only with nonconformity, but with treason. Rutherford regarded the writing of his book as "the offence which had done much to intensify the enmity of the bishop and others against him." His trial lasted three wearisome days. Hour after hour he was barraged with questions which had no connection with the charges against him, but by which they hoped to entangle him in his own words. But the unworthy schemes failed, for he "answered them not a word." When he had spoken in his own defense, some of the commissioners were so moved by his statements that they were disposed to acquit him. But the determinations of the wicked bishops prevailed and he was ordered into exile at Aberdeen. His first emotion on hearing the sentence was one of holy joy that he was "counted worthy to suffer shame for Christ's name." "There is no quarrel," he said, "more honest or honourable than to suffer for truth. That honour my kind Lord hath now bestowed upon me, even to suffer for my royal and princely King, Jesus. I go to my King's palace at Aberdeen; tongue, pen, and wit cannot express my joy!"

"Lex Rex" begins with Rutherford affirming the idea that there is a strong connection between natural law and scriptural revelation; as he put it, "The Scripture's arguments may be drawn out of the school of nature." From this concept, Rutherford derived his theory of limited government and constitutionalism. It was this belief that provoked the fury of King Charles.

Samuel Rutherford was also one of the Scots commissioners—appointed in 1643 to the Westminster Assembly. He was very much loved and respected by his fellow ministers for his unparalleled faithfulness and zeal in going about his ministry. It was during this time that he published his *Lex Rex,* and several other learned pieces, against the Erastians, Anabaptists, Independents, and others, who began to prevail and increase at the time. But none ever had the courage to take up the gauntlet and challenge this champion of the faith.

But no sooner did the restoration of Charles II to the throne take place than the course of affairs began to change. When the King saw *Lex Rex,* he said it was not even worthy of an answer. The treatise was then burnt at the cross of Edinburgh, and at the gates of the new college of St. Andrews, where Rutherford was professor of divinity. Having set their hearts against him, the clergy persuaded the parliament, in 1661, to accept an indictment against him. Everybody knew Rutherford was dying, yet in their hard-hearted inhumanity they proceeded anyway and summoned him to appear before them at Edinburgh. Rutherford was summoned to answer to a charge of high treason! But he had a call to appear before a higher tribunal, where his Judge was his Friend. Rutherford died before the time came for him to face the evil tribunal.

It is commonly said that, when the summons came, Rutherford spoke out from his dying bed and said, "Tell them I have got a summons already [to appear] before a superior Judge and judicatory, and I plan to answer my first summons, and ere your day come I will be where few kings and great folks come." When they returned and told the magistrates that he was dying, the parliament put to a vote, whether or not to let him die in the college. It was carried, "put him out," with only a few dissenting votes. The righteous Lord Burleigh said, "Ye have voted that honest man out of the college, but ye cannot vote him out of heaven." Some evil men said, "He would never win there, hell was too good for him." But Burleigh responded, "I wish I were as sure of heaven as he is, I would think myself happy to get a grip of his sleeve to haul me in."

The passage of Scripture that embodies the life and ministry of Samuel Rutherford is found in 2 Corinthians 1:3-5. "Blessed be the God and Father of our Lord Jesus Christ, the Father of mercies and God of all comfort, who comforts us in all our tribulation, that we may be able to comfort those who are in any trouble, with the comfort with which we ourselves are comforted by God. For as the sufferings of Christ abound in us, so our consolation also abounds through Christ."

"Thus died the famous Samuel Rutherford, who may justly be accounted among the sufferers of that time; for surely he was a martyr, both in his own design and resolution, and by the design and determination of wicked men. Few men ever ran so long a race without stopping. His was so constant, so unwearied, and beyond reproach. Two things rarely to be found in one man, were eminent in him; a quick invention and sound judgment; and these accompanied with a homely but clear expression, and graceful elocution; so that such as knew him best, were in a strait whether to admire him most for his penetrating wit, and sublime genius in the schools, and peculiar exactness in disputes and matters of controversy, or for his familiar condescension in the pulpit, where he was one of the most moving and affectionate preachers in his time, or perhaps in any age of the Church. To sum up all in a word, he seems to have been one of the brightest lights that ever arose on this horizon" (*Scots Worthies,* by John Howie).

In all his writings Rutherford exudes the true spirit of religion, but in his *Letters,* he touched the painful chord of human suffering, yet lovingly soothed the ache of the brokenhearted and grief-stricken. Gentle compassion and love for Christ pour out of every letter written by Rutherford to one of his fellow sufferers, and speak of the One whose comfort is ever-present and ever-faithful. (See 2 Corinthians 1:3-5.)

Key Writings of Rutherford: 1. *Plea for Paul's Presbytery in Scotland* (1642); 2. *Lex Rex, The Law of the Prince* (1644); 3. *The Trial and Triumph of Faith* (1645); 4. *The Divine Right of Church Government* (1646); 5. *Christ's Dying and Drawing of Sinners* (1647); 6. *Survey of Spiritual Antichrist* (1648); 7. *On Liberty of Conscience* (1649); 8. *Discourse on the Covenant* (1655); 9. *Life of Grace* (1659); *Letters in Two Parts* (1664); 4. *Discourse on Prayer;* 8. *Survey of Antinomianism;* 9. *Summary of Church Discipline;* 13.*Treatise on the Divine Influence of the Spirit.*

Worth Reading: *Scots Worthies,* by John Howie; *Life of Samuel Rutherford,* by Andrew Bonar (1862); *Rutherford Gathered,* by W. P. Breed (1865); *A Garden of Spices,* by Rev. Lewis Dunn (1869).

Richard Baxter *1615-1691*

English Presbyterian Puritan

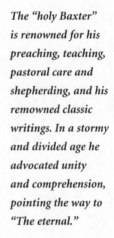

This eminent man of God lived at a time of great civil and religious strife. Within the period of his life are found the plague, the fire of London, the Long Parliament, and the rejection of two thousand of the finest ministers of the Church of England by the Act of Uniformity.

To no man among the Puritans are lovers of religious freedom under such large obligation as they are to Richard Baxter.

Baxter is so well known for his *Saint's Everlasting Rest* and other excellent, pious writings, but his eminence as a standard-bearer of the truth is found in the example of a godly life, a dedicated mind, an intrepid spirit, and an impeccable character of intense fervor and profound devotion.

In his early years, Richard Baxter was exposed to careless and ignorant clergy, and what he learned of divine truth was gathered chiefly from religious books and the example of a godly father. Richard Sibb's *Bruised Reed*, and William Perkins, *On Repentance* were of great influence to his heart and mind, but he credits the means of decisive change to *Bunny's Resolutions*. Although his family was loyal to the Church of England, Baxter was greatly influenced by the Puritans. He admired the sharp contrast between their blameless lives and many of the established church's Anglican clergy.

There are not many men that can be classed with Richard Baxter. Even among Puritans he stands alone. In many respects he was a combination of opposites. Intensely controversial, yet in heart most catholic. He was as devoted to logic as Thomas Aquinas, and soaring and ethereal as Bernard of Clairvaux.

The "holy Baxter" is renowned for his preaching, teaching, pastoral care and shepherding, and his renowned classic writings. In a stormy and divided age he advocated unity and comprehension, pointing the way to "The eternal."

The Church at Kidderminster.

"His Puritanism was intense and sincere, never eccentric, and after he had come to mature years, was always marked by a rare sobriety and ripeness of judgement. His ethical severity was tempered by tender piety as well as by lyrical devotion which often caught fire and flamed into poetic and soaring eloquence."[1]

He possessed an intellect as clear and sharp as a diamond, with the burning soul of a seraph. Though wasted and diseased in body, he worked with the energy and unweariedness of one in perfect health, uncompromising in his maintenance of the Gospel of Jesus Christ, yet with a charitable feeling to all men, even those who were opposed to him. In his theology Baxter was primarily a Calvinist, but varied on a number of issues such as his views of redemption and justification. He was primarily Presbyterian, but partly Independent—representing a precious balance known in few other man.

As a young man, Baxter taught school and studied theology. In 1641 he became pastor of the church at Kidderminster and his powerful preaching of God's Word soon transformed the town. Visiting travelers reported that instead of widespread immorality, they began to hear praise and prayer coming from every house.

With the outbreak of England's Civil War between king and Parliament, Baxter served for a time as chaplain to the Parliamentary forces under Oliver Cromwell. He often opposed the rather brutal actions of the general, and his efforts of persuasion were not often pleasantly received.

While ministering to soldiers suspended between life and death on the battlefield, Baxter wrote *The Saints Everlasting Rest*. This book has been a classic on the subject of eternal life since its introduction to the press in 1650. Baxter has made heavenly meditation important and

The Old Torn Book

(Article from 1878 edition of The Youth's Companion*)*

There was nothing in particular to distinguish the boy Dick from his mates when he played, two hundred and fifty years ago, on the banks of the Severn, or trudged to school along the roads that lead to the capital city of Shropshire. He lived in evil times, when religious persecutions were a common thing, when Bibles were dear and few, and the influential classes thought less of the Holy Volume than they did of ceremonies and liturgies.

But it is one good thing to say of those darker days, that there were then not so many (possibly none) of the cheap, vicious books and papers which have lately been let loose upon the world like Pandora's plagues. It may be owing entirely to that saving fact that Shropshire Dick was ever heard of in after years with credit to himself; for he was fond of reading, and ready to devour anything new in print that came into his hand.

His parents were respectable people, but they owned only a very scanty library, and Dick soon exhausted everything in it. One day, when he was fifteen years old, an honest fellow, a common laborer, who sometimes worked for his father, knowing the boy's tastes, offered to loan him an old book that he owned.

Dick borrowed the book at once. It was a rather dilapidated volume, with one cover gone, and some leaves badly torn or missing altogether. But Dick could make out most of the contents, and he soon read it through, for he had nothing else to read.

The title of the book was, "Bunny's Resolutions," and it was the perusal of this that first made the careless boy a serious and devout thinker, and led him to heavenly light. At that early age his earnest life began, and the foundation was laid for the long usefulness that made his memory a blessing to mankind.

It is said that he did not become a declared and active follower of Christ until after his reading of Sibbe's "Bruised Reed," a new volume, which his parents bought from a country peddler; but the true date of his awakening to his better life in Christ is from the day he finished the old torn book which the poor workman lent him.

Shropshire Dick became the great and good Richard Baxter; the man who, amidst the sufferings of life and death on the battlefields of war, wrote "The Saints Everlasting Rest."

1 *Reliquiae Baxterianae*, introd. p. viii. by J. M. Lloyd Thomas, (1925).

interesting, and at the same time truly engaging and delightful.

The English people were just emerging from the Civil War when the book appeared in print and it became standard reading in Puritan households. Baxter's famous advice that you should keep "heaven in your eye at all times" continues to strengthen the Christian's heart, amidst a dying a depraved world. In Rev. James Janeway's *Token for Children*, we have the story of a little boy, whose piety was so discovered and promoted by reading the *Saints' Rest*, as the most delightful book next to the Bible, that the thoughts of everlasting rest seemed, even while in health, to swallow up all other thoughts, so he lived in constant preparation for it. This young lad looked more like one

that was ripe for glory, than an inhabitant of this lower world. And when he was sick and near death, before he was twelve years old, he said, "I pray, please let me have Mr. Baxter's book, that I may read a little more of eternity before I go into it." Another of Baxter's books, *Call to the Unconverted,* exhorts the reader to turn away from sin and live a sanctified life in Christ.

If all Baxter writings were brought together they would number over 60 volumes, yet three of his books retain undying vitality: "Call to the Unconverted," the "Saints Everlasting Rest," and "The Reformed Pastor."

At one point he was offered the bishopric of Hereford, but he refused it rather than compromise his beliefs and betray the convictions of nearly 2,000 Puritan ministers who refused to submit to the demands of the Church of England under its edict in 1662 of the Act of Uniformity. This bill required scrupulous observance of the *Book of Common Prayer*, ordination only by bishops, and acceptance of the Apocryphal books as canon, among other things. The Puritans dissented and were thereafter labeled "non-conformists."

Later that year, Baxter was married to Margaret Charlton, a young woman residing in Kidderminster who benefited from his ministry. Their nineteen years spent together was a troubled time. If it was not for the warm affection they had for each other and the enjoyment of the "peace that passeth all understanding," there would have been little sunshine in their wedded life.

There was ever about him a keen sense of the world to come. Orme calls Baxter "unearthy" or "at the brink of the grave and the door of eternity."

As a leader among the Puritans, Baxter suffered repeated persecution between 1662-1687, and was imprisoned for eighteen months in 1685-1686 due to his non-conformity in ecclesiastical matters. Yet, his desire to preach the gospel burned in his breast, over and above Parliamentary prohibitions. Even his ever-failing health did not prevent him from preaching three or four times every week.

Baxter's balance as a leader and a theologian had a profound

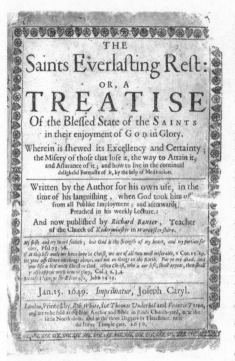

THE

Saints Everlasting Rest:

OR, A

TREATISE

Of the Blessed State of the SAINTS in their enjoyment of GOD in Glory.

Wherein is shewed its Excellency and Certainty; the Misery of those that lose it, the way to Attain it, and Assurance of it; and how to live in the continual delightful Foretasts of it, by the help of Meditation.

Written by the Author for his own use, in the time of his languishing, when God took him off from all Publike Imployment; and afterwards Preached in his weekly Lecture.:

And now published by *Richard Baxter*, Teacher of the Church of *Kedderminster* in *Worcestershire*.

My flesh and my heart faileth; but God is the strength of my heart, and my portion for ever, Psal. 73. 26.

If in this life onely we have hope in Christ, we are of all men most miserable, 1 Cor. 15. 19.

Set your affections on things above, and not on things on the Earth. For ye are dead, and your life is hid with Christ in God. when Christ, who is our life, shall appear, then shall ye also appear with him in glory, Col. 3. 2, 3, 4.

Blessed are the dead, ye that die in the Lord also, John 14. 19.

Jan. 15. 1649. *Imprimatur,* Joseph Caryl.

London, Printed by *Rob White,* for *Thomas Underhil* and *Francis Tyton,* and are to be sold at the blue Anchor and Bible in *Pauls* Church-yard, near the little North-door, and at the three Daggers in Fleetstreet, near the Inner Temple gate. 1650.

Title page to the first edition of Baxter's Saint's Everlasting Rest, published in 1650.

impact upon the church of his day. Whether Episcopalian, Presbyterian, or Independent, his example of resolute piety and conviction to truth brought about a wholesome fellowship between the clergy never before known in that vicinity.

As a writer, he has delighted, challenged and encouraged the souls of countless Christians, not only in his own day, but in all generations that followed. His friend, Dr. Thomas Manton freely expressed that he "thought Mr. Baxter came nearer to the apostolical writings than any man in the age." John Flavel affectionately says, "Mr. Baxter is almost in heaven, living in the daily views and cheerful expectation of the saint's everlasting rest with God; and is left for a little while among us, as a great example of the life of faith." Baxter possessed a keen sense of the world to come. Orme calls him "unearthy" or "at the brink of the grave and the door of eternity." In his funeral sermon on Baxter, William Bates says, "There was an air of humility and sanctity in his mortified countenance, and his conduct was as one who knew he was a stranger upon earth and a citizen of heaven."

Altogether, Baxter finished nearly two hundred distinct publications before his death on December 8, 1691.

Key writings of Richard Baxter: 1. *The Saints' Everlasting Rest* (1650). 2. *A Scripture Proof of Infant Baptism* (1653) 3. *A Call to the Unconverted* (1669). 4. *Christian Directory* (1673). 5. *The Reformed Pastor* (1674). 6. *Dying Thoughts* (1688). 7. *Reliquiae Baxterianae, A Narrative of His Life and Times* (1696). 8. *Works and Life of Baxter* (1830), 23 vols.

Worth Reading: *The Life and Times of Richard Baxter,* by W. Orme (1830); *Priest, Puritan, and Preacher,* by J. C. Ryle (1856); *A Pastoral Triumph: the Story of Richard Baxter & His Ministry at Kidderminster,* by Charles F. Kemp (1948); *Puritanism and Richard Baxter,* by Hugh Martin (1954); *A Grief Sanctified: From Sorrow to Eternal Hope: Including Richard Baxter's Timeless Memoir of His Wife,* by J. I. Packer (2000).

John Owen *1616-1683*
"Prince of Divines"

"You will find in Owen the learning of Lightfoot, the strength of Charnock, the analysis of Howe, the savour of Leighton, the glow of Baxter, the copiousness of Barrow, the splendour of Bates, are all combined. We would quickly restore the race of great divines if our candidates were disciplined in such lore." —Dr. Hamilton

"Prince of divines" is what Charles H. Spurgeon calls the famous English Puritan and theologian, John Owen. After studying at Oxford, he became a Presbyterian, but later joined the Independents. In doctrine he was a Calvinist, in philosophy an Aristotelian, and in Church government an Episcopalian. He was highly esteemed by the parliament, and was frequently called upon to preach before them. Cromwell, in particular, was so highly pleased with him, that when going to Ireland, he insisted on Dr. Owen accompanying him for the purpose of regulating and superintending the college of Dublin. After spending six months in that city, Owen returned to his clerical duties in England. But in 1650, he was again called away by Cromwell, to Edinburgh, where he spent the next six months in service to him. Subsequently he was promoted to the deanery of Christ Church college in Oxford, and soon after he was appointed to the vice-chancellorship of the university, which office he held till Cromwell's death. After the "Restoration," he was favored by Lord Clarendon, who offered him a promotion in the Church if he would conform to the Church of England, but the principles of Dr. Owen did not permit him to do so. The persecutions of the non-conformists repeatedly disposed him to emigrate to New England, but attachment to his native country always prevailed. Notwithstanding his decided hostility to the Church, the amiable dispositions and agreeable manners of Dr. Owen procured him much esteem from many eminent churchmen, among whom was the king himself. On one occasion, the king sent for Owen, and after a conversation of two hours, gave him a thousand guineas to be distributed among those who had suffered most from the recent persecution.

Owen had a great command of the English language and was one of the most polished and fair writers who have ever appeared against the Church of England. In this he handled his adversaries with far more civil, decent, and temperate language than many of his fiery brethren. He confined himself wholly to

Though Owen and Baxter disagreed on certain points of doctrine, the two formed a powerful duo of Christ-centered preaching, teaching, and writing. They stood together in fierce opposition to the formidable forces of false religion in England.

the cause without the unbecoming mixture of personal slanders and reflection.

He was a man of extensive learning, and most honorable character. As a preacher, he was eloquent and graceful, and displayed a degree of moderation and liberality not very common among the ministers with whom he was associated. His extreme industry is displayed by the more than eighty theological publications he authored. Controversies of the times often involved the differences between the Calvinists, of which Owen was a part, and the Arminians. The primary object of his work, *A Display of Arminianism,* was to give a view of the sentiments of Arminians, on the decrees of God, divine foreknowledge, providence, the efficacy of divine grace, original sin, and other leading doctrines surrounding this important controversy.

The antinomian tendency of John Owen's beliefs and writings elicited protests from fellow Non-conformists, such as Richard Baxter and John Home.

Of all his writings, Owen's work on the *Exposition of the Epistle to the Hebrews* (1668-84) is one of the finest commentaries on this particular book of the Bible.

More than sixty nobility gathered at his grave at Bunghill fields, "The Puritan Necropolis." His funeral service was a becoming end to a life spent in the active exercise of the duties of a holy life and unwearied zeal in the service of the eternal Kingdom of God.

Key writings of Owen: 1. *A Display of Arminianism* (1642); 2. *The Death of Death in the Death of Christ* (1643); 3. *Duty of Pastors* (1644); 4. *Doctrine of the Saint's Perseverance Explained and Confirmed* (1654); 5. *Vindiciae Evangelicae* (1655), *written in defense of the Deity and Satisfaction of Jesus Christ;* 6. *Mortification of Sin in Believers* (1656); 7. *The Nature of Schisme* (1657); 8. *Of the Divine Original Authority of the Scriptures* (1659); 9. *The Power of Indwelling Sin in Believers* (1668); 10. *Exposition of the Epistle to the Hebrews* (1668); 11. *Practical Exposition on Psalm 130* (1669); 12. *Vindications of the Doctrine of the Trinity* (1669); 13. *Exercitations Concerning the Name, Nature, Use, and Continuance of a Day of Sacred Rest* (1671); 14. *Discourses Concerning Love, Church Peace, and Unity* (1672); 15. *Discourse concerning the Holy Spirit* (1674); 16. *The Nature of Apostasy and the Punishment of Apostates Declared* (1676); 17. *The Doctrine of Justification By Faith Through the Imputation of the Righteousness of Christ Explained, Confirmed and Vindicated* (1677); 18. *Glorious Mystery of the Person of Christ* (1679); 19. *Phronema pneumatos; or the Grace of Being Spiritually-Minded* (1681); 20. *Work of the Holy Spirit in Prayer* (1682); 21. *Meditations and Discourses on the Glory of Christ* (1684); 22. *True Nature of the Gospel Church and its Government* (1689); *Meditations and Discourses on the Glory of Christ* (1696).

Worth Reading: *Life of Owen,* by W. Orme; *The Life of John Owen,* by A. W. Mitchell (1840); *God's Statesman: The Life and Work of John Owen,* by Peter Toon (1971); *John Owen on the Christian Life,* by Sinclair Ferguson (1987); *Communion With God. the Treasures of John Owen for Today's Readers,* by R. J. K. Law (1991); *John Owen: Prince of the Puritans,* by Andrew Thomson (1996); *Divine Discourse: The Theological Methodology of John Owen,* by Sebastian Rehnman (2002); *John Owen: The Man and His Theology,* by Robert Oliver (2003).

John Bunyan *1628-1688*

The Christian Dreamer

Only after reading Luther's commentary on Galatians did John Bunyan realize he needed to be justified by faith alone. Bunyan was so liberated by this truth that he yearned to tell the whole world about faith in Christ. He therefore became a field preacher. His words were so effective people would arrive at dawn to hear him preach at noon.

The stoutest heart might have quailed at the prospect now before the brave prisoner. His case unheard, his business almost in ruins, his wife and blind daughter, and three little ones besides, left dependent on friends or on the world's cold mercies; and the prospect of the gallows ever before him. As a prisoner his chosen work was forbidden to him, and his appeal to justice was persistently ignored. What could be more desolate? True, he might have ended it all by a vow "to speak no more nor to teach in the name of Jesus," but God forbid! He would rather lose everything. He would rather die!

In this prison John Bunyan remained, from his committal in 1660 to 1672—from the thirty-second to the forty-fourth year of his life. The period was divided by a brief interval of freedom in 1666, when he was released "through the intercession of some in trust and power that took pity upon his suffering." But he was speedily rearrested for secretly holding a religious service, and remained a prisoner until King Charles' momentous "Declaration of Indulgence" set him free.

But the work for which John Bunyan will most notably be remembered with gratitude is his immortal *Pilgrim's Progress*. He penned this literary and spiritual masterpiece from within the walls of his Elstow jail cell. No uninspired book has awakened the dead heart and impacted the mind more than Bunyan's *Pilgrim's Progress*. Nor has any written volume ever been demanded with greater eagerness by all classes of readers, or been so remarkably multiplied through the press, since it was first published and distributed in 1678.

John Bunyan was born at Elstow, a small village a mile south of Bedford, England. His father was a poor tinker, but sent him to school until he could read and write. As a lad he fell into the company of wicked companions with whom he would lie and swear; but his conscience often reproved him. He was frightened in his sleep with terrible dreams, and in his waking hours he had thoughts of his condition and future judgment.

Even at a young age, he sensed God was preserving his life. He recalls a number of remarkable instances of divine

John Bunyan had the remarkable ability to view the Christian life in allegorical forms. Even his classic and immortal **Pilgrim's Progress** *draws from experiences in his own life.*

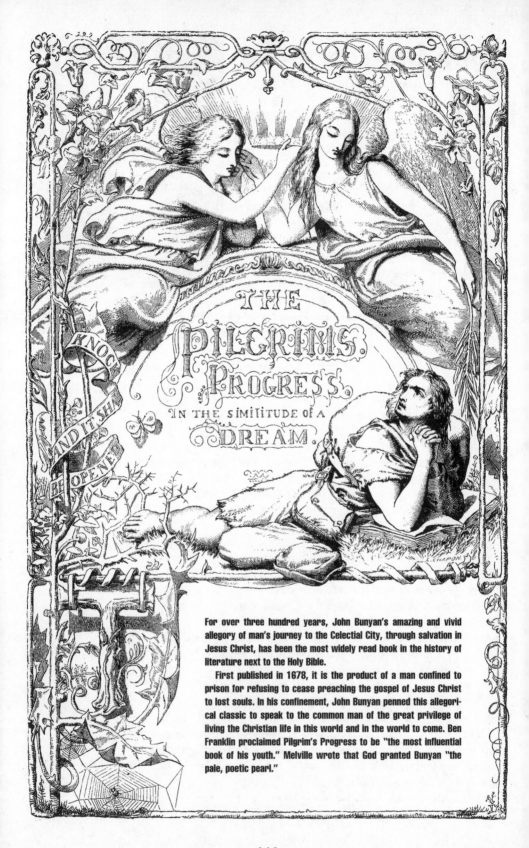

THE PILGRIMS PROGRESS IN THE SIMILITUDE OF A DREAM

KNOCK AND IT SHALL BE OPENED

For over three hundred years, John Bunyan's amazing and vivid allegory of man's journey to the Celectial City, through salvation in Jesus Christ, has been the most widely read book in the history of literature next to the Holy Bible.

First published in 1678, it is the product of a man confined to prison for refusing to cease preaching the gospel of Jesus Christ to lost souls. In his confinement, John Bunyan penned this allegorical classic to speak to the common man of the great privilege of living the Christian life in this world and in the world to come. Ben Franklin proclaimed Pilgrim's Progress to be "the most influential book of his youth." Melville wrote that God granted Bunyan "the pale, poetic pearl."

intervention: "At one time I fell into a creek of the sea and hardly escaped drowning. Another time I fell out of a boat into the river at Bedford. At another time, being drafted as a soldier to go to the siege of Leicester. One of the company desired to go in my place, who, as he stood sentinel, was shot in the head with a musket-bullet and killed."

At the tender age of nineteen, Bunyan married his first wife, a virtuous and gentle woman, whose only dowry was two Christian books left to her by her godly father when he died; *The Plain Man's Pathway to Heaven* by Arthur Dent (1599) and *The Practice of Piety*, by Lewes Bailey. Bunyan and his wife often read these books together, and the youthful husband found in their pages an echo of the deep yearnings that, despite all his recklessness, had never quite left him.

Thus it was with Bunyan until the memorable day when, on a visit to Bedford, he came upon a group of poor women whom he has since rendered immortal. They were "sitting at a door in the sun, talking about the things of God. Their talk was about a new birth—the work of God on their hearts, and also how they were convinced of their miserable state by nature. They talked how God had visited their souls with His love in the Lord Jesus. With what words and promises they had been refreshed, comforted, and supported one another against the temptations of the devil." He drew near to listen, perhaps to join in the conversation. But to his astonishment, the language of these good people was wholly strange to him. They spoke of heart experiences, mysterious conflicts and triumphs, and happy fellowship with God, of which he knew nothing. "They spake as if joy did make them speak!" There was a secret that he had not yet learned. He went away, resolved, if possible, to attain this new knowledge. He frequented the society of these poor people, learning more and more of his own deficiencies and still crying for light. "I saw that in all my thoughts about religion and salvation the new birth did never enter into my mind, neither knew I the comfort of the word and promise, nor the treachery of my own wicked heart." He turned to the Bible with new zest and found it "was sweet and pleasant to me, and I was still crying out to God that I might know the truth and the way to heaven." At length the intense contrast between what he saw in these rejoicing Christians, and what he felt himself to be, shaped themselves into a waking dream, in which we may discern as a far-off sketch of the *Pilgrim's Progress* in his heart.

"The Bedford jail was that den wherein Bunyan dreamed his dream—The Pilgrim's Progress, *a book which the child and his grandmother read together with delight; and which, more than any other work may be said to be 'Meet for all hours, and every mood of man.'"*
—Dr. Williams

Bunyan visits the pious poor women at Bedford, whom the Lord used to affect his conversion.

"The state and happiness of these poor people at Bedford was thus, in a dream or vision, represented to me. I saw as if they were set on the sunny side of some high mountain, there refreshing themselves with the pleasant beams of the sun, while I was shivering and shrinking in the cold, afflicted with frost, snow, and dark clouds. I thought also, between me and them, I saw a wall that did compass about this mountain. Now through this wall my soul did greatly desire to pass, concluding, that if I could, I would go even into the very midst of them, and there also comfort myself with the heat of their sun."

Bunyan was now a rejoicing believer, and yet the time of conflict was not over. He had crossed the Slough of Despond, and had surmounted the Hill Difficulty; but he had yet to pass through the Valley of Humiliation, to do battle with Apollyon, and to quail amid the darkness before the spectres of the Valley of the Shadow of Death. Meanwhile he found a little rest in the Palace Beautiful. Already had the teachings of the gospel been opened up to him by "Evangelist," in the person of Rev. John Gifford, the wise and saintly pastor of St. John's in Bedford.

The year Gifford died, Bunyan took a more active role in the ministry of the Church. He was asked by the brethren to give a word of exhortation at their assemblies. He consented with fear and trembling, but his gifts were recognized immediately. Little did they know what light was being kindled in their simple gatherings.

During the next five years, Bunyan found prosperity in both tongue and pen, as well as his business as a tinker. But bitter sorrow would visit his home. The wife of his youth—the gentle "Mercy"—who bore him four beautiful children, was taken from him by the angel of death. His eldest, Mary, was blind and extremely close to her father. In 1659, he married his second wife, Elizabeth, the Christiana of *Pilgrim's Progress. She* became a loving mother to his children and a brave-hearted helper to her husband.

In 1660, King Charles II recalled old laws against the Puritans and Nonconformists, requiring all people to attend parish churches or be punished. Bunyan was unable to cease preaching the Word of God and chose rather to meet secretly in homes,

The Holy War, *Bunyan's next great allegory was, like his* Pilgrim's Progress, *destined to become a classic in Christian literature by which all generations would be blessed.*

John Bunyan in his Bedford prison cell, being comforted by his blind daughter, Mary, and the compassionate jailer who released him on occasion.

fields and forests for worship. To one who questioned holding secret services he replied, "No, by no means will I stir, nor will I dismiss the meeting for this. Come, be of good cheer, let us not be daunted." After numerous arrests and warnings, Bunyan, to use his own expression, went "home to prison." He was offered freedom if he would cease preaching, but he answered, "If I am let out of prison today, I would preach the Gospel tomorrow, with God's help."

Bunyan's petition for release was placed in the hands of his wife, Elizabeth. Undaunted, this true "Christiana" made her way to court and presented her appeal with the noble wit of heroic womanhood. But all her words would not move the hard-hearted prelates and Bunyan was remanded to county prison. The jailor, however, had compassion on the preacher and allowed Bunyan to depart occasionally during the day, with the promise that he would return by nightfall.

Elizabeth Bunyan pleading for her husband's release before Judge Twisden and Matthew Hale.

He was not idle during his long and severe confinement, but diligently studied his Bible. The Scripture and *Foxe's Book of Martyrs*, composed his whole library. They were to him "pearls of great price." Bunyan's own hands also ministered to the necessity of his indigent family. But his great calling continued in preaching to all who could gain access to the jail. He spoke with a spirit and a power that pierced the hearts of his hearers.

The volume of Foxe's Book of Martyrs *that kept companion with John Bunyan in prison for so many years was sold in 1780 to the Bedfordshire Library. It is enriched with numerous annotations from the hand of the prisoner.*

It was in the Bedford jail that he composed numerous treatises, in addition to his inspiring *Pilgrim's Progress*. Through seasons of trial and persecution the Lord often works great things through his humble servants. After his release in 1672, he continued with his mighty pen to produce brilliant classics such as *The Holy War* and *The Life and Death of Mr. Badman*. John Bunyan steadfastly continued as a faithful pastor and preacher. His ministry always attracting huge crowds, and affected a great many conversions.

Key Writings of Bunyan: 1. *Grace Abounding to the Chief of Sinners;* 2. *Pilgrim's Progress;* 3. *Christian Behaviour;* 4. *Solomon's Temple Spiritualized;* 5. *The Jerusalem Sinner Saved;* 6. *The Holy War;* 7. *The Life and Death of Mr. Badman;* 8. *Come and Welcome to Jesus Christ;* 9. *The Barren Fig-Tree;* 10. *Prison Meditations;* 11. *The Heavenly Footman;* 12. *Sighs From Hell.*

Isaac Newton analyzing the ray of light in 1668. It was at this time that he discovered that white light is actually composed of a spectrum of colors.

Isaac Newton *1642-1727*

Great Christian Scientist

Newton's discovery of universal gravitation and his decomposition of light will always be rightly regarded as forming the chief turning-point in the scientific history of the world, as well as the brightest pages in the records of human reason and discovery. Throughout his life Newton cherished the doctrines of the Bible as the most sacred and highest of all truths, and attributed every one of his mathematical and scientific discoveries to the grand master design of the Master himself, the Lord God of all creation.

The very incidents surrounding Isaac's birth seemed to indicate God had some special plan for him—at least that's what Isaac Newton thought. He was born premature and sickly, but like his Bible namesake Isaac (which means "laughter"), the baby was miraculously delivered. He was so small at birth his mother remarked, "they might have placed him in a quart mug."

Isaac Newton was born on Christmas Day in 1642. He never knew his father, who died three months before his birth. It was also the same year the brilliant scientist Galileo died, and Newton sensed Galileo's mantle had fallen on his shoulders.

So weak and feeble was Isaac in his early infancy that on one occasion two women who were dispatched to bring him some strengthening medicine did not expect to find the child alive on their return. It was, however, divinely appointed that this frail and tiny child should grow to vigorous maturity, surpassing even the average of human physical existence. He also excelled the most distinguished philosophers and scientists in the multitude and magnitude of his gifts. The immeasurable grandeur and utility of Newton's discoveries demonstrate the infinite wisdom, power, and goodness of the Creator.

The peculiar giftedness of his mind was displayed early in his school days. During the play hours when the other boys were occupied with their amusements, his mind was engrossed with mechanical contrivances, either in imitation of something he had seen, or in execution of some original conception. For this purpose he always carried with him numerous little tools and gadgets. While other children were studying grammar and reading Virgil and Shakespeare, young Isaac managed to construct a windmill, a water-clock, a carriage, and a sundial. His fellow townspeople affectionately named it the "Isaac dial" .

Newton is among the greatest scientific geniuses of all times. He made major contributions to mathematics, optics, physics, and astronomy. He discovered the law of gravitation, formulated the basic laws of motion, developed calculus, and analyzed the nature of white light. Behind all his science was the conviction that God made the universe with a mathematical structure

Sir Isaac Newton is generally regarded as the most original and influential discoverer of scientific principles and laws under creation. His understanding of light and color led to the invention of his telescope. This great man of God also discovered the law of gravity, calculus, and the three laws of motion.

and gifted the minds of people to understand it.

Newton knew that the very orderliness and design of the universe reflected God's awesome majesty and wisdom. The design of the eye alone required a perfect understanding of optics, while the design of the ear required a knowledge of sounds. Newton knew the solar system itself could not have been produced by blind chance or fortuitous causes, but only by a Cause "very well skilled in mechanics and geometry," he said. Gravity itself is an active principle used by God to maintain order in the world.

Seeking to understand God's methods, Newton developed formulas for specific phenomena such as ocean tides, paths of comets, and the succession of the equinoxes (lunar eclipses).

Dr. Humphrey Newton says of Isaac's Principia *that, "After its printing, Sir Issac was please to send me several of them as present for the heads of colleges, some of whom said that they studied it for seven years before they could understand anything of it."*

Newton also spent a tremendous amount of time studying the Bible, especially the prophetic portions of Scripture. He believed history was under the dominion of the Creator, and prophecy showed how the Almighty was to establish His earthly kingdom in the end. His *Chronology of Ancient Kingdoms Amended* used astronomical data to argue that the Bible is the oldest document in the world and that Biblical history preceded all other ancient historical accounts.

Newton states, "Whence came all the order and beauty which we see in the world? How came the bodies of animals be contrived with so much art, and with what ends were their several parts designed? Was the eye contrived without skill in optics, and the ear without a knowledge of sound?"

In spite of his many discoveries and honors for scientific achievements, Newton remained a gracious and humble man. He once wrote his nephew; "To myself I seem to have been only a boy playing on the seashore, and diverting myself in now and then finding a smoother pebble or a prettier shell than ordinary, while the great ocean of truth lay all undiscovered before me."

Until Newton's arrival, philosophers and scientists had endeavored in vain to give any explanation for the differences in color. In 1668, he observed that when a beam of sunlight passing through a small round opening in a shutter was filtered through the angle of a prism, there appeared on a screen behind the prism, not a round white spot, but an elongated spectrum of seven different colors. This is now one of the most familiar facts in optics, but it was looked upon at that time as a startling discovery. Furthermore, its truth was by no means readily admitted.

But Newton's optical discoveries pale in comparison to his great discovery of universal gravitation. The former showed his skill as an experimental philosopher, the latter his transcendent powers as a mathematician and as an expounder of the secrets of nature. In the year in which he earned his B. S. degree he discovered his method of Fluxions, or what is now known as differential and integral calculus, a branch of mathematics without which any profound research into the motions of the heavenly bodies is impossible.

In 1665, the fall of an apple from a tree under which Newton was sitting is said to have given him the idea of a central force of gravitation. It's what makes a stone fall to the ground, and its the force which retains the moon in her orbit around the Earth. It is found to operate with no sensible variation even at the tops of the highest mountains.

Newton's two greatest discoveries of light and gravity were recorded in great detail in his *Optics* and his *Principia*. Few writings have influenced the advance of science, mathematics or philosophy as these two brilliant works.

It was Newton's reflecting telescope, made in 1668, that finally brought him into full view of the scientific community. His work with light and colors led him to believe that refracting telescopes, which were subject to color interference were outdated. He made his reflecting telescope entirely on his own with some parts he made specifically for that purpose. His invention made telescopes much smaller. His was only six inches long and one inch in diameter, yet it magnified over thirty times.

Newton's niece, Catherine Barton, with whom he worked very closely for years, tells how "he could not bear to hear anyone talk ludicrously of religion."

On April 16, 1705, Queen Anne, with Prince George of Denmark, and the rest of the Court, visited the University of Cambridge and conferred the honor of knighthood on Newton. This gracious mark of recognition of scientific merit on the part of royalty is the first recorded honor of the kind conferred on men distinguished for scientific attainments and discoveries. But scientific merit was not by any means the least or the sole claim Newton had to such a mark of royal favor. His high situation under government, his invaluable services rendered to the state in the recoinage of the current coin, his spotless moral character, his generous charities, and above all his unaffected piety combined to present him to the eye as an eminently worthy object of Royalty's special favor and patronage.

Shortly before leaving this world for the better, perfect one in glory, Newton summed up his life's work with these words: "I do not know what I may appear to the world, but to myself I seem to have been only like a boy playing on the seashore, and diverting myself in now and then finding a smoother pebble, or a prettier shell than ordinary, whilst the great ocean of truth lay all undiscovered before me."

The religious and moral character of Newton was exemplary. His conduct was always guided by the principles of the Christian faith which he had studied most profoundly, and believed in most sincerely. He was too deeply versed in holy Scripture and too much imbued with the Holy Spirit to judge harshly of other men who took different views than himself. Newton cherished the belief in religious toleration and freedom of worship, and he never hesitated to express his abhorrence of religious   persecution even in its mildest form. He never allowed immorality and impiety to pass in his presence unreproved, and when a colleague, Dr. Halley, ventured to state anything disrespectful of religion, Newton invariably checked him and said; "I have studied these things—you have not." Always hospitable and kind to his friends, Newton's generosity and charity to the needy had no bounds. He used to remark, "they who gave away nothing till they died, never gave at all." For the parsimonious he had a   profound contempt, and he spent by far the greater portion of his wealth in relieving the poor, in assisting his relations, and in encouraging science and learning.

Dr. Isaac Watts, in his renowned book Improvement of the Mind *says; "That wonder of our age and nation, Sir Isaac Newton." And Richard Addison says of Sir Isaac Newton in his* Defence of the New Philosophy, *"The great ornament of the present age."*

It is undeniable that in all his writings Isaac Newton appears to have looked through all the marvelous works of nature up to nature's God. It is clear that he deeply desired the world to see in his own discovered system of the starry heavens the strongest possible evidence of the wisdom, unbounded power, and goodness of the Creator. From the observed phenomena of nature, and from his investigation of its laws, Newton concludes that there must exist "a Being incorporeal, living, intelligent, omnipresent," who directs and rules the worlds and systems He has created.

There have been those partial to secular reasoning who have claimed that Newton's "religious tendencies" were only in the latter years of his life as his mental faculties were declining, but nothing could be further from the truth. His love for God and genuine trust in Jesus Christ his Savior was only strengthened during the course of his life. The more he discovered in the world around, the more convinced he became of the existence and power of the all-wise, immortal, invisible God. By effectively uniting philiosphy and religion, Newton helped dissolve much of the unholy scepticism and worldliness of his day, and added to the "cloud of witnesses" his amazing discoveries.

Key Writings of Newton: 1. *Principia* (1687); 2. *Optics* (1704); 3. *Arithemetica Universalis* (1707); *Observations Upon the Prophecies of Holy Writ*; 4. *Historical Account of Two Notable Corruptions of the Scriptures*; 5. *Chronology of Ancient Kingdoms; Optical Lectures* (1728).

Worth Reading: *Brewster's Life of Newton,* by David Brewster; *Men of Science, Men of God,* by Dr. Henry Morris (1982); *Never at Rest: A Biography of Isaac Newton,* by Richard S. Westfall (1983); *In the Presence of the Creator: Isaac Newton and His Times,* by Gale Christianson (1984); *God's Other Son, Isaac Newton: The Link Between Science & Religion,* by James Brettell (2000)

Isaac Watts *1674-1748*

Father of English Hymnody

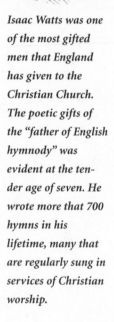

Not only was Isaac Watts a prolific writer of Christian verse of the highest style, but he is also remembered as a powerful preacher, a children's poet, and an author of timeless Christian literature. He played a vital role in preparing England for the great evangelical awakening under the Wesleys and Whitefield.

he glory of Puritanism was fading, Non-conformists were still being persecuted, worship was little more that a formality, and dead orthodoxy was spinning the Church into spiritual darkness and indifference. Such was the state of Christianity in England at the beginning of the eighteenth century. But before the great revival under Edwards, Wesley, and Whitefield came, God was pleased to prepare the way by touching the heart of Isaac Watts and lead him to move both England and America to a spiritual awakening with a humble but powerful instrument not well known in his day— the sacred hymn.

It was immediately after his academy days, when he had returned to live in his father's home, that Watts composed his first hymn. One Sunday after the morning church service he began to complain about the dull and lifeless Psalm-singing in which they had just participated, a characteristic of nonconformist worship at that time. The elder Watts replied, "If you do not like it, why do you not give us something better?" Isaac went home, opened his Bible to a place in Revelation, chapter 5 where the new song of Heaven is described, and wrote a poetic transcription of it. Two of the stanzas read:

Isaac Watts was one of the most gifted men that England has given to the Christian Church. The poetic gifts of the "father of English hymnody" was evident at the tender age of seven. He wrote more that 700 hymns in his lifetime, many that are regularly sung in services of Christian worship.

> *Behold the glories of the Lamb*
> *Amid his Father's throne:*
> *Prepare new honors for his name,*
> *And songs before unknown.*
>
> *Thou hast redeemed our souls with blood,*
> *Hast set the prisoners free,*
> *Hast made us Kings and Priests to God,*
> *And we shall reign with Thee.*

This first effort was sung at the next service in the Southampton church. It touched the hearts of those in the congregation and moved them so deeply that they encouraged him to write more songs for them. So on that day the English hymn was born.

Behold the Glories of the Lamb not only introduced a new era in public and private worship, it established a pattern followed, for the most part, by all seven hundred of Watts' hymns and by thousands of others written since his day. Taking his cue from the Psalm versions, this young man in his early twenties, sought only to make it possible for the Lord's people to sing the Word of God in the form of good poetry and pleasant tunes. Each time he wrote, he took a familiar text of Scripture and set it to words and music. And as he honored the Word of God, the God of the Word honored him.

Isaac Watts' father was imprisoned for his Non-conformist beliefs. When just an infant his mother would take little Isaac to nurse him while visiting his father's prison cell.

Isaac Watts was born at Southampton, where his father, who had previously been imprisoned for nonconformity, at the latter part of his life kept a boarding-school. Isaac was the eldest of nine children. From his earliest years, he displayed great avidity for learning. Before he was old enough to speak clearly, whenever any money was given to him, he would carry it to his mother and say, as well as he could, "A book! A book! Buy a book!" It is reported that he almost "lisped in numbers." On one occasion, his mother having chastised him for addressing her in rhyme, he unconsciously repeated the same offense in imploring her forgiveness. From this time on, she encouraged his natural gift for verse-making and gave him a small gratuity whenever his lines pleased her. Having presented him with a farthing for one of his childish efforts, he soon afterwards brought her the following couplet:

I write not for a farthing; but to try
How I your farthing poets can outvie.

Isaac Watts left his father's house in Southampton and went to London on October 15, 1696, to become tutor to the son of Sir John Hartopp, head of a wealthy Non-conformist family living in Newington Green, where many of London's richest Dissenters lived. They belonged to the upper class, the aristocracy of Puritanism in which Watts moved all the days of his life. For five years he remained as tutor to John Hartopp while continuing his own studies.

On his birthday in 1698, Watts preached his first sermon to Dr. Chauncey's congregation. On the death of Pastor Chauncey, Watts was offered to folow him. In spite of his many physical infirmities he continued to preach until he was seventy years old, and developed a considerable reputation as an expositor of the Word of God.

His preaching was described by contemporaries as weighty and powerful. There was a certain dignity and spirit in his very presence when he appeared in the pulpit, that commanded attention and awe. When he spoke, strains of Christian eloquence flowed from his lips, with a genuine passion for God. He possessed a tender concern for the everlasting salvation of his hearers. His enunciation was said to be remarkable, and he spoke with such deep gravity and sincerity, his hearers were moved to "go and do likewise" in the world for Christ.

A discourse appearing in *An Humble Attempt towards the Revival of Practical Religion* (1731), entitled "An Exhortation to Ministers," revealed his standards for the pulpit. He expressed that a preacher should have unquestioned assurance of his own salvation. He must speak plainly enough to be understood by the ignorant, but he must at the same time be able to convince the most learned. A good preacher should avoid controversy as far as possible. He ought never to read in the pulpit, unless quoting. And most of all he must lead an exemplary life before his people.

The greater part of his time was dedicated to writing on the subjects the Lord placed on his heart. In 1724, he published *Logic: or The Right Use of Reason in the Inquiry After Truth*, and its companion work, *The Improvement of the Mind: A Supplement to the Art of Logic*.

Other successful books written by Watts included *The Art of Reading and Writing English*; *The Knowledge of the Heavens and the Earth Made Easy*; and the famous *Children's Catechisms*. These "instructions in the principles of the Christian religion and the history of Scripture, composed for children and youth according to the different ages," were translated into many languages and used all over the world.

Great English hymnwriters such as Charles Wesley, Philip Doddridge, and Horatius Bonar followed in the footprints forged by Isaac Watts.

One of his finest works is *The World to Come*, written as an expression of his own meditation on and anticipation of Heaven amidst his life-long infirmities. He experienced great pain and suffering in this world, but came to enjoy a deep peace, looking forward to his heavenly mansion in the world to come. The reader of this classic work cannot help but be drawn to eternal solicitude and release from the pangs of sin and death this world sadly offers.

In order to understand the magnitude of the contribution made to hymnology by Watts, it is necessary to know something of the state of sacred song in public worship at the time he appeared on the horizon. For more than one hundred years *The Whole Booke of Psalmes*, by Hopkins and Sternhold, had dominated the churches as the official songbook, since its publication in 1562. In America, *The Bay Psalm Book* (1640) occupied a similar position. The versions of the Psalms prepared by Hopkins and Sternhold were intended to be a literal transcription of each of the one hundred and fifty Psalms, but as poetry they were harsh and crude. It was the custom to have the stanzas droned out line by line as a clerk read them to the congregation. They were hard to sing, a source of annoyance to all in the assembly, and a weariness to the soul.

This practice received a great amount of criticism, and not without justification. For example, in "lining out" the Fiftieth Psalm, the presenter would read, "The Lord will come and He will not." The people would sing this line, pause to listen to the presenter, and then sing the next line, "Keep silence but speak out." In many churches there were only three tunes in use, so it was not unusual for each member of the congregation to choose his own tune.

The reception given to the hymns of Watts was remarkable. Rev. Philip Doddridge in a letter to Watts mentioned a church service at which the congregation sang *Give me the wings of faith to rise within the veil.* Doddridge wrote, "I had the satisfaction to observe tears in the eyes of several of the people; and after the service was over some of them told me they were not able to sing, because their hearts were so deeply affected. They were most of them poor people who worked for their living, yet on the mention of your name, I found...that your Psalms and hymns were almost their daily entertainment."

Not until he was urged to make his religious poems available to the public did Watts publish some of them. The first edition was published in 1706, under the title, *Horae Lyricae.* It was followed in 1707 by a collection of 210 hymns, entitled, *Hymns and Spiritual Songs,* and in 1719 by *The Psalms of David Imitated in the Language of the New Testament.*

These latter two works formed his famous "System of Praise" which marked the beginning of a new era in English hymnody.

On both sides of the Atlantic he was held in such high esteem that sometimes if a hymn by another writer was announced, some in the congregation would sit down and refuse to sing. His tremendous popularity continued for well over one hundred years. Even today, with the accumulated wealth of hymnody of some three hundred years, the hymns of Isaac Watts are sung throughout the world. They include such noble verses as "O God Our Help in Ages Past," "Before Jehovah's Throne," "Joy to the World," "Come, Holy Spirit, Heavenly Dove," "There Is a Land of Pure Delight," and "Am I a Soldier of the Cross." And it is doubtful that such a hymn as When I Survey the Wondrous Cross could possibly be surpassed.

> *"Since in many things we offend all, and there is not a day that passes which is perfectly free from sin, let 'repentance towards God, and faith in our Lord Jesus Christ,' be your daily work. A frequent renewal of these exercises which make a Christian at first, will be a constant evidence of your sincere Christianity, and give you peace in life, and hope in death."*
> —Watts, in his Advice to Young Men

Key Writings of Watts: 1. *Horae Lyricae* (1706); 2. *Hymns and Spiritual Songs* (1707); 3. *Orthodoxy and Charity United (1707);* 4. *A Guide to Prayer* (1715); 5. *Divine and Moral Songs for Children* (1715); 6. *The Psalms of David Imitated in the Language of the New Testament* (1719); 7. *The Art of Reading and Writing English* (1721); 8. *Logic: The Right Use of Reason in the Inquiry of Truth* (1724); 9. *The Knowledge of the Heavens and the Earth Made Easy* (1726); 10. *Dissertations Relating to the Christian Doctrine of the Trinity* (1726); 11. *Treatise on the Love of God* (1729); 12. *Catechisms for Children* (1730); 13. *Short View of the Whole Scripture History* (1730); 14. *Humble Attempt Towards the Revival of Practical Religion* (1731); 15. *Proof of a Separate State of Souls* (1732); 16. *Freedom of Will in God and Creatures* (1732); 17. *Philosophical Essays* (1733); 18. *Reliquiae Juveniles* (1734); 19. *The Redeemer and the Sanctifier* 1736); 20. *Strength and Weakness of Human Reason* (1737); 21. *The World to Come* (1738); 22. *On Civil Power in Things Sacred* (1739); 23. *The Ruin and Recovery of Mankind* (1740); 24. *Improvement of the Mind* (1741); 25. *Glory of Christ and God-man Unveiled* (1746).

Worth Reading: *Select Works of Isaac Watts,* Thoemmes Press (8 vols).

John Brown *1676-1714*
Martyred Scottish Covenanter

For fifty years, during the seventeenth century, the Scottish Covenanters chose to suffer persecution with courage and fortitude at the hands of the King of England, rather than compromise their principles of civil and religious freedom. These "Martyr Warriors" as they were so often called, held fast to owning "Christ alone," as opposed to King Charles II "as head and lawgiver to the Church." As a result of their resolve they were dragged from their homes, beaten, and martyred in the name of "religion."

There are very few periods in the history of the world, since the introduction of Christianity, in which Christian heroism has been exhibited on a larger scale than among the Scotch Covenanters in the seventeenth century. There have been some Historians who choose to regard these Covenanters with contempt, and portray them as factious and seditious, receiving from the temporal power the reward they deserved. But there could not be a more false representation of the facts of history. What were these facts? The great mass of the inhabitants of Scotland were Presbyterians, worshipping God according to His Holy Word, quite unlike the fashion of the Church of England, which, at that time, seemed to be just a few steps removed from Romanism, however they may have positioned themselves.

"Now," says the temporal power to these honest, conscientious Presbyterians, "you shall not worship in this way. You must have bishops, and prayer books, and rituals, and all that sort of thing." "May it please you," replied the Coven-anters, "we will have nothing of the kind. We are content as we are." Then came the hour that "tried men's souls." The dominant parties were bent upon forcing the Scotch to receive Episcopacy. The Scotch generally were resolute in their determination to resist, if necessary, at the sacrifice of their lives. The result was that multitudes of ministers were deprived of their livings. More than this though—they were

Covenanters were dragged from their homes and places of worship by the king's soldiers to face execution.

thrust into prison, tortured in a manner almost as brutal as the Inquisition in the darkest epochs of its history. They were led to the scaffold, and many of their hearers, men and women in humble life, suffered with them. Walter Scott and the royalists, and high churchmen who sympathize with him, may draw such pictures of the Covenanters and their persecutors. Hundreds of the Scotch Presbyterians of the seventeenth century were legally murdered for no other crime than that they were Presbyterians, and that they declared that they meant to remain such, by the grace of God.

In Edinburgh the scaffold received some of the brightest ornaments that the Church ever possessed. Search the annals of history and we cannot find more praiseworthy examples of sacrifical lambs for the truth's sake, than those found in Scotland at that time. What an exhibition of heroism, for example, is there in the pious John Brown and his devoted wife. John Brown had chosen to establish a Sunday school and spread the gospel to all people, which made him stand out in the eyes of the government.

One morning in the early spring, Brown had just finished family worship and was on his way to work in the field, when a company of soldiers, with a man called Claverhouse at their head, approached him. Claverhouse was a wicked man and he hated the Scottish Presbyterians. The soldiers brought their victim back to his house, and told him to go to his prayers, for in a few minutes he would die. The godly man knelt down and prayed with so much fervor that the hardened soldiers were affected to tears. Three times Claverhouse interrupted him, saying, "I gave you time to pray, but you have begun to preach." When the doomed man rose, he took leave of his wife and children and Claverhouse ordered his troopers to fire. But they had not the nerve to carry out the deed. Enraged at this, Claverhouse, took a pistol from his saddle and shot this disciple of Christ through the head. Then turning to the woman whom he had just made a widow, he said "What do you think of your husband now?" The answer of this heroine deserves to be engraved in the deepest lines upon the tablet of Church history. "I always thought much of him, and more now than ever."

To the everlasting shame and disgrace of the prelatical party in Great Britain, four hundred and eighty of the servants of Christ in Scotland perished as martyrs without any process of law. Eighteen hundred were subjected to torture. Seventeen hundred were banished. Great numbers were sent to the colonies as slaves, and two hundred of these were drowned. Yet nothing could subdue the fortitude of these martyrs. "If I had as many lives as there are hairs on my head," said one of them, who was shot in the fields, "I would willingly suffer as many deaths for Christ and His cause."

Worth Reading: *Lives of the Scottish Covenanters,* by John Howie.

In 1638, King Charles regarded protests against the prayerbook as treason, forcing Scots to choose between their church and the King. A "Covenant", swearing to resist these changes to the death, was signed in Greyfriars Church in Edinburgh. The covenant was accepted by hundreds of thousands of Scots.

Jonathan Edwards *1703-1758*
New England Revivalist

Freedom to worship the Lord God through Jesus Christ with a pure heart and a clear conscience—this was what the Puritans who came to America in the 1630's dreamed of establishing—a Biblical society which would be an example for all nations. But within a few generations the dream faded. Their great-grandchildren were not as interested in making God the center of their lives. They were prospering in America, and these Puritan descendants felt quite capable of handling their lives and affairs independently of the God of their fathers. America was ripe for a religious revival and the Church was ready for a man to lead it.

uring the eighteenth century Puritanism retained among the colonists of North America a position relatively far more important than in the life of mother country, England. Puritan doctrine and Puritan church life, under the forms of Presbyterianism and Congregationalism, were predominant in New England throughout the eighteenth century. And the most powerful representative of New England theology and devotion was unquestionably Jonathan Edwards.

From a very early age, Jonathan was very methodical and driven in all his activities, competent in Latin, Greek, and Hebrew before he was a teenager. Just short of age thirteen he entered the Collegiate School of Connecticut (Yale University) and graduated at the head of his class. Though he was fascinated by the philosophies of John Locke and wrote profound metaphysical essays in his teens, Jonathan was primarily interested in religion as the leading interest of his life. As a child he had revolted against the sovereignty of God and thought it a horrible doctrine, but shortly before his graduation at seventeen, he said God's sovereignty, glory, and majesty became "exceedingly pleasant, bright, and sweet" to his soul. He first found this satisfactory when reading the glorious doxology in Paul's first Epistle to Timothy: *"Now unto the King, eternal, immortal, invisible, the only wise God, be honor and glory for ever and ever. Amen."* Edwards' mind was naturally contemplative and meditative, and from his youth the themes upon which he most delighted to ponder were the character and attributes of God, the plan of redemption, the work of the Spirit, and the joys and glories of Heaven. In his case religion took a tone and color quite peculiar to itself. Serenity and majesty were distinctives in his Christian life, and he was often lifted above the stormy atmosphere of human conflict, anxiety, and fear.

The glory and majesty of God became Edwards' compelling

Over two centuries after Edwards' death, the great British preacher, Dr. Martin Lloyd-Jones, said of him; "No man is more relevant to the present condition [growth] of Christianity than Jonathan Edwards."

passion in life. After studying divinity for two years, Edwards preached some and was appointed a tutor at Yale. In 1727, he became a co-pastor with his grandfather Solomon Stoddard in Northampton, Massachusetts. Stoddard, sometimes called the "Pope of western Massachusetts," had been a powerful preaching influence in Northampton and Massachusetts for over fifty-five years. When he died in 1729, the church at Northampton called its young assistant, Jonathan Edwards, to become pastor.

His early years as pastor were busy with the daunting challenge of reaching a society of people immersed in immorality and worldliness. This was the cause of great distress in the spiritually-minded pastor who was laboring for their spiritual welfare, but his preaching cut to the hearts of many, and his faithful counsels were blessed by God to the recalling of many offenders to an improved Christian life. Wicked activities were forsaken, and young and old alike began to take a deeper interest in religious devotion, particularly the condition of their souls.

Edwards usually spent thirteen hours a day in study, preparing at least two sermons a week and often additional lectures. Many of his Bible studies later resulted in published works.

Edwards took great pleasure in the loveliness and beauty of Christ. He experienced "calm, sweet abstraction of soul from all the concerns of this world." "The sense," he says, "I have of divine things would often suddenly kindle up, as it were, a sweet burning in my heart, an ardour of soul, that I know not how to express."

"I have loved the doctrines of the gospel. They have been to my soul like green pastures. The gospel has seemed to me the richest treasure; the treasure that I have most desired, and longed might dwell richly in me. The way of salvation by Christ has appeared, in a general way, glorious and excellent, most pleasant and beautiful," says Edwards from his own account of his conversion. "Holiness appeared to me to be of a sweet, pleasant, charming, serene, calm nature; which brought an inexpressible purity, brightness, peacefulness and ravishment to the soul."

It was in his sermons that Edwards' studies bore their richest fruit. From the first he was recognized as a remarkable preacher. He was as arresting and awakening as he was instructive. Under Edwards' preaching and teaching, a revival came to Northampton in 1735, and over 300 converts were gathered into the fold. Edwards recognized this was the work of God's Spirit, for only God could convert a sinful heart and transform lives of self-centeredness into lives of Christian holiness. It was during this time that Edwards preached one of the most famous and enduring sermons given to men, *Sinners in the Hands of an Angry God.*

In connection with a visit from Whitefield in 1740, another wave of religious fervor was started known as "the Great Awakening." It did not spend its force until it covered the whole land. Edwards shared the stories of the revival with correspondents in America and England, publishing *A Faithful Narrative of the Surprising Work of God* in 1737.

After a number of years of religious prosperity it became apparent to Edwards that some of the "conversions" in his midst were not sincere. Edwards forbade their participation in the Lord's Supper which caused much dissension in the people. After a sharp dispute which lasted two years, Edwards was dismissed from his pastorate in 1750.

The renowned pastor decided it was a good time to retire to a smaller pastorate outside Stockbridge. It was there that he wrote the treatises on which his fame as a theologian chiefly rests: *Freedom of the Will* (written in 1753, published in 1754), and *Treatise on Original Sin* (in the press when he died, 1758), the striking essays on *The End for Which God Created the World*, and the *Nature of True Virtue* (published 1765, after his death), and the unfinished *History of Redemption* (published 1772). No doubt he utilized material previously collected for these works. He lived practically with his pen in his hand, and accumulated an immense amount of written matter.

Shortly after publishing his excellent work, *Treatise on Religious Affections*, Edwards met David Brainerd, the young missionary who brought awakening to the Indians. In Brainerd, Edwards found the living example of all he had written concerning a Christian's transformed life of holiness and affections moved by the Holy Spirit. Brainerd was engaged to be married to Edwards daughter, but contracted tuberculosis and died in Edwards' home in 1747 at the age of twenty-nine. Edwards was deeply moved by Brainerd's young life and edited his journal for publication. His edition of Brainerd's journal, *The Life of David Brainerd*, continues to be read to this day. It has influenced countless missionaries and others to aspire to a closer intimacy with the Lord.

The heaven I desired was a heaven of holiness; to be with God, and to spend my eternity in divine love, and holy communion with Christ. My mind was very much taken up with contemplations on heaven, and the enjoyments there; and living there in perfect holiness, humility and love.— J. Edwards

Throughout his ministry Edwards was blessed to have a lovely, godly wife by his side. Sarah Pierrepont saw it as her spiritual duty to keep her home peaceful and pleasant so Jonathan could devote the maximum amount of time to his studies and ministry. That she was able to do this with eleven children is a testimony to her qualities. When the rigors of the day came to a close, Jonathan and Sarah would ride horseback through the nearby woods and Jonathan would freely share with Sarah all the spiritual riches he had mined in his studies that day.

When the evangelist George Whitefield was in the Edwards' home, he was impressed by their happiness and wrote: "I felt great satisfaction in being at the house of Mr. Edwards. A sweeter couple I have not yet seen. Their children were not dressed in silks and satins, but plain, as become the children of those who, in all things, ought to be examples of Christian simplicity. Mrs. Edwards is adorned with a meek and quiet spirit. She talked solidly of the things of God, and seemed to be such a helpmeet of her husband, that she caused me to renew those prayers, which, for some months, I have put to God, that He would be pleased to send me a daughter of Abraham to be my wife."

"President Edwards, in the esteem of all the judicious, who were well acquainted with him, either personally, or by his writings, was one of the greatest and most useful of men that have lived in this age," records Samuel Hopkins in his 1764 edition of

Edwards' biography.

"The peculiarity of Edwards' theological work is due to the union in it of the richest religious sentiment with the highest intellectual powers. He was first of all a man of faith, and it is this that gives its character to his whole life and all its products," says Rev. B. B. Warfield, the eminent Presbyterian minister.

Edwards was content to continue with his writings, but he was interrupted in the autumn of 1757 by an invitation to become the President of the College of New Jersey, at Princeton. It was with great reluctance that he accepted this call. It seemed to him to interfere with what he had thought to make his life-work, the completion of a series of volumes on the Arminian controversy. On the advice of some of his friends he accepted the call, and moved to Princeton to take up his new duties as President, in January 1758.

While in Princeton he was inoculated against smallpox on February 13, but died of this disease on March 22 in the fifty-fifth year of his life. He was acutely aware of his approaching end, and displayed a truly Christian patience and resignation under suffering and in prospect of death. Jonathan and Sarah were married thrity-one years. When Jonathan died in 1758, Sarah was still in Stockbridge preparing for the move to New Jersey, but his daughter was by his bedside. Through her he sent a most affectionate and consolatory message to his wife and his children, bidding them submit to the will of God, and encouraging them to look forward to reunion in Heaven. "Give my kindest love to my dear wife, and tell her that the uncommon union which has so long subsisted between us has been of such a nature as I trust is spiritual and therefore will continue forever."

Some of those standing by when he was about to breathe his last, spoke with concern and lamentation regarding the loss which the college and the cause of religion generally would suffer by his death. The dying man heard their conversation, and to their surprise, exclaimed, "Trust in God, and at last need not fear!" These were his words. With no sign of pain or of distress he quietly "fell asleep" in Jesus' arms. Before the year closed, first his widowed daughter, and then his widowed wife, followed their beloved and honored one into the nearer presence of the Savior.

That the distinguished light of Jonathan Edwards has not shone in vain, there are a cloud of witnesses. God, who gave him his great talents, led him into a way of improving them, both by preaching and writing, which has doubtless proved the means of converting many from the error of their ways; and of greatly promoting the interest of Christ's church, both in America and Europe.

Key Writings of Edwards: 1. *Edward's Resolutions* (1722); 2. *A Faithful Narrative of the Surprising Work of God* (1737); 3. *Thoughts On the Revival of Religion* (1742); 4. *The Life of David Brainerd* (1746); 5. *Treatise on Religious Affections* (1746); 6. *Treatise on Original Sin* (1758); 7. *Freedom of the Will* (1754); 8. *The End for Which God Created the World* (1765); 9. *Nature of True Virtue* (1765); 10. *History of Redemption* (1774).

Worth Reading: *Complete Works of Jonathan Edwards*, 7 vols. (1809); *The Life and Character of the Late Reverend Mr. Jonathan Edwards*, by Samuel Hopkins (1764); *Sixteen Lectures on Charity and its Fruits*, by Tryon Edwards (1852).

John Wesley *1703-1791*
Founder of Methodism

In the beginning of the eighteenth century England was morally and spiritually decadent. Deism, slavery, and gambling led the list of moral decay, and the Puritanism of the previous century had given way to spiritually dead clergymen. John Wesley was one such spiritually dead minister until he saw true Christianity alive in the humble and devout Moravian immigrants. By their "Methods" which he adopted and revised, he led a powerful revival that transformed the religious character of a nation—in fact, many nations.

 ll seemed well within the Wesley home as its eleven inhabitants slept soundly that frightfulful night in 1709. Little John (Jacky) was only six years old and sleeping with his brothers in a second-floor back bedroom, when in the middle of the night a malicious ex-parishioner set fire to their home.

Rev. Samuel Wesley was aroused from his sleep by the cry of fire from the street, but little imagined that the fire was in his own house. He opened his bedroom door and found the place full of smoke. The roof was already burned through and the fire was spreading rapidly. Directing his wife and two girls to rise and flee for their lives, he burst open the nursery door, where the maid was sleeping with five children. She snatched up the youngest and urged the others follow her. The three eldest did as instructed, but John did not wake up and in the chaos was forgotten. The rest of the family escaped—some through windows, others by the garden door; and Mrs. Wesley, to use her own expression, "waded through the fire."

Then great fear came over the whole assembly when crying was heard coming from the nursery. "Where is Jacky?" was the cry. Their father, Samuel, ran back into the house and made his way to the stairs, but they were so nearly consumed by the flames that they could not bear his weight. Unable to reach his beloved son his heart was filled with utter despair, and he fell upon his knees in the hall, and in agony commended the soul of the child to God. Meanwhile, John had been awakened by the smoke and flames in his room and on his bed. Finding it impossible to escape by the door, he climbed upon a chest that stood near the window, where he was heard and seen by the now large group of family and neighbors that had gathered in the yard. There was no time for finding a ladder, so one man was hoisted on the shoulders of another, and within moments, the scared little boy was taken out to safety, just moments before the roof caved in. Brokenhearted and in tears, his father made his way out of the flame-consumed

The Methodist revival cut across denominational lines and touched every class of society. England itself was transformed in the process. In 1928 Archbishop Davidson wrote that "Wesley practically changed the outlook and even the character of the English nation."

Suzannah Wesley was the mother of nineteen children. On her deathbed, she uttered to them, "Children, as soon as I am released, sing a song of praise to God." As her spirit left, her children encircled her bed in prayer and sang, "Hosannah to Jesus on high!"

structure towards his family to bear the news of Jacky's demise. But then he saw the sweet face of his child, safe in the arms of his mother, and Rev. Samuel cried out with joy and thankfulness, "Come, neighbors, let us kneel down. Let us give thanks to God! He has given me all my eight children this night. Let the house burn, for I am rich enough." Rev. John Wesley remembered this providential deliverance throughout his life with the deepest gratitude. Under one of the portraits painted during his life, is a representation of a house on fire, with the scriptural inquiry, "Is not this a brand plucked out of the burning?"

John Wesley was born at Epworth, England where his father, the Rev. Samuel Wesley was a pastor for over thirty years. Both Samuel and his wife, Susanna, came from a line of Puritan ancestors, who had endured persecution for their faith. The Wesley home was filled with numerous sons and daughters who were all quite accomplished. Brave, bright spirits and high principles were the subjects within that remote Lincolnshire parsonage. It was a home of strict and earnest religion, of much learning, of true high breeding, and of sometimes bitter poverty.

Susanna Wesley was an admirable mother and it was her custom to give each of her children an hour a week for religious conversation and prayer. It seems that John's miraculous escape from certain death awakened in her a special interest in his future, and so she dedicated a portion of each Thursday that she might converse and pray with him. Orderliness, steadfastness, authority, and tender affection, were all combined in this godly woman. And all these qualities were remarkably reproduced in her son John.

At age nine, John contracted smallpox to which his mother writes to her husband, "Jack has born his disease bravely like a man, without complaint, indeed like a Christian."

Wesley attended Oxford and made the acquaintence of

Artist's depiction of John Wesley being saved from his burnig home at age six.

pious men such as James Hervey and George Whitefield, with whom he joined the "Holy Club."

John Wesley began his work as a minister living and preaching formal religion without a renewed heart. He went to Georgia with James Oglethorpe to work as a missionary to the Indians, but soon returned to England in despair and wrote, "I went to America to convert the Indians, but O, who will convert me!" But on the ship, Wesley met some Moravian immigrants whose piety and loving confidence in divine providence impressed him, particularly amidst the perils of a storm at sea when it appeared they all might perish. All screamed in fear, but the

Moravians who remained at peace and calmly sang to King Jesus. Back in England, as Wesley struggled with his own sinfulness and need of salvation, it was Moravian, Peter Boehler, who proved to him from Scripture that faith was a spiritual act of divine operation. After repeated lessons, Wesley was thoroughly convinced of his former "Phariseeism." He writes in his journal for that day; "By Boehler, in the hand of the great God, I was clearly convinced of unbelief—of the want of that faith whereby alone we are saved." Having learned this hard lesson, he determined to act on his teacher's advice, "Preach faith, till you have it; and then because you have it, you will preach faith."

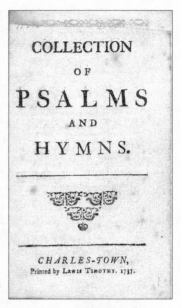

COLLECTION

OF

PSALMS

AND

HYMNS.

CHARLES-TOWN,
Printed by LEWIS TIMOTHY. 1737.

Title page of the first edition of Wesley's 1737 Methodist hymn book used in worship.

On May 24, 1738, during a private meeting at Aldersgate, Wesley exercised a true saving faith in Jesus Christ his Savior. Boehler was reading from Luther's work on Romans, regarding the change which God works in the heart through faith in Christ alone. Wesley wrote, "I felt my heart strangely warmed. I felt I did trust in Christ alone for salvation and an assurance was given to me that he had taken away my sins."

A few months later his brother Charles, who had been much disturbed by the change in his brother's views, was also convinced of the truth of the Moravian teacher's doctrine. "My brother," says John Wesley in his journal, "had a long and particular conversation with Peter Boehler. And it now pleased God to open his eyes, so that he also saw clearly the nature of that one true living faith, whereby alone, 'through grace, we are saved.'" The next day Peter Boehler left London, in order to embark for Carolina, and Wesley makes the following very remarkable entry in his journal; "Oh! what a work hath God begun since his coming into England. Such an one as shall never come to an end till heaven and earth pass away." With this the two brothers and about forty others formed the first Methodist Society. They met each Wednesday and adopted statutes which constitute the basis for the whole Methodist economy.

It did not go well with Wesley, at first. He was rejected and even physically beaten for his new "sect." But in all he reviled not and conducted himself worthy of a true soldier of the Cross. His passion as a genuine convert made him an evangelist. The passage in Romans 10:17, *Faith comes by hearing, and hearing by the Word of God,*" inspired him to become a mighty preacher and a shining light in every community he influenced.

In 1741, Wesley organized the famed "lay-preachers,"who spread the simple and powerful word of Christ in meeting rooms with wide influence and great impact on the people.

Wesley was one of the most "catholic" of men. His beautiful sermon *A Catholic Spirit* exemplified his own true spirit and practice. He thought little of doctrinal differences where there

Though his brother Charles was the more famous hymn-writer, John has about thirty ascribed to him in the Methodist hymnal. Among his most notable hymns is "Jesus, Thy Blood and Righteousness."

was the unity of Christian love in the heart. The controversies he was compelled to take part in were never raised or continued by him on high dogmatic or purely theological grounds. It was always Antinomianism breaking out in practice among those under his charge which constrained him to enter into controversy. And in his controversies he never returned railing for railing. The faith of which he spoke and wrote was always "the faith which works by love, and purifies the soul."

During his fifty-three years ministering the gospel, John Wesley traveled over 250,000 miles and preached more than 40,000 sermons.

One of the griefs of his life was the difference between Whitefield and himself in regard to the doctrines of election and predestination. But the two great evangelists were not very long in agreeing to differ. The controversy was never relieved while both were active in ministry, but they loved each other dearly. Whitefield appointed Wesley his executor, and Wesley preached his funeral sermon.

From George Whitefield, Wesley learned the importance of preaching in the open air to reach the masses. At first he could not imagine souls being saved unless they were in church, but Jesus' "open-air preaching" of the Sermon on the Mount convinced him it was biblical.

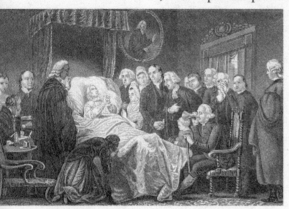

John Wesley on his deathbed in 1791.

This precious man of God left this world at age eighty-seven. His last act was to write to his friend and fellow laborer, William Wilberforce, exhorting him to persevere in his public efforts against the slave trade. Wesley was blessed to see the Methodist Society established in Europe, America, and the Indies, before his death. He also witnessed Methodist ministers numbering into the thousands.

In the end, John Wesley was mightily used of the Lord to reform England. His Methodists became a national force. John traveled over 250,000 miles to spread the gospel as only a man filled with the Holy Spirit can, telling of Jesus to all the lost souls he met. Wherever he preached, lives were changed and morality increased. It is widely agreed that John Wesley's preaching helped spare England of a revolution similar to what occurred in France.

Key Writings of Wesley: 1. *Collection of Psalms and Hymns by John and Charles Wesley* (1737); 2. *Primitive Physic* (1747); 3. *Earnest Appeal to Men of Reason and Religion* (1750); 4. *Doctrine of Original Sin* (1757); 5. *Compendium of Natural Philosophy* (1763); 6. *Calm Address to the Inhabitants of England* (1777); 7. *A Concise Ecclesiastical History History from the Birth of Christ to the Present Century* (1781); 8. *Life of Rev. John Fletcher* (1786); 9. *Journals on England and America* (1735-1790).

Worth Reading: *Beauties of Rev. John Wesley* (1802); *Works of John Wesley,* by Joseph Benson (1818); *The Life of John Wesley,* by John Telford (1887); *John Wesley the World His Parish,* by Basil Miller (1943).

George Whitefield *1714-1770*
English Revivalist and Preacher

No individual has so identified himself with the growth and spread of practical religion in England and America as George Whitefield. It was appointed by God for him to preach, which he did more than 18,000 times, often before a crowd of drowsy worldlings. Probably not since Luther and Calvin has there been such a vessel chosen for bearing the errands of mercy to the multitude. By the power of the Holy Spirit, he changed our sterile religious wastes into verdant, heavenly pastures, and sowed on good ground those seeds of practical piety, whose fruits bless and encourage us in the institutions and habits that have been handed down to us from the Christianity of past generations.

 eorge Whitefield, the eminent and pious English preacher, was born, the youngest of seven children at Gloucester, where his mother kept the Bell Inn. His father died in 1716, when George was just two years old. His youth was spent in rather "brutish," activities, as he recalls. At an early age his powers of speech were discovered, but were directed toward a point rather distant from the pulpit. The boys at school were fond of Thespian entertainments, and their master encouraged them in it. Whitefield owed much of his attractive manner in preaching, to his early attachment to theatrical entertainments. While he denounced plays from the pulpit, he unconsciously gave an added force to his impassioned words by oratorical graces and winning gestures undoubtedly transferred from the stage.

Before he went to Oxford, he had heard of the young men there, who lived "by rule and method," and were therefore called Methodists, who were generally despised. But he felt himself strangely drawn toward them, and when he heard them reviled, he defended them strenuously. Seeing them going to receive the sacrament at St. Mary's in the midst of a ridiculing crowd, he was strongly moved to follow them. For more than a year he yearned after fellowship with them, but was kept back by a sense of inferiority. One day a pauper committed suicide and Whitefield sent a woman to Charles Wesley to request him to come and minister spiritual medicine to the sufferer. She was charged not to say who sent her, but she disobeyed and told his name. Wesley, who had heard of Whitefield, invited him to breakfast next morning. An introduction to the little band followed, and Whitefield also began to live by rule, and to pay more attention to how he spent his time, that not a moment of it might be lost. At this time,

Whitefield was the most traveled preacher and one of the greatest evangelists of the eighteenth century. His diligence and sacrifice helped turn two nations back to God.

169

The first Calvanistic Methodist Conference convened in Wales in January 1743. (L-R) John Cennick, Joseph Humphries, John Powell, William Williams, George Whitefield, Daniel Rowland, and Howel Harris.

Charles Wesley gave him a little book entitled, the *Life of God in the Soul of Man*, by Henry Scougal. It was by reading this volume, says Whitefield, "God showed me that I must be born again."

He continued at Oxford after the Wesleys had gone to America, until his great devotional excesses broke down his health and laid him upon a bed of long and wearisome sickness. He was forced to move to the country to recover his strength. Soon he was able to leave his bed and there he attracted the notice of Dr. Benson, Bishop of Gloucester, who sent for him and offered him ordination whenever he should choose to accept it. Whitefield felt a praiseworthy fear and hesitancy about undertaking this sacred office, but the encouragement of the bishop and the persuasions of his friends convinced him, and he was ordained in such a spirit, that he thought he could call Heaven and Earth to witness. When the bishop laid his hand upon him, he gave himself up to be a martyr for Christ who had hung upon the Cross. His whole subsequent life proves his sincerity.

After a short time as temporary pastor to the congregation in Hampshire, Whitefield acted on the yearning of his heart to assist the Wesleys in America. When he arrived, he preached five times a week to such congregations that he could hardly make his way through the crowded aisles to the pulpit. When he preached his farewell sermon, and said to the people that they would see his face no more, the entire assembly burst into tears at his words. When he returned to London, the multitudes followed him everywhere. The churches were opened on weekdays, and constables stood at the doors to prevent too many people from forcing their way into the building. On Sunday mornings, in the latter months of the year, the streets were filled with people with lanterns, going to secure a place to hear him. The nearer the time of his departure arrived, the more intense these feelings became. They stopped him in the aisles and embraced him. They waited on him at his lodgings, entreating him to pray with them and speak words for their comfort.

His popularity was as great as ever. One day, while preaching at Bermondsey church, he knew that nearly one thousand people stood outside unable to obtain admittance, so he felt a strong inclination to go out and preach from the tombstones. This inclination led him to adopt a system of preaching in the fields, and it was soon commenced in Kingswood, near Bristol. This area of the country was filled with low and degraded beings in the most wretched state of poverty. When Whitefield first announced his intention of going to America to convert the Indians, many of his friends said, "What need of going abroad for this? Have we not 'Indians' enough here at home? If you have a mind to convert Indians there are colliers enough in Kingswood." To these lost souls he had long yearned to open the light of heavenly truth, for they had no churches. He came among them and preached one day without notice. His audience then numbered about two hundred. The second time he preached, two thousand persons assembled to hear him, and the third audience numbered between four and five thousand. The number of worshippers went on increasing until they were estimated at more than twenty thousand. Meanwhile, the clerical authorities had taken offense at him, and would no longer permit him to preach in the churches, so that what he had adopted by choice, was now become a matter of necessity.

Amidst all his success, Whitefield never forgot that he was the pastor of a little parish in Georgia, and the raising of money to build an orphan house there was the principal business he had in England. Once he received the necessary means for the orphan house, he set sail for America on August 14, 1739. He arrived in Philadelphia early in November and was at once invited to preach in the churches. But no church could hold the crowds that assembled to hear him, so he chose the gallery of the little courthouse for a pulpit, and his audiences stood around in the open space in front. Whitefield left Philadelphia and preached a while in New York, and then went south to Savannah, preaching continually in every church he came to. He arrived at Savannah, in January, 1740, and two months later he laid the foundation of his orphan house, which he called Bethesda, the House of Mercy.

In the fall of 1740, he traveled to New England, preaching everywhere with success, particularly at Boston and in the colleges at Cambridge and New Haven. Returning by way of New York and Philadelphia, he sailed from the Delaware River to Charleston, and reached Savannah on December 20th. On his way back he summed up his labors, "It is the seventy-fifth day since I arrived at Rhode Island. My body was then weak, but the

More than 18,000 sermons were preached by Whitefield in his lifetime, an average of 500 a year, or ten a week. Many of them were given over and over again. Less than ninety of them have survived in any form.

171

Lord has much renewed its strength. I was able to preach one hundred and seventy-five times in public, besides exhorting very frequently in private. I have traveled upwards of eight hundred miles, and gotten upwards of seven hundred pounds sterling in goods, provisions, and money for my poor orphans." Having arranged the affairs of the orphan house, he preached a farewell sermon and again left Savannah for England. On January 24, 1741, he crossed Charleston harbor. On March 11th he arrived at Falmouth and rode to London. On the next Sabbath day preached at Kennington Common.

Before sailing back to America, he had become impressed with Calvinistic views, which had brought about a partial separation between him and John Wesley, and subsequent occurrences tended to widen the breach. Whitefield implored Wesley not to preach against election, as he (though he believed it) agreed not preach in favor of it, to avoid division among themselves. But Wesley's position was to, "preach and print." He preached at once, but did not print till after the departure of Whitefield, who answered his publication by a sharp letter from Georgia. The Wesleys, by their powerful preaching and incessant exertions brought nearly the whole body of the Methodists over to their views. Whitefield responded with two ill-judged attacks made on England's greatest favorites—*The Whole Duty of Man*, by Allestree, and Archbishop Tillotson. This left Whitefield nearly destitute of the popularity he had once acquired. His whole work was to begin again, and he commenced with new insight into the doctrines of grace. He preached at first to one or two

Whitefield preaching at the Moorfields in London, despite much opposition from town authorities.

hundred persons, but soon his audiences grew to what they were formerly. At the invitation of some of his friends in Scotland, he went to Edinburgh and then to many places in the kingdom, preaching the gospel without allying himself to any sect. His preaching was so powerful it began a religious revival, which was continued by zealous laborers after his departure with the greatest results.

His popularity, meanwhile, increased steadily, and he was bold enough to attack Satan in his stronghold by preaching in the Moorfields during the Whitsun holidays. It was a fierce battle, and lasted all day and into the night. Whitefield displayed great generalship. He began at six in the morning, when some ten thousand people were assembled, waiting for the sport events to begin. He was attended by a throng of praying people, and when he began to preach the crowd flocked around his pulpit. Whitefield preached three times for many hours during the day, in spite of drummers, trumpeters, players, keepers of wild beasts, and their friends. Stones, dirt, rotten eggs, and pieces of dead cats and other animals were frequently thrown at him, and a recruiting sergeant marched his men through the midst of the audience in the hope of making a disturbance. Whitefield requested his people to fall back and make way for the kings officers and then close up again. This maneuver baffled them, and they found themselves trapped within the mass of worshippers. Another part of the preacher's tactics was very effective. His voice was like a trumpet, but sometimes the uproar became so great that he could not be heard. So he stopped preaching and called the praying people to his aid. At his signal they all began singing with one loud voice. And so with the singing, praying, and preaching, he kept the field. In this strange warfare he produced a very great impression. More than a thousand notes were handed up to him by persons who were "brought under conviction" by his preaching that day, and three hundred and fifty persons came to Christ and joined his congregation. On the next day he fought a similar battle in Mary-le-bone fields, a place of similar crowds. On the third day he returned to Moorfields and preached, if possible, with greater effect than the previous day.

In 1762, Whitefield went again to Scotland and with able and willing co-laborers there he set the country in a state of excitement such as the cool-blooded inhabitants had never dreamed of. Besides Edinburgh and Glasgow, it is amazing to think how many places in the west of Scotland he visited within a few weeks, preaching at every place.

All this time, Whitefield had continued to correspond with the Wesleys, and they occasionally preached in each other's pulpits. Each did justice to what he knew was good and noble in the character of the other, and there was a rivalry between them in forgiving injuries committed earlier in "hot blood." In 1765, when Whitefield returned from America to England for the last

Benjamin Franklin was fascinated with Whitefield's speaking ability and the effects his teaching had on the people. Though Franklin never openly became a Christian himself, he did become a friend of Whitefield's and his publisher in America. He was impressed with the change Whitefield's gospel preaching brought on society. Franklin wrote that "It was wonderful to see the change soon made in the manners of our inhabitants. From being thoughtless or indifferent about religion, it seemed as if all the world were growing religious, so that one could not walk through the town in an evening without hearing psalms sung in different families of every street."

time, John Wesley visited him and gives an account of the interview in his journal:

"I breakfasted with Mr. Whitefield, who seemed to be an old, old man, being fairly worn out in his Master's service, though he has hardly seen fifty years. And yet it pleases God, that I, who am now in my sixty-third year, find no disorder, no weakness, no decay, no difference from what I was at five and twenty, except that I have fewer teeth, and more gray hairs."

Whitefield could paint word pictures with such breathless vividness that crowds listening would stare through tear-filled eyes as he spoke.

The history of Mr. Whitefield's labors is unparalleled. They continued till his death, and were always effective. He made many opponents, who often convicted him of occasional error. He thanked them so earnestly when they showed him his faults. As a result those most embittered against him learned to respect and love him. His death took place in 1770, at Newburyport while on a visit to New England. He wished for a sudden death, and his desire was in some degree granted to him. His illness was but of few hours duration. When he was first seized with it one of his friends expressed a wish that he would not preach so often. He answered that he would "rather wear out than rust out." He was buried in the Presbyterian church in Newburyport, in front of the pulpit. Every mark of respect was shown to his remains. All the bells in the town tolled, and the ships in the harbor fired mourning guns and hung their flags at half mast. In Georgia, all the black cloth in the stores was bought up, and the church was hung in black. The governor and the council met at the state-house in deep mourning, and went in a procession to hear the funeral sermon. Funeral sermons were preached in all the tabernacles in England, and John Wesley preached several of them, wishing he said to show all possible respect to the memory of so great and good a man.

Of the sects which were benefited by his labors, the Presbyterians in America undoubtedly reaped the greatest from the untiring ministry of Whitefield. But who shall attempt to estimate the number of those who were awakened by his burning words to a sense of their religious wants, and encouraged by him to come to Jesus Christ, who gives us our daily bread. Scores of men who have since become shining lights in the Lord's ministry on Earth, date their first religious impressions to the time of hearing Whitefield. No doubt, the number is great of those who have blessed his memory as they felt the benefits of a religious faith in the hour of death.

Key writings of George Whitefield: 1. *Works of Rev. George Whitefield* (1771-72); 2. *Collection of Sermons* (1772).

Worth Reading: *Life and Times of George Whitefield*, by Luke Tyerman; *Memoirs of Whitefield*, by John Gilles; *Life of Whitefield*, by Dallimore.

David Brainerd *1718-1747*
Missionary to the Indians

Rev. Jonathan Edwards says of his dear friend, David Brainerd, "What is here set before us is a remarkable example of true and eminent piety, in heart and practice—tending greatly to confirm the reality of vital religion, and the power of godliness; that it is most worthy of imitation, and in many ways calculated to promote spiritual benefit to all."

David Brainerd was born in Haddam, Connecticut, the son of Hezekiah Brainerd, one of the king's counsel. At an early age his father died, and his mother followed a few years later. These bereavements seemed to have so powerfully affected his mind, that for six years he was haunted by thoughts of death and his own wickedness. He sought relief in a strict adherence to religious duties, but this did not relieve his deep distress.

In 1739, at the age of twenty, he entered Yale College, where he studied with such fervor he became quite ill. It was the time of the "Great Awakening" in New England which God used to speak to Brainerd's heart. Along with several other students David secretly held a series of religious meetings and Bible studies in various rooms of the college. He was expelled from the school in his junior year for repeatedly criticizing the faculty, referring to one as "having no more grace than a chair." There were three professors who stood behind him who resigned from their posts at Yale and helped found Princeton College.

At the age of twenty-four David received his license to preach. Commissioned by the Scotland Society for the Propagation of Christian Knowledge he preached among the Indians at Kanaumeek, a place twenty miles distant from any English settlement. Here Brainerd suffered greatly, shut out from all society. His diet was meager and unwholesome, his lodging a log hut, and his bed a bundle of straw spread on boards. He describes his condition, "I am now quite alone with no friend to take sweet counsel together. In my weak state of health, I have no bread, nor could I get any. I am often forced to go ten or fifteen miles in stormy and severe weather for all the bread I eat, and sometimes it is moldy and sour. I was almost outdone with the extreme fatigue and wet. Yet, I love to live alone in my own little cottage, where I can spend much time in prayer."

After Brainerd had been at Kanaumeek about a year, the commissioners resolved to send him to the Delaware River. He gathered the Indians around him and preached to them for the last time, then set out for his new field of labor. On the way, his trials,

David Brainerd lived only twenty-nine years but inspired many to follow Christ through his tireless missionary work in New England. His example of piety encouraged many to follow his footsteps onto the mission field, such as William Carey and Henry Martyn.

temptations, and hardships were so numerous, that on more than one occasion he was at the point of throwing himself on the ground to await the approach of death. He appeared to have met with little success, and afterwards obtained permission of the Pennsylvania governor to open a mission upon the Susquehanna River. After his first sermon at an Indian village on that river, he went from house to house, conversing with the people, and explaining to them the truths which they had just heard.

The narrative of his condition, experiences, and feelings at this time is most touching. "I rose at four in the morning and traveled with great steadiness till six at night, then made a fire and a shelter of barks. The wolves howled around us. The following night we lost our way; it was very dark—few stars to be seen. Formerly, when exposed to cold and rain, I was ready to please myself with the thoughts of enjoying a comfortable house, a warm fire, and other pleasures. I came to a lone dwelling where was one dead and laid out. Looking on the corpse, it was the youthful owner of the house, and his widow grieving for him. Death had found him out in his solitude."

David Brainerd poured out his life in ministry to these Indians, writing that he wanted "to burn out in one continual flame for God."

On returning to the Delaware River, Brainerd built for himself a small cabin and resumed his preaching and teaching to the Indians. Still he was surrounded by difficulties. At that time a number of French settlers in the neighborhood aroused the displeasure of the Indians. The tribe then rushed upon the settlers, and massacred the entire number. The horrors of this scene only added to the hardships which surrounded Brainerd.

In the spring his prospects brightened. The Indians came in considerable numbers to hear his preaching. The interpreter was converted and a chief one hundred years old soon followed. Afterwards at a great meeting held in New Jersey many hundreds were converted. Cheered by this success and resolved to make New Jersey his principal field of labor, he stationed himself at

View of the Parsonage in Cranbury, New Jersey, July 1833. Occupying the ground where Rev. Brainerd preached to the Indians in 1746.

Crossweeksung. In his journal he wrote, "It was late at night. All day I had labored with the people. My soul had longed for this hour and was transported with joy. Earth, cover not my head yet; though the thoughts of death are sweet, I would stay while this great work advances." The Indians abandoned their idolatry, and invited the missionary to their houses to hear more about Jesus.

His labors at Crossweeksung were divided between preaching, examining the new converts, and administering baptism. Some came fifty miles to hear him. "I stood amazed," he writes, "at the influence that seemed to descend upon the assembly, and with an astonishing energy bore down all, and could compare it to nothing more aptly than to a mighty torrent. The most fierce and stubborn hearts were now obliged to bow. Their concern was so great, each for himself, that none seemed to take any notice of those about them, but each prayed for himself."

So fatal had been the ravages of ill health upon his youthful frame, that in riding back and forth, six Indian companions accompanied him, and sometimes caught him in their arms as he fell fainting from his horse.

He returned to the Susquehanna, but once again saw little progress. The Indians were civil and friendly, but "bad listeners and worse believers." He was welcomed however to their wigwams. They spread before him the game they had killed, and when the warriors were hunting, he had free access to the older chiefs, the children, and the women. They were astonished at his temperate habits, and in a little while began to look upon him with a feeling of awe. After remaining at this place for a short time Brainerd returned to New Jersey.

It might be supposed that in this favorite retreat, where seventy Indians had now been baptized, the missionary would have been willing to end his days. But Brainerd's heart was firm upon spreading the gospel message to the unconverted. "I will then say, 'Farewell earthly comforts and friends, the dearest of them all; the very dearest, if the Lord calls for it, *adieu, adieu*. I'll spend my life, to my last moment in caves and dens of the Earth, if the Kingdom of Christ may be advanced.'"

The next field of Brainerd's labors was a small Dutch settlement near the Delaware. He built a hut and soon the sturdy settlers along with some Indians gathered their homes around his to listen to his instructions. Brainerd had a school and church built and found a gifted schoolmaster to teach the children. Religious instruction "was received with great solemnity and seriousness, and seemed to diffuse through their hearts great union and love toward each other." His ministry had such an affect on the people's souls that they frequently retired into the woods and spent the greater part of the night in devotional exercises. During the day they gathered around the missionary for instruction. His method of teaching was to give historical lessons from Scripture or to expound chapters of the New Testament. Then he proposed questions on what they had heard until the truth was thoroughly impressed upon the mind.

A change had come over the outward prospects of this devoted man of God. Brainerd's fame had spread, not by his wish, but because it could not be repressed. Other ministers fifty or sixty miles away often invited him to their homes. It is touching to read in his narrative how he arrived, sometimes at night, to some friendly home, where many comforts invited him to stay awhile. The kind words and tender compassions of the women, their minute attentions to his failing health, the sympathy of his brother ministers was such a blessing to his body and soul. He was encouraged, even amidst his sufferings, by the rapid progress of Christianity among his people. His unwearied efforts and entreaties by day and night, from house to house and with individual converts was a source of much consolation.

At Northampton he consulted Dr. Mather concerning his health. Dr. Mather diagnosed him with life-threatening consumption and advised him to go to Boston. His reputation had preceded him and there was great excitement at his coming. Ministers from the area visited him continually. Many gave large donations for his Indian mission. One night an overwhelming joy pervaded his mind. All the mercies of his lonely career, the days and nights of agonizing prayer, the presence and love of the Comforter, all gathered around his parting soul like swift and glorious witnesses.

Brainerd's diary influenced many missionaries in future generations, including William Carey and Henry Martyn, who went to India. It also had a huge impact on Jim Eliot, the twentieth century missionary who gave his life ministering to the Auca Indians.

David's special friend during his stay in Boston was Jerusha, the young daughter of Jonathan Edwards, to whom he was engaged. One morning she came to David's bedside and broke down into tears of grief for her would-be husband. The pain of heartsick lovers was too much for onlookers to bear. Looking earnestly at her, he expressed his grief at parting with her, and expressed the glad confidence and anticipation of meeting her in glory. During the day he lay in great agony, and expired at daybreak the next morning. He was only twenty-nine years old.

Few will read this sketch of poor Brainerd, short and imperfect as it is, without a sigh. There was never a more striking instance of the magical influence of the spirit over the frame, urging it to incredible exertions and hardships, and yet warding off the dissolution which tracked it at every step. There was something sublime in David Brainerd's life and heroic in his early departure. His weakness was made perfect in divine strength, and he continually looked to Christ with gratitude and love.

David Brainerd died in Edwards' house and was buried at Northampton, Massachusetts. Three months later his grave was re-opened, and the lovely young Jerusha who had shed bitter tears while watching her dying fiancee, and over whom eighteen summers had scarcely passed, was lowered down to sleep by his side.

Key Writings of Brainerd: 1. *Mirabilia dei inter Indicos: or the Rise and Progress of a Remarkable Work of Grace Among a Number of the Indians in the Provinces of New Jersey and Pennsylvania* (1746); *Divine Grace Displayed: or the Continuance and Progress of a Remarkable Work of Grace* (1746). Both of these works, published at Philadelphia, are commonly known as *Brainerd's Journal.*

Worth Reading: *The Life of Rev. David Brainerd* (1749), by Jonathan Edwards.

John Newton *1725-1807*

Hymn Writer, Preacher and Author

Reflecting on his former life, Newton wrote one of the world's most beloved hymns: "Amazing Grace." Newton would come to experience that amazing grace that transformed his life and made him a powerful preacher of the gospel. He never ceased to be amazed at God's miraculous work in His life.

The storm was relentless! For over a week the rain and winds had thrashed against the Greyhound on its way back to England. The sails were damaged and nearly all the food and cargo had been washed overboard. All on board the vessel had worked the pumps day and night to keep the ship from sinking, but they were losing the battle. John Newton, too exhausted to continue pumping, tied himself to the helm and steered the ship from noon until midnight. This became the Lord's time for working on the mind and heart of "the great blasphemer." Newton's mind swirled, as much as the fierce winds upon the deck, with thoughts of death, of his past, and of the things of God that he had so often profaned. Thinking himself too sinful to receive any mercy, he pleaded with the Almighty that he might obtain the faith that his sweet mother faithfully taught him in his youth.

Reflecting upon his own desperate condition, Newton wrote; "He has promised here to give that Spirit to those who ask, I must therefore pray, and if it is of God, He will make good His own word. In the gospel I saw at least a peradventure of hope, but on every other side I was surrounded with black, unfathomable despair."

Many years later, Newton wrote in his diary, "He was pleased to show me at that time, the absolute necessity of some expedient to interpose between a righteous God and a sinful soul. On that day the Lord sent from on high and delivered me out of deep waters." He knew all too well that only God's amazing grace could and would take a proud, profane, slave-trading sailor and transform him into a child of God.

John Newton was born in London, England. His father, a seafaring man, was the master of a ship in the Mediterranean engaged in Spanish trade. He was a stern, severe man. He had married a gentle and pious woman, and John was their only child. To John's early training she devoted all diligence and prayer. When barely four years of age young John could read quite well, and in his mind was stored many portions of

In his own day he was one of England's most prominent preachers. Today, John Newton is best known for his inspiring hymn "Amazing Grace," which is probably the best known hymn ever written.

Scripture. She taught him Isaac Watts' catechisms and hymns. Both of these treasures were frequently used among pious Nonconformists in England, as well as in the Presbyterian churches in Scotland. This dear woman saw with delight the quick progress of her son, and cherished the hope that she might guide him into the ministry, if the Lord should so direct his heart. Sadly she died when he was only seven years old, but the mother's training and prayers had been faithfully committed to God. The seed sown in John's young heart, though long hidden and to all appearance lost, bore fruit after many years. Few instances are more striking, and no encouragement more cheering for Christian mothers, than the life of John Newton. God alone knew the end from the beginning of that life, and the story of it is full of interest and instruction.

No instance more striking, and no encouragement more cheering for Christian mothers, could be given than the life of John Newton. God alone saw the end from the beginning of that life, and the story of it is full of interest and instruction.

When only eleven years old John's father took his son out of school to sail the Mediterranean in his ship. Before he was fifteen he had made several more voyages. During these excursions the younger Newton was introduced to the slave-trading business. Sadly, this became his chief occupation and pursuit during the next decade of his life.

John Newton became well-known and very successful in the slave-trade business. But the gnawing at his heart and conscience grew more difficult to ignore, and he felt drawn to deeper reconsideration of the religious sentiments begun on the sea during that great and terrible storm.

In 1750, Newton married his childhood sweetheart, Mary Catlett. His harsh demeanor was softened greatly by this sweet woman who possessed a gentle countenance and firm moral resolve.

Though Newton continued in his profession of sailing and slave-trading for a time, his soul was being transformed. He began a disciplined daily schedule of Bible study, prayer, and Christian reading. He tried to be a Christian example to the sailors under his command. Philip Doddridge's *The Rise and Progress of Religion in the Soul* provided much spiritual comfort, and a fellow-Christian, Captain Clunie, guided Newton further in his Christian faith.

In 1755, Newton left slave-trading all together and accepted the job of tide surveyor at Liverpool. Here he was blessed by the ministry and conversations he regularly shared with George Whitefield and John Wesley. At this time Newton dedicated himself to an arduous study of the Scriptures as well as the Hebrew and Greek languages. He read Howe, Hooker, and Matthew Henry, and it wasn't long before his heart became filled with yearnings for the Christian ministry. His mother's prayers for her son were answered, and in 1764, at the age of thirty-nine, John Newton began preaching the Gospel of Jesus Christ.

John and his beloved wife Mary (he wrote that their love "equaled all that the writers of romance have imagined") moved to the little market town of Olney. He spent his mornings in Bible study and his afternoons in visiting his parishioners. It was here that Newton blossomed as a preacher, author and hymn writer.

During the twenty-eight years of his London incumbency Pastor Newton diligently and zealously accomplished his ministerial and pastoral work. He took no public part in political affairs and was careful to avoid controversy either on doctrinal or ecclesiastical questions. Sometimes he was accused by Calvinists as being an Arminian, and sometimes by Arminians as being a Calvinist. To which he responded, "This makes me think that I am on good scriptural ground." Always courteous and tolerant towards those who differed with him on minor points, Newton was held in honor and loved by all. Before his death, Charles Wesley requested that his friend John Newton be a pall-bearer at his funeral.

Commenting on Newton's writings, Rev. F. Cunningham says, "to the young it shows the evil attendant upon a sinful course. To the established Christian it will be found to abound in edification and encouragement. And to al it will teach the power of the grace of God in subduing and turning the heart."

Newton's many gifts extended to the pen as well. He was a ready and voluminous letter writer. He was sought after by innumerable correspondents, most of whom sought advice or instruction. He devoted much of his time to the voluntary task of replying, often at considerable length, to their questions, or striving to help solve their difficulties. Many of these letters have been printed, in addition to correspondence on more general topics. In the early volumes of *The Sunday at Home* are a few of these long-treasured letters. During his life, or soon after his death, various volumes of Newton's letters were published, of which the best known are *Letters to a Wife, Letters to Captain Clunie,* and a collection of letters on many important topics of Christian life and experience under the title *Cardiphonia, or the Heart's Utterances on Sacred Subjects.*

In his hymns and sacred poems Newton has left a precious legacy to the Christian Church. Newton often composed a new hymn for each Sunday evening service, which further developed the lessons and Scripture for the evening. In 1779, two hundred and eighty of these poetic pieces were collected and combined with sixty-eight hymns by Newton's friend and parishioner, William Cowper, and published as the *Olney Hymns.* The most famous of all hymns came from his work, entitled, "Faith's Review and Expectation," known today as "Amazing Grace." Several other of Newton's Olney hymns continue to appear in church hymnals, including "How Sweet the Name of Jesus Sounds," and "Glorious Things of Thee Are Spoken."

Another notable feature in Newton's character was his immense sympathy and tenderness of heart. It was said of him that he literally wept with those that wept and rejoiced with those that rejoiced. The law of love ruled his heart, and the language of it poured forth from his lips. Whether in the pulpit, in his letters, or in sweet fellowship with him one would always experience the love of Christ. Newton possessed throughout his ministry the same compassion and kindness of his Savior.

It was in his pastoral visits, and still more in receiving the numerous strangers who came to consult him that his tender sympathy was seen. He knew how to comfort the afflicted, to confirm the wavering, to cheer the feeble-minded, and was in every way an excellent physician of souls.

Toward the end of his days, Newton's heart was cheered by the rise and progress of home and foreign missionary work, the establishment of the Bible and Tract Societies, and other agencies devoted to the extension of Christ's Kingdom. He continued also without intermission to carry on his own ministerial work, even when friends tried to dissuade him from public exertion. His friend and fellow minister, Richard Cecil, said to John shortly before he left this world, "Might it not be best to consider your work in preaching as done, and stop before you discover you can speak no longer?" "I cannot stop," John replied, raising his voice. "What, shall the old African blasphemer stop while he can speak?"

Mr. Cecil preached John Newton's funeral sermon in which he described his friend as "gradually sinking as the setting sun, shedding to the last those declining rays which gilded and gladdened the dark valley. In the latter conversations I had with him, he expressed an unshaken faith in eternal realities; and when he could scarcely utter words, he remained a firm witness to the truth he had preached."

Newton never ceased to stand in awe of God's work in his life. In his declining years, he once commented, "When I think about heaven I am amazed at three things: first, there I will see some I didn't expect; second, I will not see some I expected to see; and lastly, that I myself will be there."

William Wilberforce, a member of Parliament and a prime mover in the abolition of slavery, was strongly influenced by John Newton's life and preaching. Newton's "Thoughts on the African Slave Trade," based on his own experiences as a slave trader, was very important in securing British abolition of slavery.

Key Writings of Newton: 1. *Letters to a Wife;* 2. *Letters to Captain Clunie;* 3. *Cardiphonia;* 3. *Apologia;* 4. *Aged Pilgrim's Triumph;* 5. *Heart's Utterances on Sacred Subjects;* 6. *Review of Ecclesiastical History* (1770).

Worth Reading: *Life and Works of John Newton,* by Richard Cecil; *Out of the Depths,* an Autobiography; *But Now I See: The Life of John Newton,* by Josiah Bull (1998).

Richard Allen *1760-1831*

Founder of African Methodist Episcopal Church

Richard Allen was the pivotal leader and founder of the American Methodist Episcopal Church. He was born into slavery in 1760, gave his life to Christ, bought his freedom, and is now recognized as one of the great Christian leaders in American history.

 he story of Richard Allen is one of great adversities boldly overcome in the strength of faith in Christ. Richard was born in Philadelphia into a slave family. As a child he was sold along with his family to a Delaware farmer where the cruelties of slavery touched his life in every way. To pay off debts, Richard's master sold Richard's mother with three of her children. Richard never heard from them again.

At age seventeen, Allen received Christ into his heart after hearing a sermon delivered by the gifted Methodist preacher Freeborn Garrison. "I was awakened and brought to see myself, poor, wretched and undone, and without the mercy of God I must be lost. Shortly after, I obtained mercy through the blood of Christ. I was brought under doubts, and was tempted to believe I was deceived, and was constrained to seek the Lord afresh. I was tempted to believe there was no mercy for me. I cried to the Lord day and night…all of a sudden my dungeon shook, and glory to God, I cried. My soul was filled. I cried, it is enough for me—the Savior died." His perspective radically changed as he saw himself to be a child of God, a human being with inestimable worth, instead of the disposable property of another man.

As a "new man," Allen's heart was softened toward his persecutors. By his constant Christian example, hard work and submissive spirit, Allen's master came under conviction of sin and was also converted to the faith. Allen's owner was greatly indebted to him and allowed Richard to earn his own freedom. While working evening and weekend jobs chopping wood and driving a wagon during the Revolutionary War, Allen successfully won his freedom. After the war he furthered the Methodist cause by becoming a "licensed exhorter," preaching the gospel to blacks and whites from New York to South Carolina. His efforts attracted the attention of Methodist leaders, including Francis Asbury, the first American bishop of the Methodist Church. In 1786, Allen was appointed as an assistant minister in Philadelphia, serving the racially mixed congregation of St. George's Methodist Church. His giftedness and passion for

In 1784, the year of the first organizing conference of American Methodism, an unknown artist drew this chalk and pastel portrait of a young Richard Allen, founder and first bishop of the African Methodist Episcopal (AME) Church. Allen was twenty-five years old and an itinerant preacher at the time. The portrait was later owned by another AME bishop, Benjamin Tucker Tanner, who, nearly a century after it was painted, passed it on to his artist son, Henry Ossawa Tanner.

serving Christ was evident to all. The following year he, a friend, and fellow black preacher, Absalom Jones, joined other ex-slaves and Quaker philanthropists to form the Free African Society, a quasi-religious benevolent organization that offered fellowship and mutual aid to "free Africans and their descendants."

In 1787, the young black preacher went to pray with some other black Christians at St. George's Methodist Church in Philadelphia. They had contributed money for the construction of the very floor where they knelt to pray. But it happened to be a section reserved for whites and a church trustee demanded their removal even before they finished praying. This sad experience led Allen to form his own congregation. He gathered a group of ten black Methodists and purchased an old blacksmith's shop in the increasingly black southern section of the city, and converted it to the Bethel African Methodist Episcopal Church.

Allen and his friends began holding services in a rented storeroom. From that humble beginning the African Methodist Episcopal Church eventually emerged. It grew rapidly and has provided a spiritual bulwark to millions of black Americans. It now has over 2 1/4 million members.

Allen's decision to begin a black congregation was partly a response to white racism. Although most white Methodists in the 1790s favored emancipation, they sometimes did not treat free blacks as equals, even refusing to allow African-Americans to be buried in the congregation's cemetery.

Because of the Act of 1793, slaveowners were allowed to seize blacks without a warrant. As if to underline the importance of these political initiatives, Allen was temporarily seized in 1806 as a fugitive slave, showing that even the most prominent northern blacks could not be sure of their freedom.

Richard Allen also recognized the importance of education to the future of the African-American community. In 1795, he opened a day school for sixty children and in 1804 founded the "Society of Free People of Color for Promoting the Instruction and School Education of Children of African Descent." By 1811, there were at least eleven black schools in the city.

Richard Allen was married to Sarah Bass Allen, and together the Lord blessed them with six children: Richard Jr., James, John, Peter, Sarah, and Ann.

Allen's life as an inspirational story bears a dual significance. Not only was he the founder and leader of the African Methodist Episcopal Church, but he was one of the first slaves to be emancipated during the Revolutionary War. His experience, piety, intellect, and influence forged an identity for African-Americans that has carried to the present day.

Worth Reading: *Richard Allen,* by Martha Mathews (1963); *Richard Allen: Apostle of Freedom,* by Charles H. Wesley (1969); *The Emergence of Independent Black Churches,* by Carol George (1977); *Richard Allen: Religious Leader and Social Activist,* by Richard Klots (1991); *America's History* (1997).

Adoniram Judson *1788-1850*
Ann Judson *1789-1826*
Founders of American Modern Missions

The concept of evangelizing the heathen in foreign countries
had scarcely received much attention in Europe, and in
America, there was not even a Missionary Society—until
Adoniram and Ann Judson. They are therefore often
referred to as the Founders of Modern American Missions.

 doniram Judson suffered one
of the most horrible and difficult imprisonments a Christian
missionary has ever been called to
endure for the sake of the gospel.
The thirty-seven-year-old missionary was
arrested for preaching the Gospel of Jesus Christ and cast into a
Burmese prison. He was given very little food and water. His feet
were bound to a large bamboo pole, his hands tied to another,
and at night his feet were lifted above his head. He therefore had
to swing suspended on the small of his back with his feet tied to
a raised pole. His heroic wife, Ann, brought little bits of food to
him, although she and the baby were near death at times themselves, and eventually succumbed to the rigors of life in Burma.
Amidst severe hunger and constant sickness, Judson's burning
passion for the conversion of the Burmese people drove him to
secretly work on his translation of the Bible in their native language, hiding his work undetected in a hard pillow.

In 1812, Adoniram
and Ann Judson set
sail for India. These
first missionaries to
be sent from America
evangelized Burma
and translated the
Scriptures into the
Burmese language.

Adoniram was a son of a Congregational minister from
Massachusetts. When only four years of age, young Adoniram
seemed to foreshadow his future career. Gathering the children
of the neighborhood around him, he would mount a chair, and
go through a preaching service with marked earnestness. His
favorite hymn upon these occasions was one of Watts', commencing, "'I go, preach my gospel,' saith the Lord."

During his course of studies at Providence College, a circum-
stance occurred that changed the whole future of his life. In his
class was a young man named Ernest, to whom he was warmly
attached, and by whose influence he was led into professed infidelity, to the great grief of his devoted parents.

Starting out on a traveling tour at the close of his school,
Judson assumed another name and joined a theatrical company
in New York. Whenever the thought of a mother's tears would
occur, he tried to soothe his conscience, by saying, "I am in no
danger, I am only seeing the world, the dark side of it, as well

as the bright." After a while, pursuing his journey westward, he stopped at a country inn. As the landlord took him to his bedroom, he said: "I am obliged to place you next door to a young man, who is exceedingly ill, probably in a dying state, but I hope it will occasion you no uneasiness."

It proved, however, a very restless night; groans were frequently heard, and other sounds that made him think of eternity. Alone, and in the dead of night, he felt the conviction of his infidelity. Then he would try to shame his fears by thinking what his witty, clearminded, intellectual friend Ernest would say to such consummate boyishness.

At last, morning came and the bright flood of light which poured into his chamber dispelled all his superstitious illusions. Going in search of the landlord, he made inquiry about his fellow-lodger.

When the government refused to allow them to enter the country, they went to Burma, where they worked for six years before winning a convert. During those years they were plagued with ill health, loneliness, and the death of their baby son.

"He is dead," was the reply. "Dead!" "Yes, he is gone, poor fellow!" "Do you know who it was?" inquired Judson. "O yes, it was a young man from Providence College, a very fine fellow, named Ernest."

Judson was completely stunned. He knew not what to say or do. "Dead!" "Lost!" These were the two words that kept ringing in his head. He could go no further in his journey. This death-scene of his infidel companion was the pivot on which turned his destiny, both for time and eternity.

In 1789, Anne Hasseltine was born in Bradford, Massachusetts. Very early in life she gave signs of future distinction and usefulness. She possessed a persevering mind and a love for travel and adventure. At age nineteen her conversion from extreme worldliness to a life of piety was deep and permanent. Her ardor for learning only increased and she said, "Such was my thirst for religious knowledge, that I frequently spent a great part of the night in reading religious books." She read with deep interest, Edwards, Hopkins, and Doddridge. Edwards' *History of Redemption* was a means of instructing, quickening, and strengthening her soul. A friend once remarked about her resolve: "When reading Scripture, sermons or other works, if she met with anything dark or intricate, she would mark the passage, and beg the first clergyman who visited her home to explain it to her."

Mr. Judson, a graduate of Brown University "was an ardent and aspiring scholar." He was one of four or five young men in the then newly founded Theological Seminary at Andover, whose minds had become deeply impressed with the wants of the unconverted overseas. These young men stirred up one another's desire to go and labor among them. By their earnestness and perseverance they awakened an interest in their project, that a Board of Commissioners for Foreign Missions was appointed, and the young men were set apart as missionaries. During the two years in which Mr. Judson and his associates were busy preparing for a missionary's life, he had fallen in love with Ann Hasseltine, and made her an offer of his hand. He did not wish to blind her to the extent of the sacrifices she would make in accepting him. His manly and eloquent letter to her father, asking for his daughter's hand in marriage, is abundant evidence.

"I have now to ask you, sir, whether you can consent to part with your daughter early next spring, to see her no more in this world; whether you can consent to her departure for a heathen land, and her subjection to the hardships and sufferings of a missionary life; whether you can consent to her exposure to the dangers of the ocean; to the fatal influence of the southern climate of India; to every kind of want and distress; to degradation, insult, persecution, and perhaps a violent death? Can you consent to all this for the sake of Him who left his heavenly home, and died for her and for you; for the sake of perishing immortal souls; for the sake of Zion and the glory of God? Can you consent to all this in hope of soon meeting your daughter in the world of glory, with a crown of righteousness, brightened by the acclamations of praise which shall redound to her Saviour from heathens saved, through her means, from eternal woe and despair?"

Mrs. Ann H. Judson

After marrying Ann Hasseltine, the two set sail for the realms of heathen darkness on the *Caravan*, a ship bound for Calcutta. Mr. and Mrs. Newell, also missionaries, sailed in the same vessel, and they all became fast friends. In sharing her love and affection for her new husband Ann wrote to her sister:

"I find Mr. Judson one of the kindest, most faithful and affectionate of husbands. His conversation frequently dissipates the gloomy clouds of spiritual darkness which hang over my mind, and brightens my hope of a happy eternity. I hope God will make us instrumental in preparing each other for usefulness in this world, and greater happiness in a future world."

Their plan to minister in India was interrupted by various circumstances and eventually the Lord directed them to Burma, where their hearts were quickly burdened for the lost Buddhists.

Just as they were getting under way with their missionary work at Ava, the capital of Burma, war broke out and Mr. Judson and others were violently seized as English spies and cast into the "death prison."

For nine months, he was stretched on the bare floor, bound by three pairs of iron fetters, and fastened to a long pole, to prevent his moving. This was during the hottest season in Burma. He was locked up with a hundred prisoners in a room without any windows or ventilation. The only fresh air came through the cracks in the boards. They were all obliged to lie in

Judson was imprisoned for nearly two years, during which time Ann faithfully visited him, smuggling to him his books, papers, and notes, which he used in translating the Bible into the Burmese language. Soon after his release from prison, Ann and their baby daughter, Maria, died of spotted fever.

187

a row upon the floor, without a mattress, or even so much as a wooden block, which they begged might be granted them for a pillow. This whole period of indescribable suffering continued for one year and seven months. Yet, from this dark prison issued a hymn of praise that is still sung in churches around this world. Judson dates it, "Prison, Ava, March, 1825." It is a versification of the Lord's Prayer, and reveals the thoughts and feelings that filled his heart during his long, protracted agony.

His loving wife, knowing what the "daily bread" meant in such a prison, baked a pie of buffalo meat and plantains that looked something like a mince-pie and brought it to her husband. But when it arrived in prison, its associations brought so vividly to mind the old comforts of home, that he bowed his head upon his knees, and wept until tears flowed down to the chains about his ankles. Gratefully, Ann was also permitted to bring their infant daughter to the prison to receive a father's kiss.

After his release, Mr. and Mrs. Judson continued their incessant labor of translating the Bible and writing a Bible dictionary in the Burmese language, in addition to preaching and teaching the gospel. But the hardships, climate, and constant exposure to disease took its toll on Ann, and she went to glory in 1826, at the youthful age of thirty-seven. Adoniram's motherless child was the solace of his studies and labors. However, at just two years old, little Maria was unable to endure the rigors of missionary life in Burma, and in 1827, she succumbed to spotted fever.

Adoniram Judson married Sarah Hall Boardman in 1834, but she died in 1845, en route to America, in the arms of her husband, encouraging him to continue and carry on their life's mission. In 1846, Judson married Emily Kendrick, who became an accomplished writer under the name of "Fanny Forrester." She contributed to many religious publications, and even wrote an exceptional biography of Sarah Judson.

In 1850, Judson's health had so broken down, that his only hope for restoration was a protracted sea voyage. On April 3rd, he embarked on a vessel, bound for France. Nine days later, while out at sea, he breathed his last. All that was mortal of Dr. Judson, was committed to the ocean's deep.

As a young man, he had cried out, "I will not leave Burma, until the cross is planted here forever!" Thirty years after his death, Burma had 63 Christian churches, 163 missionaries, and over 7,000 baptized converts.

The Burmese religion of Buddhism is one of the most ancient and widespread superstitions on the face of the Earth. Its sacred divinity, or Buddha, has passed into a state of eternal unconscious repose, which they consider the summit of felicity. But this is nothing more than annihilation.

They believe in a merit system for divine approval, and that the soul after death returns in animals until enough merit is attained to become man again, or reincarnation.

Worth Reading: *The Life and Character of Adoniram Judson,* by William Hague (1851); *A Memoir of the Life and Labors of the Rev. Adoniram Judson, D. D.,* by Francis Wayland (1853); *The Lives of the Three Mrs. Jusdons,* by Arabella Wilson (1856); *The Life of Adoniram Judson,* by Edward Judson (1883); *An Hour With Adoniram and Ann Judson,* by T. W. Engstrom (1943); *Mission for Life: The Story of the Family of Adoniram Judson,* by Joan Jacobs Brumberg (1980); *Adoniram Judson: Bound for Burma,* by Janet Hazel Benge (2000).

Horatius Bonar *1808-1889*

Scottish Minister, Editor, Hymn-writer

Early on in his life as a minister, Horatius Bonar allied himself with three of the most spiritual men of his day: Thomas Chalmers, William C. Burns, and Robert Murray M'Cheyne. As a young pastor, he preached with fervor and passion in villages and farmhouses throughout Scotland. He saw evangelism in a different light from his contemporaries. "How shall we multiply conversions?" To Bonar, Christ had to come first.

The trustees had the difficult responsibility of finding a minister for their congregation, and their attention had been directed to the young assistant at South Leith, whom they understood to be "a young man of sincere piety, a ripe scholar, a well-instructed theologian, and a devoted evangelist." A delegation was sent to Leith to hear him preach. Having reported favorably, Horatius Bonar was elected minister of the North Parish in Kelso, Scotland, on September 9, 1837. He preached his first sermon on the following Sabbath from the text, "This kind can come forth by nothing but by prayer and fasting." The opening sentences define the characteristics of the man and his ministry: "I do not come to address you after the manner of man's wisdom, nor with words of human eloquence, but to speak to your souls of the things which concern your eternity; to stir you up to seek in good earnest salvation for yourselves and for others. It is a light thing that you should be attracted and pleased, but it is no light matter that you should be moved to work out your own salvation with fear and trembling, God working in you to will and to do of His good pleasure. It is a light thing that the admiration of many should be obtained, but it is no light matter that the multitudes who are now far from God should be moved to return to Him from whom they 'have revolted and gone.' The gratification of an hour is all that depends upon the one; but eternity—a sinner's eternity hangs upon the other." From the first his sermons were simple, solemn, and searching. He says himself in an autobiographical sketch, "The keynote which I struck was, 'Ye must be born again;' and that message found its way into many hearts. It repelled some, but it drew many together in what I may call the bond of regeneration."

As a teacher he was a follower of the Reformers more than of the Puritans. His strength lay in his insistence on the objective facts and truths of the gospel, rather than in an analysis of human experience, or in the skill with which he laid bare the

A man of prose and poetry, Horatius Bonar was also a man of sorrows. Five of his children and his wife died during his lifetime. Yet, his comfort was his deep faith and profound understanding of the love of Jesus. The Lord used him to lead many to saving faith in Christ.

deceitfulness of the human heart. His main teaching was, "Look away from self to Christ."

Horatius Bonar was the sixth of eleven children, and of these three others became ministers. He grew up in a godly home in which the Scriptures were always read and lived by. As he matured he expressed that there was not a moment in his life that he did not know God.

Horatius Bonar did not confine himself to the labors of the pulpit. He interested himself in Sabbath and day schools, holding Bible classes, and conducting prayer meetings, which were richly blessed in spiritual results. In the widespread revival which preceded and accompanied the "Disruption," he took a foremost part, preaching and conducting evangelistic services in many parts of Scotland and the north of England, sometimes alone, sometimes accompanied by the associates of his student days.

In 1843, Bonar married Jane Catherine Lundie, the daughter of Rev. Robert Lundie, who was for many years pastor at Kelso. Dr. Bonar had brought her back to the home of her childhood. Nine children were born to the godly couple over the years.

Later that same year, the ecclesiastical conflict known as the "Great Disruption," occured between the evangelical ministers and elders who left the Church of Scotland's General Assembly and the Civil Courts. Bonar was instrumental in answering the question in his pamphlet, *Can We Stay in the Church?* After much controversy, Bonar was one of the majority of ministers who followed the moderator, Dr. Welsh, and marched out of the Assem-bly of the Established Church and formed the new Free Church of Scotland. Since the state owned and consequently reclaimed most of the church buildings of these ministers and their congregations, splits between the members was common. Bonar's 430 members had to raise money for a new building and met in local halls for worship in the meantime.

The communion seasons, at which the services lasted over several days, were greatly looked forward to and remembered, and proved to be seasons of great power and blessing. At these times Bonar was usually assisted by one or other of his brothers and by R. M. M'Cheyne, A. N. Somerville, John Milne, or some other friends. He would share in their communion services in turn, and draw afresh "water out of the wells of salvation" for his own spiritual nourishment.

Dr. Bonar was a diligent student and a hard worker. The light burned late in his study window. He was at his desk early in the morning to begin his studies with seasons of prayer. He was physically vigorous and possessed a resolute will. The work he accomplished was marvelous. Frequently members of his house-hold heard his voice in prayer far into the middle of the night.

In the early part of 1856, in company with several friends, he spent five months making a tour through Egypt, Sinai, and the

To his firstborn he welcomed into the world with the lines:

"No night descend on thee
O'er thee no shadows come!

Safe be thy journey through
This vale of cloud and gloom.

Peace be thy gentle guest
Peace holy and divine,

God's blessed sunlight still
Upon thy pathway shine."

To his youngest son he wrote:

"My flowers have faded, and my fruit
Is dropping from the tree;

The blossoms of the golden year
Are opening all on thee;

My harvest, with its gathered sheaves,
Is almost over now;

But thine is coming up, my child,
When I am lying low."

Holy Land. Two books which were the fruit of this journey, *The Desert of Sinai* and *The Land of Promise*, attained considerable popularity.

Dr. Bonar's nature was contemplative and reserved. He made little display of emotion. He was a silent man. In the small things of life he had small interest and had few acquaintances. But those admitted to the privilege of his friendship he loved with intensity, and to them he was true till death. "He was a rock," said one who knew him well, "he was preeminently a man of God. One who lived entirely under the power of the world to come. There was a degree of sternness in his character like one of the Old Testament prophets, but withal there was a wonderful element of simplicity and playfulness that came out in his intercourse with his children." He loved his children with intense affection, and their death left scars upon his heart which time did not erase. He knew what it was to be smitten with frequent and sore bereavement. Two children died in infancy, a son at three, a daughter at four, and another daughter at seventeen.

In later life he was twice again smitten. His eldest daughter had in 1876 married the Rev. G. Theophilus Dodds, who died suddenly in 1882, and Mrs. Dodds brought her five fatherless children to live under her father's roof. Dr. Bonar wrote to a friend, "God took five children from me some years ago, and He has given me another five to bring up for Him in my old age." Two years later his wife and chief companion of over forty years was taken from his side. Mrs. Bonar passed away on December 3, 1884, at the age of sixty-three.

Dr. Bonar's literary activities began in 1831, when he was one of the original promoters of the *Presbyterian Review,* and continued to within a year or two of his death. He was the author of more than forty volumes of poetry and hymns, and wrote more than 150 religious books, tracts, and booklets.

In 1839, he began the issue of his series of 'Kelso Tracts,' which soon became famous. Some of them were extracts from ancient or Puritan authors, a few were written by his friends, but most were from his own hand. Most of Dr. Bonar's larger prose writings sprang directly out of his pastoral or pulpit work, while some originated from his interest in prophetic study.

The first volume he published was a small devotional work, *The Night of Weeping: or, Words for the Suffering Family of God,* which at once revealed him as one who possessed a rare gift of speaking straight to the hearts of men, especially in seasons of trial and suffering. A sequel to it appeared in 1850, under the title *The Morning of Joy.* From that time on scarcely a year passed without some work, large or small, being printed from the pen of Dr. Bonar. Of all his books his most widely circulated and richly blessed is *God's Way of Peace,* a book for the sufferer of anxiety, written in 1862.

Bonar also did a considerable amount of valuable editorial

> *Man's dislike at God's sovereignty arises from his suspicion of God's heart. And yet the men in our day, who deny this absolute sovereignty, are the very men who profess to rejoice in the love of God,—who speak of that love as if there were nothing else in God but love. The more I understand of the character of God, as revealed in Scripture, the more shall I see that He must be sovereign, and the more shall I rejoice from my inmost heart that He is so.*
> *—Horatius Bonar*

work. For twenty years, from 1859-1879, Dr. Bonar was editor of *The Christian Treasury*, a monthly periodical of wonderful religious writings from pious men and women of the past and present. Bonar himself wrote hundreds of editorials and articles within its pages. He also edited the *Presbyterian Review* and the *Quarterly Journal of Prophecy*.

Bonar's literary skills were not limited to prose. His poetry presented in hymns became world-renowned. He began by writing a few hymns for the children in his Sunday school classes, which were soon printed into leaflets for his friends and fellow ministers. Then he published some in the *Presbyterian Review* and *The Christian Treasury*, receiving hundreds of requests for more. And in the 1860s he published volumes of hymns in a series of volumes titled, *Hymns of Faith and Hope*.

In evangelistic work he was always deeply interested. When Mr. Moody first came to Edinburgh in 1874, Dr. Bonar stood by his side and aided him in his work. Several of his hymns were written at Ira Sankey's request, to be included in the *Sacred Songs and Solos* book published by Moody and Sankey. In the great conferences at Mildmay, Perth, and other places where Christians of many denominations met for fellowship and mutual edification, he took great interest and delight.

Dr. Bonar was the spiritual father of many great men, some who became ministers or missionaries for the Kingdom of God. He preached and ministered to his flock to the end of his days, and fell asleep in Jesus on July 31, 1889.

Glory, then, is our inheritance. The best, the richest, the brightest, the most beautiful of all that is in God, of good, and rich, and bright, and beautiful, shall be ours. The glory that fills heaven above, the glory that spreads over the earth beneath, shall be ours. But while "the glory of the terrestrial" shall be ours, yet in a truer sense "the glory of the celestial shall be ours."

—Horatius Bonar, in Joy in the Morning.

Key Writings of Bonar: 1. *Words to Winners of Souls*; 2. *Another's Righteousness for Us*; 3. *Christ the Wisdom of God*; 4. *God's Way of Peace*; 5. *Follow the Lamb*; 6. *God's Testimony Concerning Man*; 7. *Christ Died for the Ungodly*; 8. *God's Way of Holiness*; 9. *No Faith But Christ*; 10. *Divine Philosophy*; 11. *God's Will and Man's Will*; 12. *The Long Time*; 13. *How Shall I Go To God?*; 14. *The Banished One Bearing Our Banishment*; 15. *God's Purpose of Grace*; 16. *The Everlasting Righteousness*; 17. *The Christ of God*; 18. *The Rent Veil*; 19. *God's Character, Our Resting Place*; 20. *True Revivals and the Men God Uses*; 21. *Modern Hostility to Revivals*; 22. *The Root and Soil of Holiness*; 23. *Divine Compassion*; 24. *What is My Hope?*; 25. *The Blood of Sprinkling*; 26. *Instead of Me*; 27. *I Can't Let God*; 28. *Revival Men*; 29. *The Hymns of Horatius Bonar*; 30. *More Hymns by Horatius Bonar*; 31. *Select Hymns of Horatius Bonar*; 32. *The True Character of Unbelief*; 33. *The Certainty of Certainties*; 34. *Saving Faith*; 35. *Faithful and Just to Forgive*; 36. *Christ the Substitute*; 37. *The World Passeth Away*; 38. *Unbelief*; 39. *In the Place of Self*; 40. *What About You?*; 41. *Do You Rejoice in God's Sovereignty?*; 42. *What Work Must Be Done in Order to be Saved?*; 43. *God's Trees Grow Slowly*; 44. *On Biblical Reproof and Correction*; 45. *The Five Points of Calvinism*; 46. *Longing for Heaven*; 47. *How Shall I Go to God?*; 48. *Night Of Weeping*; 49. *Morning of Joy*; 50. *When God's Children Suffer*; 51. *Christ the Healer*; 52. *The Better Land*; 53. *The Unwritten Wonders of the Grace of Christ*; 54. *Hymns of Faith and Hope*; 55. *The Desert of Sinai*; 56. *The Land of Promise*.

Worth Reading: *Words Old and New: Gems from the Christian Authorship of All Ages Selected by Horatius Bonar* (1994).

Samuel Crowther *1809-1891*
Bishop and Missionary of Africa

"Servant of God, Well Done" was the hymn appropriately sung at his funeral. Samuel Adjai Crowther endured the cross as a faithful missionary to the people of his native Africa. He was the first black ordained by the Church of England. Persecutions, slavery, prejudice, sickness, threats, separation, and lonliness never daunted the spirit of the man on fire for God and impassioned for the conversion of the lost.

I n 1821, a Muslim army from Eyo, a Mohammedan Foulah town in Central Africa, came down in force on the small, peaceful town of Oshogun and ruthlessly slaughtered the inhabitants. The father of one of the families had just enough time to rush into his hut and give warning of the danger to his loved ones. He hurried back to the scene of action and died in defense of his people. The wife with her three children made an attempt to escape. One of those children was twelve year old Adjai. The boy, seizing his bow and arrows, made a show of defending his mother and her younger children. But all were captured and dragged off by the cruel marauders. A long, weary journey of twenty miles, attended by all the barbaric abuses of a slave march, brought them to Isehin. There all the captives were distributed among the tribal leaders. Adjai and his sister were separated from their mother and assigned to the chief, while the others were handed over to some of the soldiers. Soon after Adjai was brought to the slave market at Dadda, when he had the pleasure of meeting his mother. But their reunion was short. Four masters in succession had little Adjai for their slave. So far he had been spared from what he feared most of all—the bondage of the "white men." A Mohammedan woman took young Adjai down to the coast to be prepared for the Portuguese buyers. Anything seemed better than the treatment which he might expect at their hands. Several times the boy attempted to kill himself, but God intervened and his life was to be spared that he might later become a great blessing to his fellow countrymen.

In time, a purchaser was found for the boy at Lagos. He soon experienced what he had so dreaded, the "tender mercies" of the white man. Indescribable sufferings were endured, first in the slave shed and then on the slave ship. A hundred-and-eighty-seven people, some almost at the point of death, were packed together in a helpless mass. Death would have been gladly welcomed, but deliverance of another kind was at hand.

Two British men-of-war ships were cruising off the coast. They had received a commission to intercept any slaver-traders and liberate the captives. The vessel in which young Adjai was

Once a victim of Muslim slave-traders, Samuel Crowther became free indeed—not only in body, but in receiving the Holy Spirit—that he might become the first of many to minister the blessed truths of Jesus Christ to his native Africans.

confined was captured by one of the men-of-war, and the slaves were told that they were now free. They could hardly realize their liberated position. It took some time before they understood they were free. But soon their fears went and a bright future opened out for them, when they found themselves in Sierra Leone—the haven of refuge for freed slaves.

In 1807, the Bill for the Abolition of the Slave Trade was passed. In the following year the government formed a settlement of the liberated Africans at the place to which the name of Sierra Leone was given. As many as two thousand freed slaves were added annually. But, unhappily, these Africans, freed from man's slavery, were not liberated from the bondage of the world, the flesh, and the devil. The place became a home of superstition, lawlessness, and immorality. The freedom from restraint promoted release of the sinfulness of the heart. In 1816, the Church Missionary Society sent missionaries there to preach the gospel among the unlearned. The cost in precious lives was great, but the price was freely paid. In twenty years as many as fifty-three missionaries died a martyr's death in Sierra Leone. What had become the black man's sanctuary, became the white man's grave.

When the slaves were first taken aboard the "white man's" vessel they seemed prepared for fresh terrors. They spotted some pork cut up and hung in the rigging, which they mistook as the bodies of some of their comrades, ready for the white man's dinner.

The little rescued Adjai was sent to Bathurst and placed at the mission school. He proved himself an eager student. On the first day of his attendance at the school, he begged a halfpenny from a friend, and quickly ran off to buy himself a much longed-for alphabet card. In six months he could read the New Testament with ease, and soon after became a tutor. He was also trained in carpentry and masonry. His teacher, Mr. Weeks, afterwards became Bishop of Sierra Leone. Under the godly training and pious example of this man of God, Adjai came to know and love the King of the "white men," Jesus Christ. He was taught the blessed gospel that Jesus died and rose from the dead that all men might trust in Him and be saved from their sins.

In 1825, Adjai was no longer to be know by his native name, but took the name of Samuel Crowther, after his baptism in Freetown. This name has become so sweet to all friends of missions. In his newfound freedom in Christ, young Samuel eagerly availed himself of every opportunity of self-improvement, but his desire to spread the Good News to his people grew fervently within his heart.

In the year 1827, Fourah Bay College was opened. It superseded the Industrial Boarding School at Sierra Leone, called the Christian Institution. This was merged into a college for training native teachers. The very first name on the roll of students is that of Samuel Crowther. In a few months Samuel made such progress that he was appointed, at the age of eighteen, assistant teacher of the college.

Writing about this time on the subject of his captivity, Crowther expressed that God used his sufferings to lead him to a knowledge of the truth. "I call it an unhappy day, because it was the day on which I was violently turned out of my father's house, and separated from my relatives, and in which I was made a slave. But it was also the day which Providence had marked out for me to set out on my journey from the land of heathenism, superstition and vice, to a place where the Gospel is preached."

In 1829, Crowther married Asano, who had been baptized by the name Susanna. This was a girl who had also been rescued from slavery, and who was with him at Bathurst. It was a happy union which lasted for half a century, separated only at the death of Mrs. Crowther in Lagos in 1881. The couple settled in England and were blessed with many children. One was later appointed Archdeacon Crowther. Two other sons were laymen, and their daughters married African clergymen.

In 1841, the first Niger Expedition was proposed by the Church Missionary Society and Crowther along with Rev. J. F. Schon were chosen to lead the mission work. It pained both men to leave their homes, but they were blessed with the missionary spirit of selflessness.

The missionaries had set out full of high hopes, yet they returned disappointed. There was one foe that could not be overcome by their prayer, courage, and energy. "The country we are now in," writes Crowther, "with its clear air and dry atmosphere which we now enjoy, would cause us to doubt that the climate could be dangerous, were it not for the sick and dying by whom we are surrounded. I pray for them, I pray with them." The sick and dying increased in number. The captains of the vessels, the medical officers, and many of the crew members contracted the dreadful disease. Of the one hundred and fifty who formed the missionary expedition, forty-two were dead within two months.

After his return to England he attended the Islington Missionary College and became an ordained minister in 1843. He was the first on the rolls of Native African descent. Later that year he continued his passion for missions by returning to Sierra Leone and establishing the Yoruba Mission. He desired to tell his own countrymen of the precious treasure he had found in Christ.

Crowther was called to Abeokuta in 1846. He found an opportunity of sending a message to Sagbua, the new chief. The latter invited the "white men" to come up at once. The missionaries were met with a hearty welcome. The Christians, of course, being especially jubilant. Promises of help in building a church were heartily volunteered.

Three weeks after Crowther arrived at Abeokuta, an event took place which should be registered in his own words: "August 21. The text for this day in the Christian Almanac is 'Thou art the Helper of the fatherless!' I have never felt the force of this text more than I did this day, as I have to relate that my mother, from whom I was torn away about twenty-five years ago, came

"How inexcusable art thou, O man, who art living in a place where the Gospel is preached every Sabbath, yet who preferrest to live in the darkness, in ignorance of God, of Christ, and of the state of thine own soul, to being made wise unto salvation by the saving knowledge of the Gospel of Jesus Christ." Thus did Crowther reflect when he reflected on the abuse of privileges by those who were blessed with what was denied to the poor natives.

Some missionaries sealed their profession by a martyr's death. The constancy of two precious saints is especially worthy of notice. They were first approached by bribes, and then by threats of most horrible torture. "I have made up my mind," said one, "God helping me, to be in chains, if it so please the Lord, till the coming of the judgment day." The answer of the other was even more noteworthy: "You know I never refused to perform my duty; but as for turning back to heathen worship, that is out of my power, for Jesus has taken charge of my heart, and padlocked it, and the key is with Him."

with my brother in quest of me. When she saw me she trembled. She could not believe her eyes. We grasped one another, looking at each other with silence and great astonishment, big tears rolling down her emaciated cheeks. A great number of people soon came together. She trembled as she held me by the hand. We could not say much, but sat still and cast now and then an affectionate look at each other—a look which violence and oppression had long checked—an affection which had nearly been extinguished by the long space of time. My two sisters, who were captives with us, are both with my mother, who takes care of them and her grandchildren, in a small town not far from here. After all human attempts for reunion had failed, God has brought us together again, and turned our sorrow into joy." Crowther's mother became one of the first converts of Abeokuta. She was baptized by the name Hannah. After living a faithful life, she died in 1883, over a hundred years old.

Crowther's years of missionary work in Africa were blessed with many conversions. He spent twelve years in Abeokuta and then travelled to Niger on his second expedition there. Many missionaries before him were killed by the cannibals, but he was determined to see the gospel preached and translated into the native Ibo language. In 1864, Samuel Crowther was consecrated Bishop of Niger, the first native bishop ever ordained by the Church of England. He returned to his mission work in Africa, established the Niger Mission Society and trained other natives in the service of King Jesus.

The society in which he had labored so faithfully made a record of his services: "Few of Christ's soldiers and servants have ever more remarkably, from earliest years, come in contact with the wickedness of this world, and with the sad manifestations of human depravity, and few have more patiently carried on the battle against evil, and have maintained individually a more consistent course, and a more unblemished reputation. Though by no means with out natural gifts, possessing both intellectual vigor and moral force of character, Samuel Adjai Crowther was a conspicuous proof of the power of the Gospel, and of the continued presence of the Spirit of God in Christ's Church. The committee pray that all who remember him, especially in West African Christendom, may be stirred up to follow him in so far as he followed Christ."

Though his work on Earth is finished, the results of Crowther's activities in the West African mission field are not finished. Eternity alone will reveal how much the dwellers around "Africa's sunny fountains" have to bless the name of Samuel Adjai Crowther.

Worth Reading: Bishop Crowther's Journals; Bishop Crowther, His Life and Work; Samuel Crowther, by Jesse Page.

Charles Dickens *1812-1870*
English Author of Classic Literature

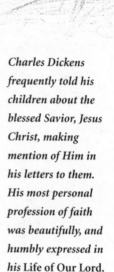

At one time early in his life he had ambitions for the theater to become a comedian, but it was God's plan to save him for greater work. The Almighty pierced his soul and called him to Himself while directing his path to write some of the most wonderful volumes of literature produced by the mind and heart of man.

ew biographers of Charles Dickens have ever written anything regarding the *true* motivation and passion behind his writing—his faith in the Lord Jesus Christ. The life of this man who wrote some of the greatest classics in literature the world has ever known, is often portrayed along side the worldly Voltaire, Cooper, Emerson, and Tennyson. But in reality, he belongs beside God-fearing authors such as Milton, De Foe, Johnson, and Bunyan.

Much of Dickens' biblical convictions are reflected in the stories he so wonderfully penned during his fifty-eight years of writing. Who cannot see the example of Christian conversion in the character of Scrooge in *A Christmas Carol*? Or the battle between mere formal religion and genuine faith in *Oliver Twist*?

There remains little written record of Dickens' Christian faith outside of his *Life of Our Lord* which he wrote himself for the private benefit of his children. He penned this classic work between the years of 1846-1849—the same time he was writing *David Copperfield*. But it did not see the light of the printing press until 1934, sixty-four years after his death.

The reason for this is best expressed in the preface of his *Life of Our Lord* written by his grandson:

"During his lifetime Charles Dickens refused to permit publication of *The Life of Our Lord* because he doubtless felt that was a personal letter to his own children, and feared that a public disclosure of so intimate a document might involve the possibility of attack and defense of his deepest religious convictions. In a letter to a clergyman he said; "There cannot be many men, I believe, who have a more humble veneration for the New Testament, or a more profound conviction of its all-sufficiency than I have. My observation of life induces me to hold in unspeakable dread and horror these unseemly squabbles about 'the letter' which drive 'the Spirit' out of hundreds of thousands.'"

A few hours before he was stricken with the attack which caused his death one day later, Dickens wrote a letter to John M. Makeham, who had accused him of irreverence in a passage of *The Mystery of Edwin Drood*. The final paragraph of that letter, perhaps the last words written by Dickens, contained this

Charles Dickens frequently told his children about the blessed Savior, Jesus Christ, making mention of Him in his letters to them. His most personal profession of faith was beautifully, and humbly expressed in his **Life of Our Lord.**

statement: "I have always striven in my writings to express veneration for the life and lessons of our Saviour, because I feel it; and because I rewrote that history for my children—every one of whom knew it from having it repeated to them—long before they could read, and almost as soon as they could speak. But I have never made proclamation of this from the housetops."

An excerpt from the ending pages of his *Life of Our Lord* might do well to affirm the love of Jesus within the breast of Charles Dickens, as expressed to his children:

"They took the name of Christians from Our Saviour Christ, and carried crosses as their sign, because upon a cross He had suffered death. The religions that were then in the world were false and brutal, and encouraged men to violence. Beasts, and even men, were killed in the churches, in the belief that the smell of their blood was pleasant to the gods—there were supposed to be a great many gods—and many most cruel and disgusting ceremonies prevailed. Yet, for all this, and though the Christian religion was such a true, and kind, and good one, the priests of the old religions long persuaded the people to do all possible hurt to the Christians; and Christians were hanged, beheaded, burnt, buried alive, and devoured in theatres by wild beasts for the public amusement, during many years. Nothing would silence them, or terrify them though; for they knew that if they did their duty, they would go to Heaven. So thousands upon thousands of Christians sprung up and taught the people and were cruelly killed, and were succeeded by other Christians, until the religion gradually became the greatest religion of the world.

"Remember!—It is Christianity TO DO GOOD, always—even to those who do evil to us. It is Christianity to love our neighbors as ourself, and to do to all men as we would have them do to us. It is Christianity to be gentle, merciful, and forgiving, and to keep those qualities quiet in our own hearts, and never make a boast of them, or of our prayers or of our love of God, but always to show that we love Him, by humbly trying to do right in everything. If we do this, and remember the life and lessons of our Lord Jesus Christ, and try to act up to them, we may confidently hope that God will forgive us our sins and mistakes, and enable us to live and die in peace."

Evening Prayer for Dickens' children:

O God, who has made everything, and is so kind and merciful to everything He has made, who tries to be good and to deserve it; God bless my dear Papa and Mamma, Brothers and Sisters and all my Relations and Friends. Make me a good little child, and let me never be naughty and tell a lie, which is a mean and shameful thing. Make me kind to my nurses and servants, and to all beggars and poor people, and let me never be cruel to any dumb creatures, for if I am cruel to anything, even to a poor little fly, God, who is so good, will never love me. And pray God to bless and preserve us all,, this night, and forevermore, through Jesus Christ our Lord. Amen.

Key Writings of Dickens: 1. *Sketches of Boz* (1836); 2. *Posthumous Papers of the Pickwick Club* (1837); 3. *Oliver Twist* (1838); 4. *Nicholas Nickleby* (1837); 5. *The Old Curiosity Shop* (1840); 6. *Barnaby Rudge* (1841); 7. *American Notes* (1842); 8. *Martin Chuzzlewit* (1843); 9. *The Christmas Tales* (1843-48); 10. *Pictures From Italy* (1845); 11. *Dombey and Son* (1846-48); 12. *David Copperfield* (1848); 13. *Bleak House* (1852); 14. *The Child's History of England* (1854); 15. *Hard Times* (1854); 16. *Little Dorrit* (1855); 17. *A Tale of Two Cities* (1859); 18. *The Uncommercial Traveller* (1861); 19. *Our Mutual Friend (1864)*

Worth Reading: *The Life of Our Lord,* by Charles Dicken's (Published posthumously, in 1934, by his grandson)

Robert Murray M'Cheyne *1813-1843*

Scottish Minister and Missionary

"Walking closely with God," exemplifies Robert Murray M'Cheyne. Though his life was a brief twenty-nine years, his impact on souls exceeded many whose heads were gray. In word, in conversation, in charity, in spirit, in faith, in purity, he ceased not day and night to labor and watch for souls, and was honored by his Lord to draw many wanderers out of darkness into the path of life.

obert Murray M'Cheyne was born at Edinburgh, Scotland. From an early age gave evidence of that mental ability and nobility of character which, "as the morning shows the day," correctly foreshadowed his brief but brilliant earthly future. His biographer, Dr. Andrew A. Bonar, informs us that at the early age of four he selected as his recreation, while recovering from illness, the study of the Greek alphabet, and was able to name, and write in a rude way upon a slate, all its letters.

At five years of age he had already taken a conspicuous place among his schoolfellows for his melodious voice and powers of recitation.

In 1821, he entered the High School in Edinburgh, where he spent six years distinguishing himself in his studies, particularly in geography and recitation. In regards to his Christian character, he was seen by his fellow students as a good, moral, and even religious young man, but as yet he knew not the Lord. And he had no higher pleasures than those which came through his love of music and singing, and from other refined aspects of society.

He entered the University of Edinburgh in 1827. Linguistic studies and poetry occupied much of his attention while at college, and in all his classes he won prizes, while he devoted much time to sketching and gymnastics.

But God in His providence had been preparing M'Cheyne to be a vessel meet for the Master's use. The first real deep spiritual impressions appear to have been brought about by the death of his eldest brother, David, in July of 1831. To this brother Robert's soul was knit by many fond and beautiful ties. For the remainder of his life, Robert was accustomed to commemorate the anniversary of his brother's death as a day of fasting and prayer.

David, the eldest of the family was of a profoundly noble, unselfish, and truthful character, and through his teachings and example made a lasting impression upon the mind of Robert.

From these impressions, the heart of M'Cheyne was gradually led on to God. But it was the *Sum of Saving Knowledge*

"Among Christian men, a 'living epistle,' and among Christian ministers, an 'able evangelist,' is rare indeed. Mr. M'Cheyne was both. And without presumption, I say he was a 'disciple whom Jesus loved,'" says his friend and fellow minister, James Hamilton.

(a Scottish addendum to the Westminster Confession of Faith) that was the instrument in God's hand of bringing him to a clear understanding of the way of salvation through Christ. Previous to this, through his brother David's influence, he had experienced some leanings towards the ministry, but now his mind was fully made up, and in the joy of his new birth he began diligently to prepare to become an ambassador of Christ.

In the winter of 1831 he entered the Divinity Hall of the Edinburgh University, under the instruction of Dr. Chalmers and Dr. Welsh. He proved himself a conscientious and diligent student in preparation for his sacred calling. He rapidly acquired a proficiency in the original languages of Scripture and his daily delight was in the study of the Hebrew Psalms, the Septuagint, and the Greek New Testament. He studied diligently Jonathan Edwards' works, and his spiritual life was nourished. M'Cheyne's evangelistic zeal was awakened by the perusal of such books as the *Lives of Brainerd, Legh Richmond and Jonathan Edwards, Rutherford's Letters,* Adam's *Private Thoughts,* and Baxter's *Call to the Unconverted.*

M'Cheyne saw no inconsistency in preaching an electing God who calleth whom He will, and a salvation free to whosoever will; nor in declaring the absolute sovereignty of God, along with the unimpaired responsibility of man. He would offer a present salvation to every one within reach of his voice.

He soon joined the Visiting Society and the Missionary Association whose object was the visitation of the needy in some neglected parts of Edinburgh. Horatius Bonar, Andrew Bonar, M'Cheyne and a number of the students met each Saturday forenoon in Dr. Chalmers' vestry, and ventured forth, after prayer and mutual consultation, to visit low courts and alleys. They also held sessions discussing various theological questions.

In 1835, at age twenty-two, M'Cheyne was solemnly licensed by the Presbytery of Annan to preach the gospel. His first sermon was preached in Ruthwell Church, near Dumfries, on "the Pool of Bethesda," and in the evening he preached in the same place on "the Strait Gate." About this time he recorded in his journal the following reflection which preachers of the gospel will in some measure understand: "It came across me in the pulpit, that, if spared to be a minister, I might enjoy sweet flashes of communion with God in that situation. My mind is entirely wrought up to speak for God."

Sixteen months after receiving his license to preach, Robert Murray M'Cheyne was ordained the minister of St. Peter's Church, Dundee, Scotland, on November 24, 1836.

His congregation at Dundee numbered 1100 hearers, one-third of whom came from distant parts of the town. The regular attendance each Lord's day was 4000. Nothing was allowed to interfere with his holy hour of morning devotion. He rose early, so as to secure time for private communion with God before breakfast. "A soldier, of the cross," he observed, "must endure hardness," and no matter how wearied he was with the previous day's labors, he would awaken early "morning by morning" to; "bear what the Lord God would speak" through His Word, and to plead with Him for His blessing upon the engagements of the coming day. At breakfast, plans were formed for the day, and nothing delighted M'Cheyne more than to have his hands full of work. His health, however, was not particularly robust, and the demands of the ministry taxed him very heavily and soon began to take it's toll upon him.

He found the people of his charge in a very low spiritual condition, and so he formed evening classes for Bible study and the catechism at his home, and held weekly prayer meetings in the church. His efforts paid off with many being saved. It was in his daily walk that he excelled. He was very careful of his every word and act. He wished to be always in the presence of God. In riding or walking he seized opportunities to speak about Christ or give a useful tract. His visits to friends were occasions when he sought to do good to souls. Dr. Bonar says he found written on a leaf in one of his notebooks the following words worth remembering: "When visiting a family, whether ministerially or otherwise, speak particularly to the stranger about eternal things. Perhaps God has brought you together just to save that soul."

Thus he spent his first few years at Dundee, blessing others by his words and example, and receiving blessings from God. M'Cheyne's health continued to decline and finally gave way at the close of 1838. He was forced to desist from his labors, and to take rest. His enforced retirement led him to entertain more serious views of life and death, and of the necessity sharing Christ yet more abundantly, "seeing that the time was short." He writes to a friend in reference to the enforced rest: "I hope this affliction will be a blessing to me."

St. Peter's (Free) Church, Dundee, built 1836, where the late Reverend R. M. M'Cheyne ministered and beside which his body lies interred.

M'Cheyne, Bonar, and others had a burning desire to spread the gospel to the unconverted, especially the Jews. They spent many months on a missionary trip that took them through many lands, such as Jerusalem, Samaria, Hebron, Carmel, Galilee, Smyrna, Beyrout, Constantinople, Poland, and Prussia, where they saw many conversions.

Dr. Bonar says that there were two things M'Cheyne never ceased from: the cultivation of personal holiness, and the most anxious efforts to save souls. His preaching was expository. His sermons were full of scriptural illustration and quotations, as well as sound doctrine. They were so full of Christ and His love. "It is strange," he wrote to a friend, after preaching on Revelation 1:15, "how sweet and

precious it is to preach directly about Christ, compared with all other subjects of preaching." His sermons displayed a deep knowledge of human nature, with keen analysis of human motives, and are rich in pointed application to the human heart. His aim was to secure immediate results. Convinced "that the glad tidings were intended to impart *immediate assurance* of eternal life to every sinner that believes them," he focused all his energies on bringing souls into direct and saving contact with the Savior *while he spoke,* and God honored his believing efforts in a very wonderful manner. Dr. Bonar says, "During the six short years of his ministry, he was the instrument of saving more souls than many true servants of God have done during half a century [of ministry]."

During a passionate open-air service M'Cheyne preached on, "The Great White Throne." (Revelation 20:11.) In concluding his address, he told his audience "that they would never meet again till they all met at the judgment seat of Christ; but the glorious heavens over their heads and the bright moon that shone over them, and the old venerable church behind them, were his witnesses that he had set before them life and death."

His burden for the people of God and the salvation of souls, pressed him to pick up the pen when he was unable to attend in person, especially due to his ill health. He had a Samuel Rutherford-type ministry to many under his care and abroad, who benefited greatly from his letters of comfort, exhortation and encouragement in Christ.

We saw that M'Cheyne returned to his flock from a preaching tour on March 1, 1843, much exhausted in body. Typhoid fever was prevailing in his parish, and though very weak he visited many of those attacked with the disease. His last sermons, on Sunday, March 12, were noted for their power and the peculiar solemnity of their delivery. In the morning he preached upon Hebrews 11:15, and in the afternoon from Romans 11:22,23. These were his last discourses to his people. In the evening he went down to Broughty Ferry, and preached upon Isaiah 60:1, "Arise, shine..." After his death a letter was found unopened, for it had come to him while he was sick with the fever. It said:

"I hope you will pardon a stranger for addressing to you a few lines. I heard you preach last Sabbath evening, and it pleased God to bless that sermon to my soul. It was not so much what you said as your manner of speaking that struck me. I saw in you a beauty of holiness that I never saw before. You also said something in your prayer that struck me very much. It was, 'Thou knowest that we love Thee.' Oh, sir, what I would give that I could say to my blessed Savior, 'Thou knowest that I love Thee!' "

On the morning of Saturday, March 25, 1843, the soul of Robert Murray M'Cheyne passed within the veil. His last action was to raise his hands in benediction to his King.

Key Writings of M'Cheyne: 1. *This Do in Remembrance of Me* (1840); 2. *I Love the Lord's Day* (1840); Daily Bread (1841); *Communion With Brethren of Other Denominations* (1841); *Narrative of a Mission to the Jews from the Church of Scotland in 1839,* (1842); *Another Lily Gathered* (1842); *Songs of Zion* (1843).

Worth Reading: 1. *Gems of M'Cheyne,* by James Hamilton (1843); *Memoir and Remains of M'Cheyne,* by A. Bonar (1845); *Sermons of M'Cheyne* (1850)

John Charles Ryle *1817-1900*
"Man of God, Man of Granite"

When the Church of England was moving futher away from the Word of God in practice and worship the Lord providentially sent J. C. Ryle, a man after his own heart, to plainly and effectively preach, teach, and write that salvation through Jesus Christ is more than liturgy and repetitions, but a dedicated holiness in thought, word, and life.

Twenty-year-old John Charles was out hunting with a group of men, including his friend Algernon Coote. During the course of the day, Coote's father, a committed Christian, heard Ryle swearing, and rebuked him for his inappropriate language. Ryle never swore again, but he did develop a life-long friendship with Algernon and received spiritual blessing amidst the godly Coote family. Ryle said of his friend: "He was the first person who ever told me to think, repent and pray." Although he did not become a Christian at that time in his life, he became aware that his own standard of life did not measure up to that of the Christians he knew. Thus, the foundations were being laid for the Master's call.

Shortly before he was to take his final exams in school, he developed a serious illness in his lungs. He was frightened and began to read the Bible and pray. The Lord heard his prayers and he was able to complete his exams. To this he credits his "time with God." But his illness gave him time to think and reflect on life, death, and religion. He came to realize that this Jesus he read about was not part of his life, and he wanted to know more.

So one Sunday afternoon in 1837, he went to a service in one of the parish churches. He remembered nothing particular about it, not even the sermon or the man who delivered it. But his soul was awakened when he heard read the passage from Ephesians, chapter two. When the eighth verse was reached, the reader laid emphasis on it with a short pause between each phrase. *"By grace are ye saved—through faith—and that not of yourselves—it is the gift of God."*

Reflecting on his conversion, Ryle said, "Nothing to this day appeared to me so clear and distinct as my own sinfulness, Christ's preciousness, the value of the Bible, the absolute necessity of coming out of the world, the need of being born again, and the folly of the doctrine of baptismal regeneration."

Even though J.C. Ryle was raised in a nominal Christian home, he once believed that Christianity must be one of the most disagreeable occupations on Earth—or in Heaven.

After the collapse of his family's fortune in 1841, Ryle applied himself to Christian service and was ordained a minister in

J. C. Ryle is known as one of the most practical writers of Christian truth. Though dead he still speaks with poignant accuracy to the heart and mind of any who dare to read his books. The reader cannot help but be affected by Mr. Ryle's candid, yet urgent appeal to holy living.

the Church of England. After thirty-nine years as rector, he was ordained Bishop of Liverpool in 1880. He was affectionately known as "the working man's bishop." And as a bishop he adopted one single text for his official work; *"Thy word is truth"* (John 17:17).

During his fifty-nine-year ministry, he remained in the Church of England, but opposed, and exposed in his writings, many of the errors of doctrine and life that crept into the Church.

Commenting on his very deliberate writing style, he said, "In form and composition, I frankly avow that I have studied as far as possible to be plain and pointed and to choose what an old divine calls 'picked and packed words.' I have tried to place myself in the position of one who is reading aloud to others." He credits Thomas Guthrie, the Scot; John Bright, the Quaker orator; John Bunyan, Puritan and author of *Pilgrim's Progress;* Matthew Henry, the great biblical commentator; and William Shakespeare, of course, as influences on his pen.

J. C. Ryle was a theological giant. He never suffered from what he called a "boneless, nerveless, jellyfish condition of soul." His convictions were not negotiable, though he demonstrated a pleasant demeanor and a teachable spirit. Indeed, his successor described him as "that man of granite." Charles Spurgeon said he was "an evangelical champion...One of the bravest and best of men." Ryle simply observed, "What is won dearly is priced highly and clung to firmly." And his fortitude was not limited to doctrinal matters. His godly character is displayed not only in what he wrote, but how he lived and ministered to the people of God.

As so many eminent Christians before him, such as Huss, Luther, and Calvin, the discovery of justification of faith had a profound effect upon Ryle's heart. By the mighty hand of God, he had become a Christian, and would unreservedly uphold reformed principles his entire life.

J. C. Ryle died in 1900 at age eighty-three. At his funeral, "The graveyard was crowded with poor people who had come in carts and vans and buses to pay their last honors to the old man who had certainly won their love." Canon Hobson, speaking in Ryle's memorial sermon, said, "Few men in the nineteenth century did so much for God, for truth and for righteousness among the English-speaking race, and in the world, as our late Bishop."

From his conversion to his burial, J. C. Ryle was immersed in the holy Scriptures. "It is still the first book," he said, "which fits the child's mind when he begins to learn religion, and the last to which the old man clings as he leaves the world."

Key Writings of Ryle: 1. *Assurance* (1850); 2. *Home Truths,* Series 1-7 (1850-59); 3. *The Young Man's Christian Year* (1853); 4. *Startling Questions* (1853); 5. *The Priest, Puritan and Preacher* (1855); 6. *Plain Speaking* (1855); 7. *Spiritual Songs* (1855); 8. *Expository Thoughts on the Gospels,* 7 vols. (1856-59); 9. *Only One Way of Salvation* (1860); 10. *Hymns for the Church on Earth* (1864); 11. *Coming Events and Present Duties* (1867); 12. *Bishops and Clergy of Other Days* (1868); 13. *Christian Leaders of the Last Century* (1868); 14. *The Two Bears, and Other Stories for Children* (1868); 15. *Knots Untied* (1874); 16. *Old Paths* (1875); 17. *Holiness; Practical Religion* (1878); 18. *Light From Old Times: or Protestant Facts And Men* (1890); 19. *Thoughts for Young Men* (1886); 20. *Duties of Parents* (1880); 21. *A Call to Prayer*

Worth Reading: *Walking With God* (condensed from *Practical Religion*)

Elizabeth Prentiss *1818-1878*

Daughter of Consolation

Daughter of the eminent Edward "Praying" Payson, Elizabeth Prentiss carried her father's torch of exemplary godliness and effective ministry amidst the fiercest trials of pain, suffering, and sorrow. To this day her writings are among the most cherished by members of the Christian family. Parents and children alike have been blessed for generations.

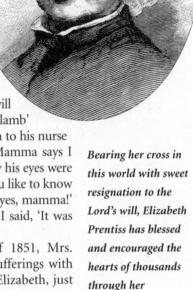

 knelt by the side of the cradle, rocking it very gently, and he asked me to tell him a story. I asked what about, and he said, 'A little boy,' on which I said something like this: 'Mamma knows a dear little boy who was very sick. His head ached and he felt sick all over. God said, I must let that little lamb come into my fold then his head will never ache again, and he will be a very happy little lamb.' I used the words 'little lamb' because he was so fond of them. Often he would run to his nurse with his face full of animation and say, 'Marget! Mamma says I am her little lamb!' While I was telling him this story his eyes were fixed intelligently on my face. I then said, 'Would you like to know the name of this boy?' With eagerness he said, 'Yes, yes, mamma!' Taking his dear little hand in mine, and kissing it, I said, 'It was Eddy.'" (Excerpt from *Stepping Heavenward*.)

During early motherhood, in the winter of 1851, Mrs. Prentiss entered into the fellowship of Christ's sufferings with the loss of two children. Edward, age three, and Elizabeth, just one month old. Though the anguish of this mother's heart was great, these times of affliction wrought a deep impression upon her perspective of life and death, so that she could say, "It is well with my child." In her writings, the ministry of this "daughter of consolation" continues to bless generations of God's people.

Elizabeth Prentiss was the fifth of eight children blessed to Reverend and Mrs. Edward Payson ("Praying Payson") of Portland, Maine. Like her father she experienced long seasons of physical illness and suffering which she battled against all her days. This "thorn"gave her wonderful insight into the blessedness of trials in the lives of God's people, which she shared in so many ways in her life and especially in her writings.

Elizabeth carried a special affection her father, who died at age forty-five after sundry afflictions. Once, when just four years old, she found him prostrate on his study floor, lost in prayer. The remembrance of this scene influenced her ever since. Her youthful character was one of brightness and enthusiasm combined with deep sympathy. Her father once commented that

Bearing her cross in this world with sweet resignation to the Lord's will, Elizabeth Prentiss has blessed and encouraged the hearts of thousands through her precious, Christ-centered writings.

"she will be in danger of marrying a blind man, or helpless cripple, out of pure sympathy."

At age sixteen, she began her literary career as a regular contributor to *The Youth's Companion* magazine. All of her contributions were later collected and published as a book, *Only a Dandelion*.

In her twenty-first year Elizabeth Payson passed through a period of deep spiritual experience, or rather "harrowing exercises of soul," which resulted in an ultimate firmness of faith which made clear to others as well as to herself the "need-be" for the trial. Bunyan's "Slough of Despond" would never be forgotten by her. The Holy Spirit was opening her eyes to see "the exceeding breadth" of the divine law, which is "holy, just, and good." She writes at this time: "I felt so guilty, and the character of God appeared so perfect in its purity and holiness, that I knew not which way to turn."

In September, 1840, she became a teacher in a boarding school for girls in Richmond, Virginia. The discipline of school life to one who was so often a sufferer must have tried her greatly, but her Christian experience was surely deepened. Her aspiration was ever: "Oh, that we might be enabled to go onward day by day, and upward too!" When writing of the battle with "irritability and pride," she says, "I have felt my pride tugging with all its might to kindle a great fire when some unexpected trial has caught me off my guard," she then adds: "I am persuaded that real meekness dwells deep within the heart, and that it is only to be gained by communion with our Savior, who, when He was reviled, reviled not again."

In 1845, Miss Payson was married to the Reverend George Lewis Prentiss. Her husband's parish was in New Bedford, Massachusetts, and in it she found her chief interest and joy. "I only hope," she writes, "I shall enter soberly and thankfully on my new life, expecting sunshine and rain, drought and plenty, heat and cold, and adapting myself to alternations contentedly." The union of wedded love consecrated Mrs. Prentiss to a new mission. If she had never given a printed line to the world, her labors as a pastor's wife would have entitled her to honorable mention among the representative women of Christendom. Her husband's parish was filled with "our people." Elizabeth Prentiss possessed a great, warm heart, ready sympathies, a love for little children which always led them into her arms, and a great efficiency as nurse and housewife. Elizabeth firmly loved the household of faith and exuded tender sympathy for the irreligious. These qualities along with a genuine womanliness and tact that never failed her, fitted and endowed her royally for the position in which her marriage placed her. With gain of years and confidence in her own talents she became a leader in church enterprises. Her Bible readings before large female audiences won plaudits from those best qualified to be judges of such

I am sure that He who has so sorely afflicted you accepts the patience with which you bear the rod, and that when this first terrible amazement and bewilderment are over, and you can enter into communion and fellowship with Him, you will find a joy in Him, that, hard as it is to the flesh to say so, transcends all the sweetest and best joys of human life. You will have nothing to do now but to fly to Him.
—Thoughts Concerning the King, by E. Prentiss

exercises.

"I was impressed," says an eminent clergyman, "with her ability to combine rarest beauty and highest spirituality of thought with the uttermost simplicity of language and the plainest illustrations. Her conversation was like the mystic ladder which was 'set up on the earth, and the top of it reached to Heaven.'"

In 1846, her first child, Una, was born. Two years later, Edward, came into the nursery, bringing much delight to the domestic scene. But in late 1851, the dark cloud of death swept fast upon the household, as first little Eddy, and then baby Elizabeth left this world for heaven above. Of baby Elizabeth she says, "I had her in my arms only twice. Once, the day before she died; and once while she was dying. I never saw her little feet." A scrap of paper was found among her manuscripts entitled:

"My Nursery, 1852."
"I thought that prattling boys and girls
Would fill this empty room;
That my rich heart would gather flowers
From childhood's opening bloom.
One child and two green graves are mine,
This is God's gift to me;
A bleeding, fainting, broken heart—
This is my gift to Thee."

In 1854, *The Flower of the Family* was published. It had a cordial welcome in America, and was issued in France as *La Fleur de Famille*, and in Germany as *Die Perle der Familie*.

From this time her pen was seldom idle and the prosperity of her books grew, but she confessed to a friend:

"I long to have it do good. I never had such desires about anything in my life, and I never sat down to write without first praying that I might not be suffered to write anything that would do harm, and that, on the contrary, I might be taught to say what would do good. And it has been a great comfort to me that every word of praise I ever have received from others concerning it has been: 'It will do good.' This I have had from so many sources that, amid much trial and sickness ever since its publication, I have had rays of sunshine creeping in, now and then, to cheer and sustain me."

Her most prominent work, by far, is *Stepping Heavenward*, which was written in 1869. "Every word of that book was a prayer, and seemed to come of itself," she tells us. No doubt, it is an angel of mercy to thousands of homes; balm and benediction to hundreds of thousands of Christian women. The story of Katy's loves and mistakes, her aspirations and her despairs, her frolics and her bereavements; of her steady progress in the way that grew less steep as she learned to walk, and not run, toward the brightening and widening horizon, was read with tears and laughter. Sobbed thanksgivings for strength received by weary

"I was impressed," says an eminent clergyman, "with her ability to combine rarest beauty and highest spirituality of thought with the uttermost simplicity of language and the plainest illustrations. Her conversation was like the mystic ladder which was set up on the earth, and the top of it reached to Heaven."

hearts through the practical spirituality of its teachings."

In the *Life and Letters of Elizabeth Prentiss,* her husband George summarized the effect of her books: "Thus eminently fitted for her office of consoler, she exercised it, not only through her books, but also through her personal ministries in those large and widening circles which centered in her literary and pastoral life. Those who were favored with her friendship in times of sorrow found her a comforter indeed. Her letters, of which she was prodigal, were to many sore hearts as leaves from the tree of life. She did not expect too much of a sufferer. She recognized human weakness as well as Divine strength. But in all her attempts at consolation, side by side with her deep and true sympathy went the lesson of the harvest of sorrow."

In the last year of her life, Elizabeth was well aware that she was soon to be taken from this world, but "her magnetic influence held all hearts in breathless attention." At the close of her days she alluded to the trials of life and the shortness of them in light of eternity. "We are all passing away, one after another. And we should not allow ourselves to be troubled, lest when our time comes we may be afraid to die. Dying grace is not usually given until it is needed. Death to the disciple of Jesus is only stepping from one room to another and a far better room in our Father's house. And how little all the sorrows of the way will seem to us when we get to our home above!"

"As the end drew near," recalls her husband, "we all knelt together, and my old friend Dr. Poor commended the departing spirit to God, and invoked for us, who were about to be so heavily bereaved, the solace and support of the Blessed Comforter. The breathing at length became gentle, almost like that of one asleep, and her distressed look changed into a look of sweet repose."

At her graveside, her own sweet hymn, written from a bereaved heart, "More Love, O Christ, to Thee," was sung to the glory of Christ, with whom she now enjoys eternal fellowship.

"Dying grace is not usually given until it is needed. Death to the disciple of Jesus is only stepping from one room to another and a far better room in our Father's house. And how little all the sorrows of the way will seem to us when we get to our home above!"

—Elizabeth Prentiss

Key Writings of Prentiss: 1. *Little Suzy's Six Birthdays* (1853); 2. *Only a Dandelion, and Other Stories* (1854); 3. *Henry and Bessie; or, What They Did in the Country* (1855); 4. *Little Suzy's Six Teachers* (1856); 5. *Little Suzy's Little Servant's* (1856); 6. *The Flower of the Family* (1856); 7. *Peterchen and Gretchen* (1860); 8. *The Little Preacher* (1867); 9. *Little Threads; or Tangle Thread, Silver Thread, and Golden Tread* (1868); 10. *Little Lou's Sayings and Doings* (1868); 11. *Fred, Maria, and Me* (1868); 12. *The Old Brown Pitcher* (1868); 13. *Stepping Heavenward* (1869); 14. *Nidworth and His Three Magic Wands* (1869); 15. *The Percys* (1870); *The Story Lizzie Told* (1870); 17. *The Six Little Princesses and What They Turned Into* (1871); 18. *Aunt Jane's Hero* (1871); 19. *Golden Hours: Hymns and Songs for Christian Life* (1873); 20. *Urbane and His Friends* (1874); 21. *Griselda* (1876); 22. *The Home at Greylock* (1876); 23. *Pemaquid: A Story of Old Times in New England* (1877); 24. *Gentleman Jim* (1878); 25. *Avis Benson; or Mine and Thine, with Other Sketches* (1879); 26. *Thoughts Concerning the King* (1890, published by her husband after her death).

Worth Reading: *The Life and Letters of Elizabeth Prentiss,* by George L. Prentiss (1882); *Our Famous Women* (1883).

"Fanny" Crosby 1820-1915
Blind Christian Hymn Writer

Though blind from infancy, Fanny Crosby became the most prolific Christian hymn-writer in the history of the Church. She witnessed over 8,000 of her poems set to music and over 100,000,000 copies of her songs printed. Many different pen names were attributed to her works by hymn book publishers so the public wouldn't know she wrote so many of them. She produced as many as seven hymns or poems in one day. On several occasions, upon hearing an unfamiliar hymn sung, she would inquire about the author, and find it to be one of her own!

rancis Jane Crosby was born in a one-story cottage into a family of strong Puritan ancestry in upstate New York. When Fanny was six weeks old, she caught a slight cold in her eyes. The family physician was away, so another country doctor was called in to treat her. He prescribed a hot mustard compress to be applied to her eyes. The infection did clear up, but scars formed on her eyes, and the baby girl became blind for life. A few months later, Fanny's father became ill and died. Mercy Crosby, widowed at age twenty-one, hired herself out as a maid to support the family, while Grandmother Eunice Crosby took care of little Fanny.

Fanny never felt any bitterness, but believed her blindness was permitted by the Lord to fulfill His plan for her life. As a young girl she was once asked by her mother if she resented being blind, and she repied, "Mother, if I had a choice, I would still choose to remain blind...for when I die, the first face I will ever see will be the face of my blessed Savior."

A wise mother set about immediately to prepare her daughter for a happy life, in spite of this great handicap. When only five years old she was taken by her mother to consult the best eye specialist in the country, Dr. Valentine Mott. Neighbors and friends pooled money together in order to send her. But, the dreaded answer came, "Poor child, I am afraid you will never see again." Fanny did not think she was poor. It was not the loss of sight that bothered her young heart. It was the thought that she would never be able to get an education like other boys and girls.

Grandmother's careful teaching helped develop Fanny's descriptive abilities. By becoming the little girl's eyes she vividly described the world around her. But grandmother also nurtured Fanny's spirit. She read and carefully explained the Bible to her, and she always emphasized the importance of prayer. When Fanny became depressed because she couldn't learn and play as other children, her grandmother taught her to pray to God for knowledge.

A stack of twenty hymnals together could hardly contain the number of Christian hymns written by Fanny Crosby in her lifetime! Though many have been forgotten today, a large number still remain favorites of Christians all over the world.

Fanny began to devour the Scriptures. It is said that as a child, she could repeat from memory the Pentateuch, the Book of Ruth, many of the Psalms, the books of Proverbs, Song of Solomon, and much of the New Testament! This furnished the themes, inspiration, and words for her imperishable gospel hymns.

In 1843, she was invited to recite some of her poetry before the U. S. Congress. She delivered no stirring oration, but simply recited some poems about the tender care of a loving Savior, bringing to tears many in the assembly.

When Henry Clay visited the school, Miss Crosby was elected to recite a poem in his honor. When she had finished, Clay took her by the hand and said, "This is not the only poem for which I am indebted to this lady. Six months ago, she sent me some lines on the death of my dear son." Young Clay was killed in a battle in Mexico. Standing there, the great statesman and the blind poet wept together.

Fanny married her lifelong love, Alexander Van Alstyne, who was also blind. He was especially fond of music and was captivated by her poetry. They enjoyed a happy marriage until his death in 1902.

She was forty-four years old when her hymn writing career officially began. Under the encouragement and assignment of the famous composer William Bradbury, she wrote her first hymn for a prison service, "Lord, Please Don't Pass Me By." In her own day, the evangelistic team of Dwight L. Moody and Ira D. Sankey effectively brought Fanny Crosby's hymns to the masses. The great crowds who thronged the Moody-Sankey revivals sang her songs until they became part of the heritage of that generation.

"Safe in the Arms of Jesus" was considered by some to be her greatest hymn. When Bishop James Hannington was brutally murdered in Uganda, Africa, his diary was recovered. In it, he tells of being dragged away to be murdered while singing *Safe in the Arms of Jesus.*

Many of her hymns, "Blessed Assurance," "All the Way My Savior Leads Me," "To God Be the Glory," among others, continue to draw souls to their Savior for both salvation and comfort, and have blessed Christian congregations and family firesides for almost 150 years!

At age ninety she declared, "My love for the Holy Bible and its sacred truth is stronger and more precious to me at ninety than at nineteen." Asked about her long years, she said her secret was that she guarded her taste, her temper, and her tongue. Fanny's famous saying through the years was, "Don't waste any sympathy on me. I am the happiest person living." Though her hymn writing declined in later years, Fanny was active in speaking engagements and missionary work among America's urban poor almost until the day of her death in 1915. She sought to bring others to her Savior not only through her hymns but through her personal life as well. What happened when Fanny died? Perhaps one of her later hymns tells it best:

> *When my lifework is ended and I cross the swelling tide,*
> *When the bright and glorious morning I shall see,*
> *I shall know my Redeemer when I reach the other side,*
> *And His smile will be the first to welcome me.*

Worth Reading: *Fanny J. Crosby: An Autobiography; Fanny Crosby,* by Bernard *Ruffin (1976); Fanny Crosby: A Woman of Faith,* by George Rice (1991).

Charles Spurgeon 1834-1892
The Prince of Preachers

Within just a few years of becoming the pastor of New Park Street Church in London, Charles Haddon Spurgeon became recognized as one of the greatest of preachers. Though he preached to thousands each Sunday, his beneficent activity included authoring dozens of books, establishing of a Pastor's College, and the creation of orphanages; all in the name of his Savior, Jesus Christ.

The Reverend Richard Knill, a saintly man, had come to preach at Stambourne at the invitation of Reverend John Spurgeon. His heart was easily knit to children, and when he heard the young grandchild of his host, Charles, read the Bible with charming emphasis, his heart went out to the boy, and an agreement was made that they should go around the garden together on the following morning before breakfast. They talked together much of Christ and of His service, and they knelt together in the great arbor, and Pastor Knill poured out a vibrant and earnest intercessory prayer on behalf of his young friend. Before he left the manse, Mr. Knill uttered a remarkable prophecy destined to be literally fulfilled. He called the family together, drew the child to his knee and said, "I do not know how, but I feel a solemn presentiment that this child will preach the Gospel to thousands, and God will bless him to many souls. So sure am I of this, that when my little man preaches in Rowland Hill's [Surrey Music Hall] Chapel, as he will do one day, I should like him to promise me that he will give out the hymn commencing—

'God moves in a mysterious way, His wonders to perform.'"

In 1856, Pastor Knill's declaration was fulfilled, and the hymn was afterwards sung on Mr. Spurgeon's first visit to the Chapel, and again when he preached in Mr. Hill's first pulpit at Wootton-under-Edge. Since then, Charles Haddon Spurgeon has become well known in all evangelical circles, and he is recognized by many as "the Prince of Preachers."

Charles was born at Kelveton on June 19, 1834. The Spurgeon family belonged to the Nonconformists, under whose faithful teaching they were raised. His grandfather and father were both faithful Independent ministers, but it is well said that much of his success may be attributed to the influence of his mother's prayers. They are referred to in at least one amusing passage of arms between mother and son, in which she said; "Ah, Charlie,

The world has come to know Charles Spurgeon as the "Prince of Preachers," but he was also a gifted teacher, counselor, author, and philanthropist. More than any other individual of his time, he revived a sybaritic English society into God-fearing, Christ-serving people.

211

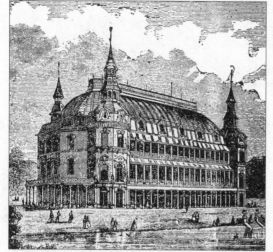

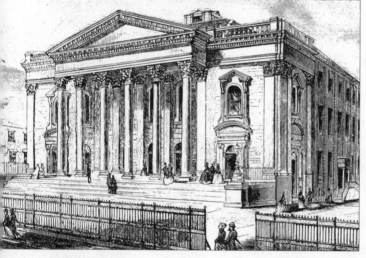

(top) Surrey Music Hall, where Spurgeon first preached held 14,000 people. (bottom) Metropolitan Tabernacle held over 8,000 worshippers each Lord's Day. Spurgeon was pastor there from 1864 until his death in 1892.

I have often prayed that you might be saved, but never that you should become a Baptist." To which he replied, "God has answered your prayer, mother, with His usual bounty, and given you more than you asked." Thrift, self-denial, contentment with a frugal lot, the touch of quaint humor, and godly training were among the earliest impressions which the Spurgeon family of ten children received in that quiet home at Kelveton.

John Spurgeon was very devoted to his grandson, Charlie, and the two had a remarkable relationship. "It was his custom to allow him to read the Scriptures at family worship, and strangers who were occasionally present were moved to remark on the unerring correctness with which the youthful reader went through the exercise."

Charles was remarkable also for his force of character and precocity. "When he was six years old he overheard his grandfather deploring the habits of one of his flock, who was accustomed to go to a public-house for a mug of beer and a quiet pipe. Little Charles said, 'I will kill him!' and shortly afterwards told his grandfather that he had done the deed. 'I've killed old Rhodes. He will never grieve my poor grandfather any more.' 'What do you mean, my child?' asked the minister. 'I have not been doing any harm, grandfather,' was the reply, 'I've been about the Lord's work, that is all!' The mystery was eventually explained by old Rhodes himself. He told Mr. Spurgeon that the lad had come to him in the public-house and said to him: 'What doest thou here, Elijah? Sitting with the ungodly, you a member of a church, and break your pastor's heart! I'm ashamed of you! I would not break my pastor's heart, I am sure.' Old Rhodes was angry for a moment, but came to the conclusion that the child was in the right, and went no more to the tap-room."

212

As a teenager, Spurgeon yearned to know the way of salvation and here records the circumstances of his conversion: "At last, one snowy day, I was obliged to stop on the road, and it was a blessed stop to me,—I found rather an obscure street, and turned down a court, and there was a little chapel. It was the Primitive Methodist Chapel. I had heard of these people from many, and how they sang so loudly that they made people's heads ache; but that did not matter. I wanted to know how I might be saved, and if they made my head ache ever so much I did not care. So, sitting down, the service went on, but no minister came. At last a very thin-looking man came into the pulpit and opened his Bible, and read these words, 'Look unto Me, and be ye saved, all the ends of the earth.' Just setting his eyes upon me, as if he knew my heart, he said, 'Young man, you are in trouble.' Well, I was, sure enough. He said, 'You will never get out of it unless you look to Christ.' And then lifting up his hands, he cried out, as only I think a Primitive Methodist could do, "Look, look, look!" 'It is only look,' he said. I saw at once the way of salvation. Oh, how I did leap for joy at that moment! I know not what else he said: I did not take much notice of it,—I was so possessed with that one thought. I had been waiting to do fifty things, but when I heard this word, 'Look,'—what a charming word it seemed to me! Oh, I looked until I could almost have looked my eyes away, and in heaven I will look on still in my joy unutterable." And he adds, "I now think I am bound never to preach a sermon without preaching to sinners. I do think that a minister who can preach a sermon without addressing sinners does not know how to preach."

In 1852, when he was eighteen years old, Charles received an invitation to become minister of the little church at Waterbeach, near Cambridge, to which he looked back afterwards as his "Garden of Eden." The congregation soon crowded the old thatched chapel to its utmost extent, and as the result of his ministry, a great revival broke out and spread throughout the neighborhood. The poor people became devotedly attached to him, and the boy-preacher was in great demand for conducting special services in all parts of the county.

In 1853, Spurgeon took the call to minister at the famous New Park Street Chapel. His first sermon was attended by only 200 people, but the good news spread and within a very short

> *"The old truth that Calvin preached, that Augustine preached, that Paul preached, is the truth that I must preach today, or else be false to my conscience and my God. I cannot shape the truth. I know of no such thing as paring off the rough edges of a doctrine. John Knox's gospel is my gospel. That which thundered through Scotland must now thunder through England."*
>
> —*C. H. Spurgeon*

One of the schoolrooms of the Stockwell Orphanage.

time the walls could barely contain the throngs that gathered to hear the Word of God from the mouth of the gifted young preacher. All who heard him united in eulogium of that wonderful voice, so full and sweet and musical, as to awaken a response in every soul that could be touched by sound. That voice withstood nearly forty years of incessant use with very little loss to either its music or its power.

Within a year, the Chapel became inadequate to house the large congregation gathered to hear Spurgeon, and the deacons therefore moved the church to the Surrey Music Hall which housed over 10,000.

In 1856, Mr. Spurgeon married Miss Susanna Thompson, daughter of Mr. Robert Thompson, of Falcon Square, London. She became a most loving and devoted helpmeet. Mr. Spurgeon's home life was ideal. No one could be an hour under his roof without perceiving the fragrance of domestic affection that pervaded the house.

Spurgeon's vision to have a permanent place of worship was begun in 1856, and after three years or labor and prayer, the Metropolitan Tabernacle was completed. It is a noble edifice, and from the commencement of his ministry until his death multitudes thronged, aisles, passages, doorways, often amounting to 5,500 or even 6,000 people.

The sanctuary of the Metropolitan Tabernacle was filled with over 8,000 worshippers each Lord's Day.

It was the spirit-attended enunciation of the simple gospel of the grace of God, together with the clearness of style and freshness of thought, that gave his sermons the power they had.

Time would fail to tell of the impact Spurgeon had on every institution and agency he founded, besides the church. In 1864, he founded the Pastor's College for training men for the ministry, which could maintain eighty men at a time. He also opened the Stockwell Orphanage for boys and girls in 1867. The greatness of this effort, which provided for the education of more than five hundred orphans, received the commendation even of those hostile to the Christian faith. In addition, his Book Fund supplied the needs of multitudes of pastors. In these philanthropic agencies we have the outworking of Spurgeon's belief in the close connection between the doctrines of grace and good works.

As an author, Spurgeon was as prolific and gifted as he was in the pulpit. He spent significant hours rewriting his sermons for publication in his magazine *The Sword and the Trowel,* to which now more than 1,900 messages are in print! His first book was *Saint and His Saviour.* He spent twenty years on his *Treasury of David,* which is arguably his finest writing. He is also well known for his *Morning and Evening* devotional, *John Plougman* series, *Lectures to My Students,* and *Feathers for Arrows.* Some of his books will last as long as the English language, and be of constant interest and value. They are distinguished by the clearness of their style; their terse proverbs; their sparkling epigrams; their homely references; and their clear evangelical teaching. Christl Christl It was always Christ; and eternity alone will reveal the millions of souls that have been quickened, directed, saved, by the words of one whom they were never privileged to see or hear. He himself says of his published sermons: "It is a great trial to be unable to preach in the pulpit, but it is no small comfort to be able to preach through the press."

Charles' parents,
John and Susie Spurgeon

His Puritan convictions and Reformed conservatism brought him to sever any connection with the Baptist Union, whose more liberal view of the Scriptures carried much grief to his soul in latter years.

For years he had suffered the ravages of a troublesome disease aggravated by his incessant labors. In the summer of 1891, he became dangerously ill, and for weeks lay at the door of death. All the nation watched around that sick couch. Royalty telegraphed for the last bulletin, the highest ecclesiastics called at his house; daily prayer-meetings, thronged with people, were held at the Tabernacle for his recovery; and his health was a daily item in the newspaper. He regained sufficient health to travel with his wife to the sunny shores of the Mediterranean, where for twenty years he had recruited his exhausted energies by one or two months' journey, and he at his old quarters in the hotel de Beau Rivage, where he was accustomed to occupy a little bed-room, with its single iron bed and simple furniture. It seemed as though he was going to recover during his last affliction, but all hopes were dashed with disappointment as tidings came of the recurrence of the disease. On Sunday, January 31, 1892, he gently "fell asleep, and was gathered to his fathers."

"Let me briefly tell once more the old, old story of Jesus and His love. Jesus Christ died in the stead of sinners. We deserved to be punished for our sins. Under the law of Moses there was no pardon for sin except through the blood of a sacrifice. Jesus Christ, the Son of God, is the one Sacrifice for sins forever, of which the thousands of lambs slain under the law were but types. Every man who trusts to the death of the Lamb of God, may know that Jesus Christ was punished in his stead; so that God can be just, and yet forgive the guilty. He can, without violating His justice, remit sin and pardon iniquity, because a Substitute has been found, whose death has an infinite value because of the Divine nature of the Sufferer. He has born the iniquities of all who trust Him. 'He that believeth on the Son hath everlasting life,'" wrote Spurgeon, shortly before his death.

So the "prince of preachers" passed away, leaving a gap not only among his own people, but throughout all of Christianity, which it will be hard, if not impossible, to fill. As long as the English tongue is spoken, among the most treasured of its names will be that of the Essex boy, who bore for fifty-seven years, unblemished and unstained, the name of Charles Haddon Spurgeon.

> "If ministers of the gospel, instead of giving lectures, and devoting so much time to literary and political pursuits, would preach the Word of God, and preach it as if they were pleading for their own lives, ah, then my brethren, we might expect better success."
> —C. H. Spurgeon

Key Writings of Spurgeon: 1. *The Metropolitan Tabernacle Pulpit,* (49 vols., 1856-1904); 2. *The Saint and his Saviour* (1857); 3. *Morning by Morning; or Daily Readings for the Family or the Closet* (1866); 4. *Evening by Evening* (1868); 5. *John Ploughman's Talk* (1869); 6. *John Ploughman's Pictures* (1880); 7. *Our Own Hymn Book* (1866); 8. *Treasury of David, an Exposition of the Psalms* (1865-1855); 9. *Lectures to My Students;* 10. *Sermon Illustrations;* 11. *Feathers for Arrows.*

Worth Reading: *The Life and Works of Rev. Charles H. Spurgeon* (1892 Memorial Edition); *Morning and Evening Devotional; Salt Cellars.*

Dwight L. Moody *1837-1899*
Founder of Modern Evangelism

"Not by might, nor by power, but by my Spirit, saith the Lord," was a common phrase from Reverend Moody as he opened his revival meetings. His brokenness for the lost and his deep love for his Savior, were the driving forces behind the passion and power of this blessed man of God, who, together with his friend and co-laborer, Ira D. Sankey, spread the gospel across two continents and effected the conversion of thousands.

A dying Sunday school teacher had to return east because of his health but was greatly concerned about the salvation of the girls in his class. Moody rented a carriage for himself and the teacher and went to each girl's home to share the love of Jesus, winning them all to Christ. The next night the girls gathered together for a farewell prayer meeting to pray for their sick teacher. This so moved Moody that soul-winning seemed to be the only important thing for him to do from then on. He made a vow to tell at least one person about the Savior each day, even though it sometimes meant getting up out of bed in the middle of the night! He became the first evangelist since George Whitefield to move two continents for Christ.

Born on a small New England farm, Dwight Lyman Moody was the seventh of nine children. He was only four when his father, Edwin, died suddenly at age forty-one, leaving his mother, Betsy a widow at only thirty-six. Their uncle, the local Unitarian pastor came to their aid at this time of great need.

On his seventeenth birthday (1854), Dwight Moody went to Boston to seek employment. He became a clerk in his uncle's retail store. His manner was rough and his temper short. One of his uncle's requirements was Dwight's attendance each Sunday at the Mount Vernon Congregational Church, pastored by Edward Kirk. Moody would often sleep in the upper pews, but one day one of the deacons discovered him in slumber and abruptly awakened him to pay attention. As he listened he heard Pastor Kirk's sermon as though he was speaking directly to his own sad condition. From then on he grew more sensitive to spiritual things.

In 1856, he moved to Chicago and went to work for his Uncle Calvin. He joined the Plymouth Congregational Church. He rented four pews there to provide lonely boys like himself a place of worship. He then joined a missions-minded group at the First Methodist Church, visiting and distributing tracts at hotels and boarding houses. He loved to see the faces of the lost light up when he shared the good news of the gospel.

In the fall of 1858, he started his own Sunday school in an

Moody traveled in Europe and America, holding revival campaigns, and personally speaking with over 750,000 individuals. He preached to more than 100,000,000 people, and saw over 1,000,000 converted to Jesus Christ.

abandoned freight car, then moved to an old vacant saloon on Michigan Street. A visiting preacher reported his favorable impressions...watching Moody trying to light the building with a candle in one hand, a Bible in the other, and a child on his knee teaching him about Jesus.

It was in June, 1860, that Moody decided to abandon secular employment and go into the Lord's work full time.

In 1861, Moody became a city missionary for the Y.M.C.A., to which he commented that he "was more indebted to this organization for his success as an evangelist than any other organized means of grace." Throughout his life, he gave much of his service and time to the Y.M.C.A. His missionary work among Chicago's youth became so well known that he was in demand as a speaker at various conventions throughout American cities.

Luther gave us the Reformation, Wesley gave us a Church on every corner, and Moody gave us the Young Men's Christian Association.

He married Emma Charlotte Revell on August 28, 1862, when he was twenty-five, and she was only nineteen. The Lord blessed them with three children, Emma (1864), William Revell (1869), and Paul Dwight (1879). His wife shared in his passion for evangelism and proved to be a wonderful helpmeet to him in all aspects of his ministry.

With the advent of the Civil War, Moody found himself doing personal work among the soldiers. He was on battlefields on nine occasions serving with the U.S. Christian Commission.

Ira D. Sankey, friend and co-laborer with Moody.

Back and forth, between Chicago and the various camps and battlefields, with tireless vigor and jubilant faith he toiled and traveled during the four terrible years of war. In large measure, through the work of the Christian Commission, the battlefields were transformed from four great harvests of death into four great harvests of souls for the garner of the Lord of the harvest. Wave after wave of patriotism and Christian devotion swept over the land, while love of country and love of Christ were mingled so that it became hard to distinguish where one ended and the other began.

In 1867, primarily due to his wife's asthma, the couple went to England. He was eager to meet C. H. Spurgeon and George Mueller. Moody traveled to Scotland as well. The Chicago Y.M.C.A. was moving ahead rapidly, as Moody rose to its presidency from 1866 to 1869. He had a part in erecting the first Y.M.C.A. building in America when he supervised the building of Farwell Hall in 1867, seating 3,000.

In 1870, the great evangelism team of Moody-Sankey was formed. The preacher and the singer met for the first time while attending a YMCA convention in Indianapolis. When Moody first heard the melodious voice of Ira Sankey praising Jesus with the hymn, "There Is a Fountain Filled with Blood," his heart was "filled with joy." He was over-whelmed with the heart and passion of this gospel singer, who quickly became a kindred spirit. Moody invited Sankey to join him in the work of evangelism, setting the pattern for a twenty-nine-year ministry that reached hundreds of thousands of people around the world.

On Sunday night, October 8, 1871, while preaching at Farwell Hall, which was being used because of the increased crowds, Moody asked those present to evaluate their relationships to Christ and

Moody preaching in England.

return next week to make a committment to Him. That crowd never regathered. While Sankey was singing a closing song, the din of fire trucks and church bells scattered them all, for Chicago was on fire. The Y.M.C.A. building, church, and parsonage were all to be lost in the next twenty-four hours. But the earlier words of Moody clung to the hearts of the people, and the Holy Spirit moved many to rebuild the building and the ministry.

Being invited to Scotland to preach, the evangelists began in Edinburgh on November 23. For hundreds of years only psalms had been sung there with no musical instruments. Now Sankey began "singing the gospel" and crowds packed out the 2,000-seat auditorium. The Christian Convention, now so familiar as one of Mr. Moody's methods of work, was tried in Edinburgh with wonderful success. In thousands of Christian households the deepest interest was felt by parents for their children, and by masters and mistresses for their servants; and so universal was this, that Dr. Horatius Bonar declares his belief "that there was scarcely a Christian household in all Edinburgh in which there were not one or more persons converted during this revival."

Moody's first city-wide crusade in America was in Brooklyn beginning October 31, 1875, at the Clermont Avenue Rink, seating 7,000. Only non-church members could get admission tickets since 12,000 to 20,000 people were turned away.

After a summer of rest in 1876, Moody and Sankey, along with a considerable number of trained gospel workers began the Chicago revival campaign. By the end of the campain it was estimated that over 6,000 people committed their lives to Christ.

They also conducted numerous Christian Conventions in Boston, Philadelphia, Buffalo, Atlanta, Chicago, Kansas City, and Manhattan over the next twenty years; in addition to his revivals in Europe—experiencing similar results which brought thousands into the kingdom of God.

In 1883, several Chicago residents began weekly prayer meetings with Miss Emma Dryer to ask the Lord to send Mr. Moody

To Moody the Word of God "is food, drink, lodging, and clothing. He climbs by it toward heaven as a sailor climbs the rigging. It is an anchor to hold him; a gale to drive him; it is health, hope, happiness, eternal life."

back to Chicago to start a training school for young men and women. In God' providence, Miss Dryer's persistent message had taken hold in 1886. Mr. Moody addressed the gathering…"I tell you what I want, and what I have on my heart: I believe we have got to have gap-men. Men to stand between the laity and the ministers, men who are trained to do city mission work. Take men that have the gifts and train them for the work of reaching the people." Thus the Chicago Evangelization Society was formed.

For a time the work of the Society consisted mainly of home visitation and services held in tents and missions. Each May the society sponsored a week-long series of training sessions known as "May Institutes." One evening as Mr. Moody waited for the start of a service at the Chicago Avenue Church he encountered an usher, John Morrison, outside the building. "Is that you, Morrison?" Moody asked. "Do you see that empty lot? Let's pray to the Lord to give it to us for a school." After a brief prayer they went into the service. The lot remained empty.

An eminent pastor says of him: "His running expositions are as full of richness as a Bartlett pear. They teach us ministers how to squeeze honey out of the word." "I like to go all round a text," said Mr. Moody, "to see what's after and before. I find often it is like a little diamond set in pearls."

In 1889, Moody was speaking at the largest and most elaborate "May Institute" yet. The board of trustees saw the success of the sessions and decided to move ahead with the purchase of the lot Moody and Morrison prayed for, as well as a second vacant lot, along with three houses.

Immediately the houses underwent remodeling and construction began on the main office building. Moody realized that the new school in Chicago needed a resident leader. He selected evangelist and good friend Ruben Archer Torrey as superintendent. Dr. Torrey arrived September 26, 1889, the day the year-round school began. After the death of Moody, the trustees changed the name of the Chicago Evangelization Society to the Moody Bible Institute of Chicago.

Moody's last crusade was only hours before he was called home to be in glory. He became very ill after preaching to thousands in Kansas City. Shortly before his death he was heard saying, "I see earth receding; heaven is opening. God is calling me. This is my triumph. This is my coronation day. It is glorious. God is calling and I must go. Mama, you have been a good wife…no pain…no valley…it's bliss."

Key Writings of Moody: 1. *Men of the Bible* (1898); 2. *Commending the Faith: The Preaching of D.L. Moody*; 3. *The Way to God*; 4. *The Overcoming Life*; 5. *Prevailing Prayer*; 6. *The Secret of Success in the Christian Life*; 7. *Still Waters*; 8. *Secret Power*.

Worth Reading: *D. L. Moody and His Work*, By Rev. W. H. Daniels (1876); *The Life and Labors of Moody and Sankey*, by Robert Boyd (1876); *The Life of Dwight L. Moody*, by William R. Moody (1900); *The Life and Work of Dwight L. Moody*, by Rev. J. Wilbur Chapman, D.D. (1900); *The Life Story of D L Moody. A Prince of Evangelists.*, by Rev. W. Ross (1900); *D. L. Moody: The Greatest Evangelist of the Nineteenth Century*, by Faith C. Bailey (1985); *The Moody Collection: The Highlights of His Writings, Sermons, Anecdotes, and Life Story*, by James Bell (1997); *A Passion for Souls: The Life of D. L. Moody*, by Lyle W. Dorsett (1997).

J. R. Miller *1840-1912*
Presbyterian Minister and Author

If all the letters hidden away in the desks and files of those who received them from the hand of Dr. Miller could be gathered together, no doubt volumes of rich comfort and blessing could be filled. Indeed thousands of souls received Jesus the day the postman delivered each jewel to its intended recipient. Today's generation can glean much from Dr. Miller to spread words of comfort and cheer to its fellow man through that blessed means of pen (or keyboard) which has all but been lost.

To those who knew him, none would be surprised to find that James Russell Miller came from the Scottish line of William Wallace. His love of men, his love for God, and his ceaseless sacrifice for the work to which he was called is worthy of his ancestry. In preparing a short biography of this eminent man of God, his own words elucidate the challenge of such a task. "We need not trouble to keep diaries of our good deeds or sacrifices, or to write autobiographies with pages of record for things we have done. We may safely let our life write its own record, and let Christ be our biographer. He will never forget anything we do, and the judgement day will reveal everything. The lowliest services and the obscurest deeds will then be manifested" says J. R. Miller in his devotional, *Come Ye Apart.*

James Russell Miller was born in Pennsylvania, into a devout Christian home. As a boy, James and his sisters would sit around the dinner table as their father would read from Matthew Henry's commentary, and expound Scripture. The children learned the Westminster Shorter Catechism together, by taking turns asking and answering each other the questions.

In 1857, seventeen-year-old Miller committed his life to Christ while attending Beaver Academy. The young convert dedicated a large part of his time to prayer and meditation, and attended various worship services throughout the week.

Miller served as a field agent for the Christian Commission, during the Civil War at Gettysburg. This "field of blood" as he called it, was a severe training ground for his future calling in ministry, and helped form the character of a man who would be greatly used by God.

In 1870, Dr. Miller married Louise King. She was a loving helpmeet to him in all his various labors. Her love for Christ was manifested in her tender care for her three children and warm affections for her husband, and all to whom he ministered.

Throughout his life Miller was known for his pastoring, preaching, and publishing. All who knew him marveled as they saw how full his days were with varied service. When someone would tell him he was doing the work of three men he would

Dr. J. R. Miller wrote more than seventy books, edited more than a dozen Christian periodicals, and pastored in a number of congregations. His ministry reached the hearts of hundreds of thousands and continues to reach millions more since his death in 1912.

insist that this was not true, responding; "It is only one man's work. Most ministers have their 'free Mondays' and their evenings for symphony concerts, and all that sort of thing, or sitting down at home. I give up every hour to activity of some sort. I am very busy at the office all day and my people are there with their troubles all the time. In the evening I go out visiting sick people and others. At about 9:30 I return and have an hour with my family before they scatter off. And I think my evenings save me from growing old. I feel younger every year."

"A very little love for our neighbor wrought out in a bit of everyday kindness is worth a great deal more than talk about love which finds no expression in act."—Dr. Miller in his book, Finding the Way.

After he left the war, Dr. Miller devoted himself to the ministry of the pen, where he could reach hundreds of thousands, instead of a few hundred who alone might benefit from him in the pulpit. As he prayed for direction, the Lord blessed him with the joy of combining his pastoral and editorial labors. Over the years he ministered and preached to the Lord's people in New Wilmington, Bethany Church, Philadelphia, and Rock Island. He wrote numerous articles for various Christian publications, including a leading weekly, *The Presbyterian.* In 1880, he was asked to become assistant editor at the Presbyterian Board of Publication (PBP), where he wrote for numerous periodicals such as *The Westminster Teacher, The Sabbath School Visitor* and *The Presbyterian Monthly Record.* Miller's dedication to the Sunday school teacher is clearly evidenced in his writings for these publications, which became very popular in the United States and England. The Board's number of publications increased dramatically, primarily due to the work of Dr. Miller. In the thirty-two years that he served in writing, editing, and publishing for the Board, more than 66 million issues were published and distributed. His publications became models of excellence in content and appearance for generations to come, and elevated the status of the PBP to one of the premier magazine and book publishers within the Christian community. Dr. Miller's editorials in particular became the noted standard for all publishers of like periodicals in the United States.

J. R. Miller in 1868, age 28.

Professor Brenton Greene, of Princeton Seminary, and chairman of the Board's editorial committee honored Miller, saying; "'God is love,' and J. R. Miller was God's own child, to a very remarkable degree reflecting the likeness and reproducing the majestic but quiet force of Him who is set before us as 'the express image' of our heavenly Father; so that in his career, we come to see how practical and potent genuine love is, how fit for harnessing to the wheels of daily life and modern enterprise, how skillful in adjusting effort to human machinery and providential occasion."

During the years between 1880-1912, Dr. Miller had published seventy books and booklets with a circulation totaling more than two million. He was widely acclaimed as the most read devotional writer in the world. Any reader of Miller's books discovers that sweet love of Jesus that pours out of every chapter. His relationship with his King was truly exemplified in his writings that reflect his simple lifelong creed, "Jesus and I are friends." His gift for such comforting communication began as early as his days in the Civil War. His messages to the front lines and those struggling in the infirmary were imbued with words of cheer, consolation, and the love of Jesus.

In 1863, he wrote in *The United Presbyterian*, "*A Study on Sorrow*," in which he said: "I had spent the afternoon of Wednesday with two or three, sore sufferers. In conversation with them I had spoken freely of their trials and their comforts. Comfort is one of life's best blessings. Even the comfort of earthly friends is soothing and sweet. But the real comfort which the Holy Spirit brings to the heart of the Christian mourner is infinitely better. It is better to go into the furnace and get the image of Christ out of the fire, than to be saved from the fire and fail of the blessed likeness." In another war time article, entitled *A Word of Comfort,* he gives this illustration: "When a hard frost comes after a rain it catches the silvery drops that fasten upon the trees, and freezes them solid, and holds them there in beautiful crystals which no wind can shake off. So death catches all the beauty and sweetness of those we love and fixes it in solid crystals which will hang upon the tree of memory forever."

Letter writing played a tremendous role in Dr. Miller's pastoral work. In his ministry the discouraged would receive a letter of cheer and encouragement, the young Christian would read a message of counsel or direction, the sick would have their day brightened by sweet words of comfort amidst affliction, and the new or struggling convert would find a pastor who possessed an understanding of their heart and filled it with peace and joy. In fact, it was a self-imposed rule of his life that each day he would send a letter of cheer to at least one person who was in need—a vow he kept his entire life.

"Every station occupied by the Commission on this field of blood is worthy of a special record. Suffice it to say that at every point of this field, as at others of like character, the effort to relieve temporal wants was blended with Christian counsel and consolation, and as ever before, so here, the Holy Spirit attended such ministrations with the divine blessing."

United States Christian Commission headquarters during the Civil War. Dr. Miller seated at the left.

A letter from a stranger attracted Dr. Miller's special attention because it gave him the hint for which he was always looking—the hint that a letter from him would be helpful. So he wrote: "Your stationery shows that you are in sorrow. I may not inter-meddle with your grief, but I may say at least that my heart goes out in sincere sympathy to you, whatever the grief may be which has touched your life. No doubt you have learned that sorrow is a great revealer. We never should see the stars in the sky, if the sun kept shining always; and the Bible is like a sky full of stars—stars of comfort, of divine revealing, of spiritual help, of which we never should know experimentally did not the sun go down for us and the darkness come on. Very much of the Bible remains like a sealed book to God's children until they are called to pass into the shadows of grief. That is what our Master meant in the Beatitude for sorrow, 'Blessed are they that mourn, for they shall be comforted.' Comfort is one of God's highest and best bless-ings. But we never can have comfort till we mourn."

In "letting Christ's love pour out" through his pen, his preaching, and his pastoring he made no distinctions among people. No matter who they were, or where they lived, if they needed the help and he could give it, it was given.

One morning a message came to his editorial office telling of the accidental death of the young daughter of a woman not a member of his church. Dr. Miller took the next train and remained with the mother until she was calm and comforted.

Some ministers might not appreciate such pastoral interven-tion, but never when Dr. Miller was the caller. His spirit was so thoroughly understood and appreciated that pastors of all denominations welcomed his presence among their parishio-ners. They knew that his life was ordered in accordance with the plea once made by him in public: "In the great central truths of Christianity all evangelical churches are agreed. Let us not waste a moment's time or a breath of energy in strife with other believ-ers. Let us rather unite all our energies in doing good, in hon-oring Christ by telling the story of His love to all men, and by carrying the joy and cheer of the gospel everywhere. The church that shows the world the most love, and that lives the most sweetly, the most joyously, the most helpfully, is the church that comes the nearest to the Master's thought. That is the sort of church that every Christian should strive to make his to be."

But at last his labors proved too heavy, and the pastor resigned his last charge. In telling the church session of his pur-pose, he said: "It has been a dream of mine that I might continue in the work, in the co-pastorate which has brought to me such joy and such delightful fellowship, ending my days at St. Paul's. None but myself can ever know how dear the people are to me. They have been gathered one by one with thought and love. In many homes I have been in times of suffering or sorrow and with hundreds I have walked in experiences of joy or of pain which have bound them to me in very sacred ties. The church has come to be to me, in a very real sense, like my own family, and I have thought that it would be a joy to spend my last days among the people and be buried among them. But the condition of my health in recent months is such that I cannot hope to carry any important part of the work hereafter. It seems wise, therefore, that I should resign my position at an early day."

His last official message was sent to the elders of the church on Christmas day, 1911. He closed with these words: "May the Christmas Day mean more to you than any Christmas before has meant. May it be the real coming anew of Christ into your heart, not as a mere sentiment, but as a living power, transforming you more and more into the divine beauty, and imparting to you divine strength, which shall make your life henceforth a richer influence, a greater power than ever it has been before. You have a large responsibility in your position, and you will meet it with faith and courage."

Dr. Miller closed the last chapters of his *The Book of Comfort*, and the final volume of his *Devotional Hours with the Bible*, ready to be joined forever with his Friend, his Joy, his Peace, and his Comfort—closing his eyes in this world and opening them in the next on July 2, 1912.

"What a tremendous sight it would be if all the millions of people who have been helped by you could gather in one company to give greeting to you as you enter on another decade of service! What messages they would send if they could speak! How they would tell of comfort received, of courage renewed, of inspiration given, of new visions of life, of 'glimpses of the Master' all through the life that God has so richly blessed during the nearly half a century of your ministry. I am glad that I, as one of this vast company, have the opportunity to tell you how I thank God for the association with you which has become one of the greatest joys of my life."—Letter received from a pastor.

Key Writings of Miller: 1. *Week Day Religion* (1880); 2. *Home Making* (1882); 3. *In His Steps* (1885); 4. *The Wedded Life* (1886); 5. *Silent Times* (1886); 6. *Come Ye Apart* (1887); 7. *The Marriage Altar* (1888); 8. *Practical Religion* (1888); 9. *Bits of Pasture* (1890); 10. *Making the Most of Life* (1891); 11. *The Everyday of Life* (1892); 12. *Girls: Faults and Ideals* (1892); 13. *Young Men: Faults and Ideals* (1893); 14. *Glimpses Through Life's Windows* (1893); 15. *The Building of Character* (1894); 16. *Secrets of Happy Home Life* (1894); 17. *Life's Byways and Waysides* (1895); 18. *For a Busy Day* (1895); 19. *Dr. Miller's Year Book* (1895); 20. *Family Prayers for Thirteen Weeks* (1895); 21. *The Hidden Life* (1895); 22. *The Blessing of Cheerfulness* (1896); 23. *Things to Live For* (1896); 24. *Story of a Busy Life* (1896); 25. *A Gentle Heart* (1896); 26. *Personal Friendships of Jesus* (1897); 27. *By the Still Waters* (1897); 28. *The Secret of Gladness* (1898); 29. *The Joy of Service* (1898); 30. *The Master's Blesseds* (1898); 31. *Young People's Problems* (1898); 32. *The Gates of Heaven* (1898); 33. *Unto the Hills* (1899); 34. *Strength and Beauty* (1899); 35. *The Golden Gate of Prayer* (1900); 36. *Loving My Neighbor* (1900); 37. *The Ministry of Comfort* (1901); 38. *Summer Gathering* (1901); 39. *How? When? Where?* (1901); 40. *The Story of Joseph* (1901); 41. *The Upper Currents* (1902); 42. *Today and Tomorrow* (1902); 43. *In Perfect Peace* (1902); 44. *The Lesson of Love* (1903); 45. *The Face of the Master* (1903); 46. *Our New Eden* (1904); 47. *Finding the Way* (1904); 48. *The Inner Life* (1904); 49. *Manual for Communicant Classes* (1905); 50. *The Beauty of Kindness* (1905); 51. *When the Song Begins* (1905); 52. *The Blossom of Thorns* (1905); 53. *A Gentle Heart* (1906); 54. *Looking Forward* (1906); 55. *The Best Things* (1907); 56. *Glimpses of the Heavenly Life* (1907); 57. *Morning Thoughts for Every Day in the Year* (1907); 58. *Counsel and Help* (1907); 59. *Evening Thoughts* (1908); 60. *A Help for the Common Days* (1908); 61. *The Gate Beautiful* (1909); 62. *The Master's Friendships* (1909); 63. *The Beauty of Every Day* (1910); 64. *The Beauty of Self-control* (1911); 65. *Learning to Love* (1911); 66. *The Book of Comfort* (1912); 67. *The Joy of the Lord* (1912); 68. *Devotional Life of the Sunday School Teacher* (1913); 69. *Devotional Hours with the Bible*, (8 vols.); 1909-1913.

Worth Reading: *The Home Beautiful* (1912); *The Life of Dr. J. R. Miller*, by John T. Faris (1912); *In Green Pastures: Devotions for Every Day of the Year* (1913); *The Shining Life: Daily Readings in the Works of Dr. J. R. Miller* (1915).

Amy Carmichael at age twenty-four, relaxing at Broughton Grange in 1892.

Amy Carmichael *1861-1951*
Christian Missionary and Author

Amy Carmichael was the author of thirty-five books. Even as a young girl, Carmichael had showed great promise as a writer. Obedience, love, commitment, and selflessness were the marks of Amy Carmichael's life. Even after a tragic accident that left her confined to the Dohnavur Fellowship compound, Amy flourished as a Christian woman and writer. Her works, centered around her life, afflictions, and ministry to the needy remain a source of comfort and inspiration to thousands of Christians around the world.

O n March 6, 1901, a course of events began that would define for Amy Carmichael the ministry to which the Lord would have her dedicate her earthly life.

Pearleyes was just seven years old. She lived in the small village of Great Lake in India where her father was a Hindu landowner. One day her mother was persuaded to allow her daughter to visit the local temple dedicated to Perumal. The women of the temple led her gently by the hand into their inner sanctum intending to train her in their wicked customs: a life of iniquity and heathen sacrifice. But Pearleyes saw it for what it was and rejected it. Even at a young and tender age she possessed a certain purity of spirit and instinctively recognized the horror before her. In fear she fled from the evil temple and embarked on the treacherous two-day journey back to her mother's new home in Tuticorin. Exhausted and hungry, the courageous little girl found her way home and fell into her mother's arms. But the temple women had tracked her down and threatened the mother with wrath from the Hindu gods if she refused to give up her child. Pearleyes clung to her mother's neck for safety, but fear seized the woman and she tore her little girl's arms from her neck and handed her over to the evil women.

Back at the temple, Pearleyes was to be "married" to the god, Perumal, in a special ritual. It was common in temples such as this to keep the children for the vilest purposes imaginable. Overhearing their plan, she set herself for another escape. The hand of the Lord guided her to leave the temple unnoticed and into the hands of an elderly Christian woman outside a church. The kind woman took her in for the night, and then to Amy and her companions the next day, saying, "An evil place is that temple house. It is good you are back home."

In her book *Gold Cord,* Amy comments on the incident: "The child told us things that darkened the sunlight. It was impossible to forget those things. Wherever we went after that day we were constrained to gather facts about what appeared a great secret traffic in the souls and bodies of young children, and we searched for some way to save them, and could find no way. The helpless little things seemed to slip between our fingers as we stretched out our hands to grasp them, or it was as though a great wave

Though she carried within her many "thorns in the flesh," Amy Carmichael committed her entire life to spreading Christ's love to those living in utter darkness.

Her prose and poetry continue to bring joy and comfort to the brokenhearted and suffering children of God.

swept up and carried them out to sea. In a kind of desperation, we sought for a way. But we found that we must know more before we could hope to find it. If we were to do anything for these children it was vain to graze on the tips of facts; it took years to do more than that." Amy Carmichael (Amma, as she was called by the children) was brokenhearted over these precious children and it was her great love for them that God used to raise up the Dohnavur Fellowship in India as a place of safety and refuge for former temple children. During her fifty-six year ministry, Amy

saw more than a thousand children rescued from persecution and abuse, often at the cost of extreme exhaustion and personal danger.

Amy Beatrice Carmichael was born in Northern Ireland in to a large, faithful Presbyterian family. She was the oldest of seven children in a happy Christian family.

When a child of three, Amy learned a wonderful lesson about how God answers prayer. Bishop Houghton records the incident in his biography of her: "Amy's favorite color was blue. She loved the blue Lotus flowers, the blue sky, and the blue in her mother's eyes. But Amy had brown eyes, and wanted more than anything to have blue eyes. So she prayed that night that God would change her eyes to blue. In the morning, fully believing that God had answered her prayer, she jumped out of bed then and ran to the mirror. Her mother heard her wail in disappointment. It took Mrs. Carmichael several minutes of careful explanation before Amy understood that 'no' was an answer too. He sometimes makes us wait or says 'no' but

Amy with Lola and Leela in 1910. The children called her Amma.

he is never heedless of our prayers." God meant Amy to have brown eyes for a reason, and her sweet mother encouraged her to remain content with God's will.

As a young girl, the Lord gave Amy a glimpse of the future work to which He would send her. One day when the family was returning home from church, they encountered a poor old woman struggling with a heavy bundle. Amy and her brothers were filled with pity, and took her by the arms and helped her while all the "respectable" neighbors looked on in horror. When she returned home, Amy shut herself in her room, talked to God, and settled on her future occupation. She realized that God was giving her a love for those whom the world deems unlovely.

In 1892, Amy wrote to her mother of her overwhelming desire to give herself to missions, and her mother consented:

"My precious mother, have you given your child unreservedly

to the Lord for whatever He wills? . . .Oh may He strengthen you to say "Yes" to Him if He asks something which costs."

"Darling Mother, for a long time as you know, the thought of those dying in the dark—50,000 of them every day, while we at home live in the midst of blazing light—has been very present with me, and the longing to go to them, and tell them of Jesus, has been strong upon me. Everything, seemed to be saying "Go," through all sounds the cry seemed to rise, "Come over and help us." Every bit of pleasure or work which has come to me, has had underlying it the thought of those people who have never, never heard of Jesus. Before my eyes, clearer than any lovely view has been the constant picture of those millions who have no chance, and never had one, of hearing of the love which makes our lives so bright." Her mother responded:

"My own precious child; yes, dearest Amy, He has lent you to me all these years. He only knows what a strength, comfort and joy you have been to me. In sorrow He made you my staff and solace, in loneliness my more than child companion, and in gladness my bright and merry-hearted sympathizer. So, darling, when He asks you now to go away from within my reach, can I say nay? No, no, Amy, He is yours—you are His—to take you where He pleases and to use you as He pleases. I can trust you to Him, and I do—and I thank Him for letting you hear His voice as you have done."

Though Amy suffered from an incurable nervous disorder (neuralgia) she looked forward to realizing her calling and was overjoyed when the time had finally come. In 1893, she was sent to Matsuye, Japan, by the director of Keswick missions. Upon arriving in Japan, Amy did not wait to learn the language, but went straight out to tell people about Christ. Amy and Misaki San (her translator) were asked to send an evil spirit out of a violent and murderous man. Village priests had tried their formulas and tortures without success. Trusting that the Lord could drive demons away, the two girls prayed and went boldly into the man's room. As soon as they mentioned the name of Jesus, the man went into an uncontrollable rage. If he had not been tied down, he would have attacked them. The two girls were thrust from the room. They assured the man's wife that they would pray until the spirit left, and asked her to send a message when it was gone. Within an hour they had word. The next day, the man himself summoned them, and over the next few days they explained the way of Christ to him and he became a Christian.

The two years she spent serving the Lord there was fertile training ground for the next and final mission call of her life. In 1895, she was commissioned by the Church of England Zenana Missionary Society to go to Dohnavur, India, where she served the people and spread the blessed love of Christ for fifty-six years, without a furlough.

From prayer that asks
that I may be
Sheltered from winds
that beat on Thee,

From fearing when
I should aspire,
From faltering when
I should climb higher,

From silken self, O
Captain, free
Thy soldier who would
follow Thee.

From subtle love of
softening things,
From easy choices,
weakenings,

(Not thus are spirits
fortified,
Not this way went the
Crucified)

From all that dims
Thy Calvary
O Lamb of God,
deliver me.

Give me the love that
leads, the way,
The faith that nothing
can dismay,

The hope no disap-
pointments tire,
The passion that burn
like fire;

Let me not sink to be a
clod: Make me
Thy fuel, Flame of God.

—Amy Carmichael

When Amy began her ministry she soon became aware of the wicked Hindu practice of child abuse within the temples. She often had to move about disguised as a Hindu in order that her purposes might remain secret. It then became apparent to her why God gave her brown eyes. Had her eyes been blue, she would have been immediately noticed as a foreigner.

Lord Jesus, for me crucified,
Let not my footsteps from Thee slide.

For I would tread where Thou hast trod,
My spirit tender of the glory of God.

That glory which meant all to Thee,
Let it mean all, my Lord, to me.

So would I tread where Thou hast trod,
My spirit tender of the glory of God.

—Amy Carmichael

Her heart was broken for these innocent children and she resolved to "save" them from such evil. The Lord blessed her efforts, but the Hindu authorities were extremely agitated and managed to have charges of kidnapping brought upon Amy—punishable by seven years in prison. After a long struggle, Amy was proven innocent of the charges. Free to pursue her mission work, she established the Dohnavur Fellowship, raising up an orphanage to care for the lost and lonely little victims of the temple.

In 1932, Amy Carmichael suffered a severe injury as a result of a tragic accident. A band of mischievous Hindus dug a hole outside her home into which she fell and received serious injury. It was hoped by all that she would recover speedily and return to her active ministry, but for the remainder of her life she became an invalid who rarely left her home. One might consider this a sad ending to a fruitful and active life, but not Amy. She knew well that God has a plan of victory for his children even amidst apparent defeat. It was at this point in her life that she entered into an intimate fellowship with Christ and His sufferings.

Though she was confined to Dohnavur because of her ailments, she saw the blessing behind the dark cloud. Her time was well spent writing more than thirty books of lasting interest and benefit to the souls of millions. Her prose and poetry have been an immeasurable blessing to encourage the heart of the suffering Christian. To this day, Amy Carmichael remains a bright and ever burning example of one whose sole existence was devoted to her beloved Lord and Savior.

Key Writings of Carmichael: 1. *Beginning of a Story* (1908); 2. *Lotus Buds* (1909); 3. *Continuation of a Story* (1914); 4. *Walker of Tinnevelly* (1916); 5. *Made in the Pans* (1917); 6. *Ponnammal: Her Story* (1918); 7. *From the Forest* (1920); 8. *Dohnavur Songs* (1921); 9. *Nor Scrip* (1922); 10. *Ragland, Spiritual Pioneer* (1922); 11. *Tables in the Wilderness* (1923); 12. *The Valley of Vision* (1924); 13. *Mimosa* (1924); 14. *Raj* (1926); 15. *The Widow of the Jewels* (1928); 16. *Meal in a Barrel* (1929); 17. *Gold Cord* (1932); 18. *Rose from Brier* (1933); 19. *Ploughed Under* (1934); 20. *Gold by Moonlight* (1935); 21. *Toward Jerusalem* (1936); 22. *Windows* (1937); 23. *If* (1938); 24. *Figures of the True* (1938); 25. *Pools and the Valley of Vision* (1938); 26. *Kohila* (1939); 27. *His Thoughts Said...His Father Said* (1941); 28. *Though the Mountains Shake* (1943); 29. *Before the Door Shuts* (1948); 30. *This One Thing* (1950); 31. *Edges of his Ways* (1955).

Worth Reading: *Amy Carmichael of Dohnavur*, by Frank L. Houghton (1953); *A Chance to Die: the Life and Legacy of Amy Carmichael*, by Elizabeth Elliot (1987); *Amma: the Life and Words of Amy Carmichael*, by Elizabeth Skoglund (1994).

Karl Barth *1886-1968*
Leading Theologian of the 20th Century

Karl Barth was a German Protestant theologian who was active in the resistance to the Nazis. The sacrifice of position and prestige he experienced as a result mattered little to Barth. He was driven to see traditional Christianity restored into a modern Protestant Church that had all but abandoned truth as it was found in the Bible.

It is appropriate that the swastika looks like a cross that is bent out of shape, for that is exactly what Hitler did to the truths of the Christian faith—he bent them and twisted them to conform to his mission for world dominance and control of the life and work of the Church of Jesus Christ. When the National Church was formed under Nazi control in 1933, most clergy succumbed to the pressure to unite, but a small band of ministers rejected Nazi threats and insisted that the Bible was still the ultimate authority and the Church must obey Christ apart from political influence. This Pastor's Emergency League, as it was named, was joined by Karl Barth and Dietrich Bonhoeffer among others, all who suffered persecution for their steadfast commitment to Christ as revealed in Scripture.

Karl Barth was born in Basel, Switzerland, where his father was a Swiss Reformed minister and professor of New Testament and Church History. After receiving his degree in Theology he served as a pastor in Safenwil in 1911. It was there he met and married Nelly Hoffman, a talented violinist and committed Christian. The couple had five children together.

In 1934, Reich-bishop Müller issued a decree which he pretended was needed to restore order in the German Evangelical Church. This decree became known as the "Muzzling Order," because it forbade ministers to say anything in their sermons about the Church controversy. Müller ordered churchmen to preach nothing but "the pure gospel," as defined by Hitler.

But faithful ministers would not allow themselves to be kept out of politics by such an order—not when politics violated the deepest principles of Christianity. In fact, the very day that Müller issued his decree, three hundred and twenty elders and ministers were already gathered at Barmen, calling themselves the First Free Reformed Synod. They accepted Karl Barth's "Declaration on the Correct Understanding of the Reformation Confessions in the Evangelical Church..." More meetings were held and in April, pastors who opposed Hitler formed the Confessing Church, which they called the "Legal Protestant Church of Germany."

Karl Barth is considered by some to be the greatest Protestant theologian of the 20th century and possibly the greatest since the Reformation. More than anyone else, Barth inspired and led the renaissance of theology that took place from about 1920 to 1950.

Barth was a forty-eight-year-old professor of theology at the University of Bonn when the Gestapo burst into his lecture and forcibly deported him to his native Switzerland. During the course of his life, Barth demonstrated that the Church's best theology often emerges from its worst suffering.

Theologian Karl Barth, world-famous for a commentary he wrote on the Apostle Paul's letter to the Romans (1919), issued a refutation of Unified Church doctrines. He said that the source of the errors of the German Christians was that they asserted that German nationality, history, and politics was a source of revelation equal in weight with Scripture.

Also in his commentary, Barth stressed the discontinuity between the Christian message and the world. He rejected the typical liberal points of contact between God and humanity in feeling, consciousness, or rationality, as well as Catholic tendencies to trust in the church or spiritualism.

According to Paul, argues Barth in His Commentary on Romans, God condemns all human undertakings and saves only those people who trust not in themselves but solely in God. Barth argued that in Scripture we find "divine thoughts about men, not human thoughts about God." In this book Barth stressed the lack of continuity between the Christian message and the world. God is known only in revelation. Human task is to reshape himself or herself to God's design, not the other way around.

The main characteristic of Barth's work is known as neoorthodoxy and crisis theology. It concentrates on the sinfulness of humanity, God's absolute transcendence, and the human inability to know God except through revelation. The critical nature of his theology came to be known as "dialectical theology," or "the theology of crisis." This initiated a trend toward neoorthodoxy in Protestant theology. The neoorthodoxy of Karl Barth reacted strongly against liberal Protestant neglect of historical revelation. He wanted to lead theology away from the influence of modern religious philosophy, with its emphasis on feeling and humanism, and back to the principles of the Reformation and the teachings of the Bible. He viewed the Bible, however, not as the actual revelation of God but as only the record of that revelation. God's single revelation occurred in Jesus Christ.

From 1932 to 1967, he worked on his *Church Dogmatics*, a multi-volume work that he never finished. It consists of four volumes, totaling more than 9,000 pages. He continued to champion the cause of the Confessing Church, of the Jews, until the end of the war. After the war, Barth was invited back to Bonn, where he delivered the series of lectures published in 1947 as *Dogmatics in Outline*. He spoke at the opening meeting of the Conference of the World Council of Churches in Amsterdam in 1948. Barth went home to his Savior in 1968.

Key Writings of Barth: 1. *Epistle to the Romans (1919, 1933)*; 2. *The Word of God and the Word of Man (1928)*; 3. *Church Dogmatics (1932-1969)*; 4. *The Humanity of God (1960)*; 5. *Evangelical Theology (1962)*.

Worth Reading: *The Triumph of Grace in the Theology of Karl Barth*, by G. C. Berkouwer (1956); *Karl Barth*, by Herni Broulliard (1957); *Portrait of Karl Barth*, by Georges Casalis (1963); *Karl Barth and the Christian Message*, by Colin Brown (1967); *Theology of Karl Barth*, by Hans Urs von Balthasar (1971); *Introduction to the Theology of Karl Barth*, by G. W. Bromiley (1979).

C. S. Lewis *1898-1963*
Christian Author, Scholar, Apologist

C. S. Lewis was famous both as a fiction writer, a Christian thinker, and a defender of the faith he so cherished. Few Christians can go through life without reading something by Lewis. His writings have encouraged the faith of Christian men and women and warmed the hearts of children for half a century.

onstantine was converted on the battlefield; Whitefield, by reading, *Life of God in the Soul of Man,* by Scougal; Chuck Colson, founder of Prison Ministries, asked God into his life while weeping in a car on a roadside; and C. S. Lewis (Jack, as he preferred to be called) came to Christ on a motorcycle on his way to the zoo. Indeed, the Lord often chooses to save His children under unusual circumstances, and the conversion of C.S. Lewis was no different.

"When we set out I did not believe that Jesus is the Son of God, but when we reached the zoo, I did." Jack recalls. He had already become a theist, but his conversion on a motorcycle was the result of serious meditation on the soul-searching discussion he'd had three days earlier with two Christian friends, J. R. R. Tolkien and Hugo Dyson.

Tolkien, who was soon to write the most intriguing fantasy of our century, *The Lord of the Rings,* argued that even some myths can originate in God and preserve truth, however distorted they may appear in content and presentation. He felt myths and allegories can present holy truths even as Bunyan's *Pilgrim's Progress* did for millions of readers since its introduction over 300 years before. Lewis doubted myths embodied truth at all. The three argued until 3 A.M. when Tolkien went home. Dyson and Lewis walked and talked some more. Dyson entered more deeply into the gospel with Lewis. He insisted that Christianity works. It puts the believer at peace with God, frees him from the guilt of sin, and provides comfort for a heart that is empty without Christ. Throughout most of his adult life Lewis had been an atheist, and he defended and argued for this philosophy with all the considerable energy, intellect, and wit at his disposal. But in 1929, Lewis humbled himself before God and with childlike faith surrendered his heart to Jesus.

Clive Staples Lewis was born in Belfast, Ireland in 1898, to Albert James Lewis and Flora Augusta Hamilton Lewis. In 1905, the Lewis family moved to a new home on the outskirts of Belfast. Lewis' life came crashing down when his mother became sick with cancer and died in 1908. Lewis' older brother Warren

C. S. Lewis published 52 books, 153 essays, and a great many prefaces, letters, and book reviews. To this day, he remains one of the world's most popular Christian authors, with more than 1.5 million copies of his works sold each year.

"Warnie" who was born in 1895, helped his younger brother through this devastating loss. The two brothers maintained a close bond throughout their lives.

To Lewis' great advantage, while a youth in their Belfast home, books overflowed everywhere. Lewis wrote in his autobiographical book *Surprised by Joy,* "There were books in the study, books in the drawing-room, books in the cloakroom,

books (two deep) in the great bookcase on the landing, books in a bedroom, books piled as high as my shoulder in the cistern attic, books of all kinds reflecting every transient stage of my parents' interests—books readable and unreadable, books suitable for a child and books most emphatically not. Nothing was forbidden me. In the seemingly endless rainy afternoons I took volume after volume from the shelves..." When little more than a toddler he read constantly the things of history, philosophy, and literature. His favorites were *Treasure Island* by Robert Louis Stevenson, Lew Wallace's *Ben Hur*, and *The Secret Garden* by Frances Hodgson Burnett. Before her death, his mother schooled him in French and Latin, and a teacher added Greek. At age sixteen he was sent to a school that prepared young people for university scholarships. In addition to his regular academic workload, Jack spent six hours a day with an agnostic tutor who taught young Jack "to think." God, in His providence, used this agnostic tutor to prepare Lewis for his future Kingdom work.

(Above) Warnie, Albert Lewis, and Jack in 1910. (Below) Jack and his toy at age 3.

On Christmas Day, C. S. Lewis joined the church and took communion. He had lacked a sense of direction for his talent, and finally felt that faith had given him a solid footing.

After a two-year tour of duty in the armed forces in World War I, from 1917-1919, Lewis enrolled in Oxford and in 1923, he received his degree in English.

In 1931, Lewis, Tolkien, and other literary-minded professors founded a literary dining club they called, "The Inklings." They met regularly on Monday mornings at a pub called "The Bird and the Baby." Membership in "The Inklings" grew throughout the years. During their term at Magdalen College the group met regularly two evenings a week. They read writings aloud and discussed them. Henry Dyson, Arthur Barfield, and Warnie were members of this group as well. (After his marriage to Joy, Jack tried to include her in these meetings but the old Inklings made excuses to avoid her attendance.)

By the middle of 1932, Jack had written the first of the many books. He became a greatly loved 20th century author and

Christian apologist. *The Pilgrim's Regress* is an account written in the style of John Bunyan about Jack's own spiritual journey to Christian faith. This was undoubtedly precipitated by his earlier life-changing talk with Tolkien and Dyson.

Initially, when Lewis first turned to writing children's books, his publisher and some of his friends tried to dissuade him, but thankfully he didn't listen to any of them. His first children's book, *The Lion, the Witch and the Wardrobe,* was a huge success. Lewis followed with six more volumes to the story of *The Chronicles of Narnia.* At first, they were not well received by critics and reviewers, but the books gained in popularity through word of mouth. The Narnia books have since sold more than 100 million copies and are among the most beloved books of classic children's literature.

In 1942, he penned his famous *Screwtape Letters,* which is a series of letters from the main character, Screwtape, who is an experienced devil, written to his young nephew Wormwood, a junior tempter on his first assignment. The reader is often confused at first by the idiomatic style of conversation between the two devils, but soon realizes the brilliance of Lewis in exposing the insidiousness of temptation in the human heart.

His most popular book on Christian apologetics is undoubtedly *Mere Christianity.* A book that many can say they read when first converted, it gives simple, yet profound insights into the natural tendencies of man to reject God, and the practical, miraculous intervention of God in the person of Jesus Christ. One of the most widely quoted statements used by Christian apologists comes from the pages of this book: "A man who was merely a man and said the sort of things Jesus said would not be a great moral teacher. He would either be a lunatic—on the level with a man who says he is a poached egg—or else he

would be the devil of hell. You must make your choice. Either he was and is the Son of God, or else a madman or something worse. You can shut him up for a fool, you can spit at him and kill him as a demon; or you can fall at his feet and call Him Lord and God. But let us not come with any patronizing nonsense about his being a great human teacher. He has not left that open to us. He did not intend to."

(top) C. S. Lewis with his wife, Joy. (bottom) Some of the Inklings: (L-R) Commander James Dundas Grant, Colin Hardie, Dr. R.E.Harvard, C. S. Lewis, and Peter Havard.

"This book proved to be especially popular. His writing mirrored his ability to recognize human failings, to be able to analyze their 'annoyingness,' as well as being able to accomplish this with a keen sense of satire and a vivid sense of humor." (*C.S. Lewis A Biography,* A. N. Wilson, p.177)

THE WEEKLY NEWSMAGAZINE

OXFORD'S C.S. LEWIS

Time September 8, 1947, featured C.S. Lewis in recognition of his popularity with Americans. The devil is the main character in his book, The Screwtape Letters, which was a collection of letters of instruction from an older devil (Screwtape) to a younger one (Wormwood), on how to trip up Christians in their walk with Christ.

It seemed as though Lewis would remain a bachelor for his entire life, until at age fifty-eight, he met an American woman, Joy Davidman Gresham, who opened his eyes to love. Her quick mind and spirited personality greatly attracted Lewis. It became obvious to those around them that God had brought soulmates together. They were married in 1956. Sadly though, Joy succumbed to a long battle with cancer and died in 1960. The death came as no surprise to Lewis since he had known she was terminally ill when he married her. His mourning found expression in *A Grief Observed,* a book that expresses his deeply broken heart and addresses questions of suffering and death. The story of her dying and his grief has twice been filmed as the movie *Shadowlands.*

C.S. Lewis never truly recovered from the pain of Joy's death and he followed her to a reunion in glory a few years later in 1963. C. S. Lewis' death was overshadowed by the assassination of President John F. Kennedy, who died the same day as Lewis.

Key Writings of Lewis: 1. *The Pilgrim's Regress;* (1933) 2. *The Allegory of Love: A Study in Medieval Tradition* (1936); 3. *Out of the Silent Planet* (1938); 4. *The Problem of Pain* (1940); 5. *The Screwtape Letters* (1942); 6. *A Preface to Paradise Lost* (1942); 7. *The Great Divorce* (1946); 8. *The Abolition of Man* (1947); 9. *The Chronicles of Narnia* (1950-56); 10. *Surprised by Joy* (1955); 11. *A Grief Observed* (1961)

Worth Reading: *C.S. Lewis: A Biography,* by Roger Lancelyn Green and Walter Hooper (1974); *The Inklings,* by Humphrey Carpenter (1978); *Shadowlands: The Story of C.S. Lewis and Joy Davidman,* by Brian Sibley (1985); *C.S. Lewis and the Search for Rational Religion,* by J. Beverluis (1985); *Clive Staples Lewis,* by W. Griffin (1986); *The C.S. Lewis Hoax,* by Kathryn Lindskoog (1988); *C.S. Lewis: A Biography,* by A.N. Wilson (1990); *The Fiction of C.S. Lewis,* by K. Filmer (1993); *The Chronicle of Narnia,* by C.N. Manlove (1993); *The Man Who Created Narnia,* by M. Coren (1996); *C.S. Lewis: Christian and Storyteller,* by B. Gromley (1998); *Sleuthing C.S. Lewis: More Light in the Shadowlands,* by Kathryn Lindskoog; *Most Reluctant Convert,* by David C. Downing (2000).

Martin Lloyd-Jones *1899-1981*

Welsh Preacher and Author

Dr. Martin Lloyd-Jones saw the Christian church falling prey to the spirit of the twentieth century syncretism and relativism. Yet, he believed that even in increasing secularism, people still respond to uncompromising truth. His power and passion in his preaching and writing greatly influenced evangelicalism in Europe and America.

he world of medicine was his life. When he was but fourteen years old, Martin attended Medical School at St. Bartholomew's Hospital, one of the finest teaching hospitals in London, where he received his MD in 1921. He was well liked and very successful. He became chief assistant to Sir Thomas Horder, who described Jones as "the most acute thinker I ever knew."

By age twenty-six he was already on his way to a brilliant and lucrative career in medicine. But then he began, slowly at first, to read the Bible. The influence of the gospel in the human heart is powerful when moved by the Holy Spirit, and Dr. Jones was gripped by the message of Jesus Christ. He says that he did not have any dramatic conversion, only that the truths of Scripture increasingly burned in his conscience to the point that he committed himself to Christ.

As the gospel message penetrated his life he found that as he treated patients for all kind of physical infirmities, he was convinced that their souls needed treatment more than their bodies. He saw that the anxieties experienced by the sick and dying around him could be truly relieved by only one thing—the saving blood of Jesus Christ within their hearts.

His passion for the lost grew and he resolved that the best way he could use his talents would be to become a minister of the gospel.

He felt compelled to return to his native Wales, where he saw a great need for spiritual revival, and in 1926 was called as the pastor of Bethlehem Forward Movement Mission Church in Sandfields, Aberavon. The next year he married a former fellow medical student, Bethan Phillips. They had two daughters, Elizabeth and Ann.

Lloyd-Jones has been called the last of the Calvinist Methodist preachers because he combined Calvin's love for truth and sound reformed doctrine with the fire and passion of the eighteenth-century Methodist revival. For thirty years he preached three sermons a week from the pulpit at Westminster Chapel in London.

"From the beginning to the end, the life of Martyn Lloyd-Jones was a cry for depth in two areas—depth in biblical

When Dr. Martin-Lloyd Jones preached, young and old, rich and poor, men and women, bright and dull, were transformed by hearing the message of Jesus Christ put forward with a power and authority not often matched.

doctrine and depth in vital spiritual experience. Light and heat. Logic and fire. Word and Spirit. Again and again he would be fighting on two fronts: on the one hand against dead, formal, institutional intellectualism, and on the other hand against superficial, glib, entertainment-oriented, man-centered emotionalism. He saw the world in a desperate condition without Christ and without hope; and a church with no power to change it. One wing of the church was straining out intellectual gnats and the other was swallowing the camels of evangelical compromise or careless charismatic teaching. For Lloyd-Jones the only hope was historic, God-centered revival." (John Piper, from sermon delivered to Bethlehem Conference for Pastors, 1991)

In his book, *Joy Unspeakable*, Jones illustrates the difference between normal, everyday Christian experience and the experience of baptism with the Spirit by telling a story from the eminent puritan Thomas Goodwin:

*In retirement he used to take his older grandchildren on in argument. They were like young cubs going for an old lion, daring where no one else would dare, thrown back by a growl, but bounding in again at once.
—Christopher Catherwood (Lloyd-Jones' grandson), in* Chosen by God.

"A man and his little child are walking down the road and they are walking hand in hand, and the child knows that he is the child of his father, and he knows that his father loves him, and he rejoices in that, and he is happy in it. There is no uncertainty about it all, but suddenly the father, moved by some impulse, takes hold of the child and picks him up, fondles him in his arms, kisses him, embraces him, showers his love upon him, and then he puts him down again and they go on walking together.

That is it! The child knew before that his father loved him, and he knew that he was his child. But oh! The loving embrace, this extra outpouring of love, this unusual manifestation of it—that is the Spirit bearing witness with our spirit that we are the children of God."

When J. I. Packer, well-known Christian author, was a 22-year-old student he heard Lloyd-Jones preach each Sunday evening during the school year of 1948-1949. He said that he had "never heard such preaching." It came to him "with the force of electric shock, bringing to at least one of his listeners more of a sense of God than any other man he had known."

This was the effect Dr. Martin Lloyd-Jones had, and continues to have on countless thousands. By some he is simply known as the "greatest preacher of this century."

Key Writings of Jones: 1. *Why Does God Allow War?* (1939); 2. *Truth Unchanged, Unchanging* (1951); 3. *Authority* (1958); 4. *Studies In The Sermon On The Mount* (1960); 5. *Preaching And Preachers* (1971); 6. *Why Does God Allow Suffering?*; 7. *God The Father, God The Son*; 8. *Reflections*; 9. *A Treasury of Daily Readings*; 10. *Alive in Christ: A 30-Day Devotional; Commentaries on Romans, Ephesians, Philippians, Colossians, 2 Timothy, 2 Peter, and 1 John.*

Worth Reading: *D. Martyn Lloyd-Jones: The First Forty Years, 1899-1939,* by Iain Murray (1982); *D. Martyn Lloyd-Jones: The Fight Of Faith, 1939-1981,* by Iain Murray (1990); *D. Martyn Lloyd-Jones: Letters 1919-1981,* compiled by Iain Murray (1996); *Martin Lloyd-Jones: Chosen By God* (1986); *Martyn Lloyd-Jones; A Family Portrait,* by Christopher Catherwood (1995).

Dietrich Bonhoeffer *1906-1945*

WWII Christian Martyr

Bonhoeffer was a well-known Christian author, theologian, and teacher. The integrity of his Christian faith and life, and the fortitude in which he suffered martyrdom for the sake of Jesus, have led to a broad consensus that he is the one theologian of his time to lead future generations of Christians into the new millenium.

 t was a cool April morning when Bonhoeffer was led out of his prison cell at the Flossenbürg concentration camp in Nazi Germany to stand before his executioners. He went calmly and peacefully to his death, as one observer states. The prison doctor who knew Dietrich said: "Through the half-open door I saw Pastor Bonhoeffer still in his prison clothes, kneeling in fervent prayer to the Lord his God. The devotion and evident conviction that I saw in the prayer of this intensely captivating man moved me to the depths." The prisoners were ordered to strip off their clothes. Naked under the scaffold, Bonhoeffer knelt for one last time to pray for strength to the Lord to endure this trial as a martyr for the gospel's sake. Five minutes later, he entered into the presence of his Savior and King.

Dietrich Bonhoeffer was one of the few Church leaders who stood up against the Hitler in courageous opposition to his inhuman practices and anti-Christian beliefs.

Dietrich Bonhoeffer was born the sixth of eight children to Karl and Paula Bonhoeffer in Breslau, Germany, along with his twin sister, Sabine. In 1927, he graduated from the University of Berlin with his dissertation *Sanctorum Communio*. He moved to New York in 1930 in order to pursue a divinity degree from Union Theological Seminary.

Bonhoeffer is best known for his work as an author and theologian, but the passion of his heart was to teach and preach the Word of God, especially words of life and hope to the post-World War I German people. In 1931, he returned to Germany and joined the theological faculty at the University of Berlin, where his father had previously taught.

By 1933, Nazism had taken such a foothold in the hearts and minds of the people that Bonhoeffer found himself opposing more and more of his friends as well as the growing anti-semitism of the German people. He became frustrated with the complacency of the German Church and wrote to Karl Barth of his decision that "it was time to go for awhile into the desert."

Shortly after moving to London, he became a founding member of a new church, called the Confessing Church. Bonhoeffer's theologically rooted opposition to National Socialism made him a leader, along with Martin Niemueller and Karl Barth, in the Confessing Church, and an advocate on behalf of the Jewish and Christian refugees. During the next few years, Bonhoeffer increasingly opposed the policies and ideals of Nazism, in his teaching and writings. In his essay *The Church and the Jewish Question* written in 1933, he challenged the German Church to stand up against the unbiblical and inhumane policies and practices of the Nazi regime. In turn, his Confessing Church dedicated itself to remaining free of Nazi influence. But it fell under pressure from the Gestapo in 1935, forcing Bonhoeffer to leave London and return to Germany.

In the same month that Bonhoeffer was hanged, on April 30, 1945, Hitler committed suicide. Seven days later Germany surrendered.

The Confessing Church leaders met in Steglitz, outside Berlin to discuss the controversy. Bonhoeffer became disgusted with his Church's failure to stand up for the "non-Aryan" Jews, and left Steglitz to teach some of his students at Finkenwalde Seminary. The next month, the school was closed by the Gestapo and twenty-seven of Bonhoeffer's former students were arrested.

In the years 1937-39, he traveled secretly within various German towns supervising his students work. But he was found out and banned from Berlin along with his Confessing Church.

With fewer options and more and more distaste for the German state and the German church, Bonhoeffer left Germany in 1939 for New York. But in a subsequent letter he wrote; "I have come to the conclusion that I made a mistake in coming to America...I shall have no right to take part in the restoration of Christian life in Germany after the war unless I share the trials of this time with my people." Bonhoeffer returned to Germany the following month.

He became known as one of the few figures of the 1930s with a comprehensive grasp of both German and English-language theology. His works resonate with a prescience, subtlety, and maturity that continually surpass the youth of their author.

In a letter smuggled out of prison Bonhoeffer showed no bitterness but rather explained how, "We in the resistance have learned to see the great events of world history from below; from the perspective of the excluded, the ill treated, the powerless, the oppressed and despised...so that personal suffering has become a more useful key for understanding the world than personal happiness."

Bonhoeffer was arrested and condemned by the Nazis for his involvement in "Operation 7," a rescue mission that had helped a small group of Jews escape over the German border and into Switzerland. The 39-year-old theologian had also been involved in planning an unsuccessful assassination attempt on the life of Adolf Hitler. His participation in the murder plot conflicted with his position as a pacifist, but as he writes to his sister: "If I see a madman driving a car into a group of innocent bystanders, then I can't, as a Christian, simply wait for the catastrophe and then comfort the wounded and bury the dead. I must try to wrestle the steering wheel out of the hands of the driver."

Key Writings of Bonhoeffer: 1. *Sanctorum Communio;* 2. *Act and Being: Transcendental Philosophy and Ontology in Systematic Theology;* 3. *Creation and Fall;* 4. *Discipleship;* 5. *Life Together;* 6. *Prayerbook of the Bible;* 7. *Letters and Papers from Prison.*

Worth Reading: *Dietrich Bonhoeffer: A Biography,* by Eberhard Bethge (2000); *Bonhoeffer's Works,* English Edition, by Fortress Press (2002); *A View from the Underside: The Legacy of Dietrich Bonhoeffer,* by Al Stagg.

Billy Graham *b. 1918*
International Evangelist

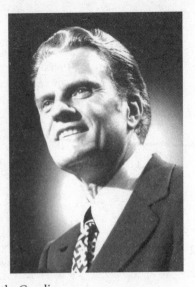

He has been a minister and friend to the the Queen of England, several prime ministers, leaders of foreign countries, and every president from Dwight Eisenhower to George W. Bush. He was the first Christian to preach in public behind the Iron Curtain after World War II, and he has been used by God in more countries than anyone ever before, to win souls for Christ.

ordecai Fowler Ham, an eighth generation, fifty-one-year-old Baptist preacher from Kentucky, was invited by the Christian Men's Evangelical Club in 1934 to lead a twelve-week revival campaign in Charlotte, North Carolina. The revival was incited due to Charlotte's intention to revoke the city's "Blue Laws" and concerns over prostitution. Ham did the preaching and his friend William Ramsey lead the praise. Together, like the Moody/Sankey team of the late nineteenth century, the Ham/Ramsey team was used by God in a mighty way to pierce the hearts of many lost souls during the revival. One such soul was a sixteen-year-old high school student destined to become one of the greatest evangelists of the twentieth century. During that revival in 1934, Billy Graham, alongside his friend, Grady Wilson, went forward and committed himself to Christ.

William Franklin Graham, Jr., known as Billy Graham to most of the world, was born on November 7, 1918, near Charlotte, North Carolina, to William Franklin and Morrow Coffey Graham. Billy, the first of four children, was raised in a Christian home and his family attended the Associate Reformed Presbyterian Church.

He began his education at Bob Jones University, but finished his training in divinity at Wheaton College, where he met and married Ruth Bell, the daughter of a missionary. It was there that Graham accepted his first and only position as a local pastor.

In 1945, Graham became a representative of a dynamic evangelistic movement known as Youth for Christ International. He toured the United States, Great Britain, and Europe, teaching local church leaders how to organize youth rallies. He also developed friendships with dozens of Christian leaders who would later provide critical assistance for his crusades when he visited their cities.

Though his fellow evangelists seemed to fall one by one to justified criticism in the 1970s-80s, Billy Graham maintained his integrity and the sincerity of his message. Far from publicly condemning other ministers, Billy spoke of them and with them regarding their souls. He even visited Jim Bakker in prison.

Like D. L. Moody, and John Wesley before him, Graham's methods of evangelism were extremely organized and effective.

Renowned evangelist and Baptist clergyman Billy Graham has been touching audiences around the world for more than fifty years. As a master of modern media, Graham has preached the Christian gospel through radio, television, film, and the printed word.

He surrounded himself with gifted men and women who possessed a passion for evangelism. He sent them out two by two or in small groups to spread the Word of God and establish cell groups or ministry centers. He developed effective public promotion of events and activities. He included men and women who were singers, counselors, and prayer leaders, all involved in the various aspects of the ministry.

In the 1980s he became a preacher of world peace, urging reconciliation with Russia and China, where his wife Ruth, the daughter of missionaries, was born.

Few developments in the ministry of Billy Graham have been more controversial and impactful than his success in penetrating the Iron Curtain. In 1978, he was given access to virtually every Soviet-controlled country. Graham used these visits to preach, to encourage Christian believers, and to explain to Communist

Billy Graham Preaching in Trafalgar Square in London on April 3, 1954.

leaders that their persecution of Christians and restriction of religious freedom was counterproductive to peace and prosperity in their own land, as well as hampering their relationship with America.

Time magazine says in its *Time 100, Most Important People of the Century* issue (Time's web poll ranked him 4th on the list): "He is the recognized leader of what continues to call itself American evangelical Protestantism, and his life and activities have sustained the self-respect of that vast entity. If there is an indigenous American religion—and I think there is, quite distinct from European Protestantism—then Graham remains its prime emblem."

Many have questioned, "Who is the next Billy Graham?" Since 1996, Billy's son, Franklin, has been taking up his father's mantle to evangelize the world for Jesus Christ. Or maybe it won't be a single person, but a generation of Christians who have been transformed internally and externally to follow King Jesus and carry forth the precious truth of his love and grace to a lost and sinful world.

Key Writings of Graham: 1. *Calling Youth to Christ* (1947); 2. *Revival in Our Times* (1950); 3. *America's Hour of Decision* (1951); 4. *Peace With God* (1953); 5. *The Secret of Happiness* (1955); 6. *World Aflame* (1965); 7. *The Challenge* (1969); 8. *The Jesus Generation* (1971); 9. *Angels: God's Secret Agents* (1975); 10. *How To Be Born Again* (1977); 11. *A Biblical Standard for Evangelists* (1984); 12. *Hope for the Troubled Heart* (1991); 13. *Just as I Am* (1997).

Worth Reading: *Billy Graham: The Man and the Ministry,* by Mary Bishop (1978); *Its My Turn,* by Ruth Graham (1982); *To All the Nations,* by John Pollack (1985); *Rebel With a Cause,* by Franklin Graham (1995).

Joni Eareckson Tada *b. 1950*
Champion of the Christian Faith

When seventeen-year-old Joni was seriously injured in a diving accident in 1967, she became a quadriplegic. But her life has become a wonderful example of faith and perseverance through tribulation. Though at first she became depressed and lost the will to live, she slowly grew into a deeper relationship with Christ, and found a new purpose for her life. Joni developed a ministry reaching out to others who were struggling and suffering.

In 1967, Joni Eareckson was just like any other Amercian teenager. She was very active in her school and community, loved playing sports, especially horseback riding and swimming, and enjoyed her times with friends and family. But on one bright summer day her life was turned into darkness and despair in an instant. Joni, her sister Kathy, and some friends were swimming in the Chesapeake Bay. Without knowing how shallow the water was, Joni dove in headfirst and crashed on the bottom. Moments from drowning, she was rescued by her sister and rushed to the hospital. After many tests, she received the devastating news that her neck had been broken in the dive, and she was paralyzed from the shoulders down.

As the Lord worked in her life from that moment on, she has inspired literally millions of people around the world. Her life of perseverence, courage, and faith has, in many ways, redefined "bearing the cross for the sake of Christ." Her strength, usefulness, and resourcefulness, amidst severe suffering has ministered the love of Jesus to more than the physically challenged.

Joni Eareckson Tada was born in Baltimore, Maryland, to John and Lindy Eareckson. She was the youngest of four sisters who adored each other very much. Her family was very close and enjoyed hiking, tennis, and camping together.

But in one sense, her life didn't *really* begin until her accident in 1967. What left her physically devastated, was used in a most profound way to awaken her spiritually. There is no substitute for Joni's own words as she shared her testimony to a large audience of Christian women in 1993:

"It hardly seems that twenty-six years ago I was lying on a hospital bed in suicidal despair, depressed, discouraged, after the hot July afternoon when I took that dive into shallow water, a dive which resulted in a severe spinal cord injury, which left me paralyzed from the shoulders down, without use of my hands and my legs. Before that time, I didn't even know what you called people like me. That spinal cord injury changed all that. There I was lying in the hospital bed in the summer of 1967, desperately trying to make ends meet, desperately trying to turn my right

The name "Joni" is recognized around the world. Overcoming the suffering and challenges of her paralysis, the remarkable life and example of Joni Eareckson Tada has ministered to the hearts and souls of millions of people over the past thirty-five years.

side down emotions, right side up. In my pain and despair, I had begged many of my friends to assist me in suicide. The source of my depression is understandable. I could not face the prospect of sitting down for the rest of my life without use of my hands, or my legs. All my hopes seem dashed. My faith was shipwrecked.

"I was sick and tired of pious platitudes that well-meaning friends often gave me at my bedside. Patting me on the head, trivializing my plight, with the sixteen good biblical reasons as to why all this has happened. I was tired of advice and didn't want any more counsel. I was numb emotionally, desperately alone, and so very, very frightened. Most of the questions I asked, in the early days of my paralysis, were questions voiced out of a clenched fist, an emotional release, an outburst of anger. I don't know how sincere my questions really were. I was just angry. But after many months those clenched fists questions became questions of a searching heart. I sincerely and honestly wanted to find answers.

"Now I knew, in a vague sort of way, that answers for my questions about my paralysis were probably hidden somewhere between the pages of the Bible, but I had no idea where. I needed a friend who would help me sort through my emotions, who would help bring me out of the social isolation, who would help me deal with the anger. A friend who would point me somewhere, anywhere, in God's Word to help me find answers. I found a friend, a young man named Steve [Estes], who knew absolutely nothing about emptying leg bags or pushing wheel chairs and he had no idea what to call people like me, whether we were physically challenged, differently abled, or mobility impaired.

"I remember my friend Steve. He was just a young teenager, who had a caring, compassionate heart, a love for God, and a halfway decent knowledge of the Bible. At my bedside, I cornered him one day, and said, 'I just don't get it! I trusted God before my accident. I wasn't a bad person. This possibly couldn't be a punishment for any sin that I've done. At least, I hope not. I don't get it, Steve? If God is supposed to be all-loving and all-powerful, then how can what has happened to me be a demonstration of His love and power? Because, Steve, if He's all-powerful, then surely He should have been powerful enough to stop my accident from happening? If He's all-loving then how in the world can permanent and lifelong paralysis be a part of His loving plan for my life? I just don't get it! Unless I find some answers, I don't see how this all-loving and all-powerful God is worthy of my trust and confidence. Who is in control? "Whose will is this anyway?" I said to him.

"My friend Steve took a deep sigh, and he was wise enough to discern that my questioning, again, was not voiced out of a clenched fist, but out of a searching heart. He knew I sincerely wanted to find an answer. And so he said, 'Joni, those are tough questions and theologians have been trying to answer them for hundreds of years. I can't pretend to sit at your bedside and

"Joni Eareckson Tada has a unique gift for stating the profoundest wisdom in the most vivid and warmhearted way. Theologically, spiritually, and humanly, her modeling from her wheelchair of healthy hope for the Christian's homeland is pure gold, as powerful as it is poignant."
—J. I Packer, on her book, Heaven.

know why and how. I can't pretend to explain the loving nature of God and how your accident is a demonstration of His power. But when it comes to the question about who is control, and whose will is this anyway, I think I can show you some answers.'

"Huh, well! I wanted to see this! So I waited to see what he would say. I thought he might quote to me the sixteen good biblical reasons as to why all this has happened. I thought surely he might lay out before me the blueprint of my life. I thought for sure he'd give me a lot of advice, a lot of his counsel, but no, Steve didn't do that. Then he opened up his Bible and he pointed me to the example of Jesus Christ. He told me that in the life of Christ I could find the answers about God's will. But he went even more specific. He showed me Christ on the Cross and he challenged me with a couple of hard hitting questions. Saying, 'Joni, whose will do you think the cross was?' Well, I obediently remembered all those good Sunday school lessons I had learned growing up and I easily voiced in response, 'God's will, of course, it's God's will. Everybody knows that.' But then Steve said, 'Joni, think it through, because you better believe that it was the devil who entered the heart of Judas Iscariot who handed over Jesus for a mere thirty pieces of silver. And you've got to know that it was Satan who instigated that mob on the streets to clamor for Christ's crucifixion, and for sure, Joni, it had to be the devil who prodded those Roman soldiers to spit on Jesus and slap Him and mock Him. Even the devil inspired Pontius Pilate to hand down mock justice in order to gain political popularity. How can any of these things be God's will? Treason, injustice, murder, torture?'

Tada is a highly sought-after conference speaker both in the United States and internationally and is also a columnist for Moody Magazine, the United Kingdom's Christian Herald, and several European Christian magazines. In 1993, she was honored as "Churchwoman of the Year" by the Religious Heritage Foundation.

"Well, I nodded and agreed. None of it seemed to be God's will. But what about all those Sunday school lessons I had learned as a little girl? That the Cross was God's plan and purpose for all of mankind? My friend Steve turned to a verse in the Bible which helped answer that question about God's will. He turned to Acts chapter 4:28 and it says there that certain men—that is Pontius Pilate, Judas Iscariot, the mob in the streets, the cruel Roman soldiers—these men did what God's power and will had decided before hand should happen. In other words, the Cross was no mistake. Somehow, some way, God was in control. Heaven and hell participated in the exact same event when Christ died on that cross.

"Steve closed his Bible at my bedside and didn't say much after that. He let the message sink in. It didn't take long for me to understand the parallel between what happened at the Cross of Christ and my own disability. I began to see that in the accident in which I became paralyzed, Heaven and Hell were participating in the exact same event, but for different reasons. When I took that reckless dive into shallow water that caused me to be a quadriplegic, no doubt, the devil absolutely wrung his hands in delight, thinking to himself, 'Aha, I have now shipwrecked this girl's faith. I have dashed her hopes. I have ruined her family.

I have destroyed her dreams and I am going to make a mockery of all her beliefs in God.' That, I'm certain, was the devil's motive. Remember, we have an all-wise, all-powerful, all-loving God who reaches down into what otherwise would be horrible evil, and wrenches out of it positive good for us and glory for Himself. I am convinced that God's motive, God's purpose, His plan in the accident in which I became paralyzed, His purpose was to turn a headstrong, stubborn, rebellious kid into a young woman who would reflect something of patience, something of endurance, something of longsuffering—who would get her life values turned from wrong-side-down to right-side-up and would have a buoyant and lively optimistic hope of heavenly glories above.

"I wouldn't dare list sixteen good biblical reasons as to why this accident happened to me. No, I wouldn't dare do that because suffering is still a mystery. I can't explain it all and my friend Steve couldn't explain it all by my bedside either. It's a mystery, but not a mystery without direction. We know for one thing in this mystery, nobody is glorifying suffering. There is no inherent goodness in cerebral palsy, muscular dystrophy, multiple sclerosis, cystic fibrosis, brain injury, stroke, heart disease, manic depression. No, No, No! There is no inherent goodness in disease or disability, but like I said, "God can reach down to what would seem like a terrible difficulty and wrench out of it positive good for us and glory for himself."

Joni Eareckson Tada is the author of over thirty books. Her best-selling and award-winning works cover topics ranging from disability outreach to heaven. The book, A Christmas Longing, *includes reproductions of Joni's best-loved Christmas paintings.* The Life and Death Dilemma *addresses the tough issues of assisted suicide.*

With her new found faith, Joni was led to share her experience publically. Her popularity quickly developed into a devotional speaking ministry that has reached millions of people.

During her years of rehabilitation, Joni did not sit around, but amazingly, she learned how to paint with a brush between her teeth. Her paintings are exceptional and are used as cover art for many of her books. Her most popular book is her first, *Joni*, where she recreates her life's story. *Joni* has been translated into fifteen languages as well as a full-length film.

In 1979, Joni founded Joni and Friends, a Christian organization ministering to the disability community, that has affected the lives of thousands of disabled and their families. One of the most successful programs is Wheels for the World, that has distributed tens of thousands of wheelchairs to needy disabled children and adults around the world.

In 1982, Joni married Ken Tada. He was a teacher for thirty-two years, but retired to serve alongside his wife as a member of the board of directors of the Joni and Friends ministry.

Key Writings of Tada: 1. *Joni* (1979); 2. *All God's Children: Ministry with Disabled Persons* (1993); 3. *The Amazing Secret* (2000); 4. *Glorious Intruder* (1991); 5. *Heaven: Your Real Home* (1995); 6. *Friendship Unlimited*; 7. *Secret Strength*; 8. *A Quiet Place in a Crazy World*; 9. *Diamonds in the Dust*; 10. *More Precious Than Silver*; 11. *Holiness in Hidden Places*; 12. *Extraordinary Faith*; 13. *A Step Further*.

Select Bibliography

The main source of information used to write this book was my private library of antiquarian Christian books. Dozens of volumes spanning four centuries supplied most of the individual biographical material. Most of these books have been out of print for many years. Though it is not possible to list everything, below is a list of general references used to help gather information on these Christian men and women of the past and present.

1. *Allibone's Dictionary of English and American Writers* (3 vols.)
Richard Allibone (1870)
2. *Nicene and Post-Nicene Fathers of the Christian Church* (3 vols.)
Philip Schaff (1890)
3. *The New Schaff-Herzog Encyclopedia of Religious Knowledge* (6 vols.)
Funk and Wagnalls (1908)
4. *Lives of Eminent Christians*
John Frost (1868)
5. *Biographies for the People* (10 vols.)
The Religious Tract Society, London (1878)
6. *Great Men and Famous Women* (8 vols.)
Selmar Hess Publishers (1894)
7. *After Jesus: The Triumph of Christianity*
Reader's Digest Association *(1992)*
8. *Sketches of Church History*
Banner of Truth (1980)
9. *Foxe's Book of Martyrs*
S. W. Partridge & Co., London (1871)

The Christian History Institute: *www.gospelcom.net/chi/index.html*
The Christian Classics Ethereal Library: *www.ccel.org*
The Hall of Church History: *www.gty.org/~phil/hall.htm/*

My Father's Business
Doing Business God's Way
by Peter Tsukahira

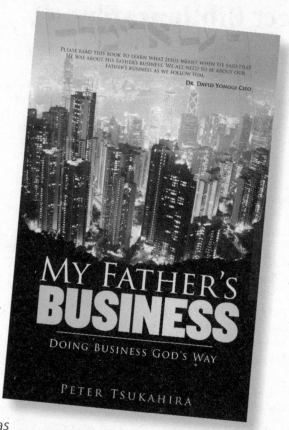

*A*uthor Peter Tsukahira is a Japanese-American-Israeli pastor and former businessman. He says, "This means I have a Japanese face, an American voice, and an Israeli passport. I have experienced the call of God that crosses national, ethnic, and religious boundaries as I have lived, done business, and ministered in the United States, Japan, and Israel." Peter now pastors on Mount Carmel, but he was once an executive in a multinational computer company. He wants people to know that God's calling is not limited to ministry in the church; it includes the marketplace as well. My Father's Business is organized into very readable, concise chapters that will help the reader to become an agent of change in society and the marketplace.

The POWER of the BUSINESS WORLD to ADVANCE GOD'S KINGDOM

ISBN: 978-088270-871-3
TPB / 172 pages

Prayers That Change Things

by Lloyd Hildebrand

More than 160,000 copies have been sold. These mass-market paperbacks contain prayers that are built from the promises of God and teaching that is thoroughly scriptural.

978-1-61036-105-7
MMP / 192 pages

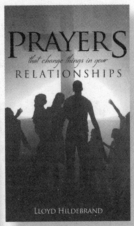

978-0-88270-012-0
MMP / 232 pages

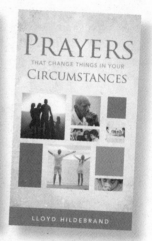

978-0-88270-743-3
MMP / 232 pages

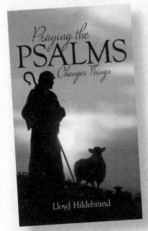

978-1-61036-126-2
MMP / 216 pages

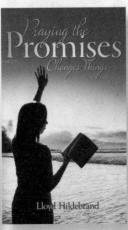

978-1-61036-132-3
MMP / 248 pages

978-1-61036-141-5
MMP / 256 pages

Pure Gold Classics

Timeless Truth in a Distinctive, Best-Selling Collection

An Expanding Collection of the Best-Loved Christian Classics of All Time.

AVAILABLE AT FINE BOOKSTORES.

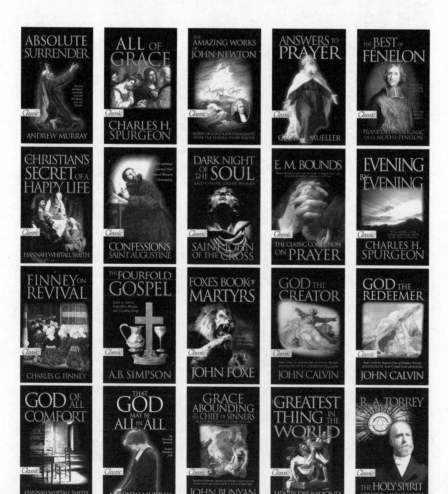

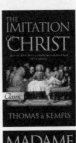

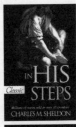

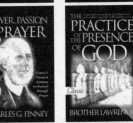
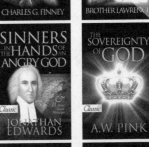

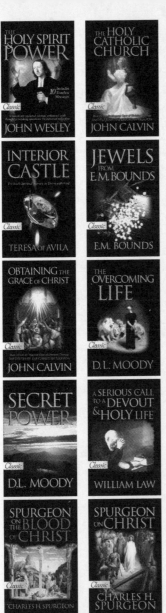

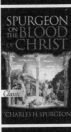

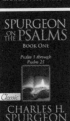
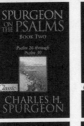

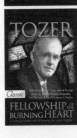

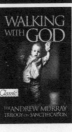

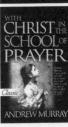